Culture and Rights
Anthropological Perspectives

D0172051

Do people everywhere have the same, or even compatible, ideas about multiculturalism, indigenous rights or women's rights? The authors of this book move beyond the traditional terms of the universalism versus cultural relativism debate. Through detailed case studies from around the world (Hawai'i, France, Thailand, Botswana, Greece, Nepal and Canada) they explore the concrete effects of rights talk and rights institutions on people's lives.

JANE K. COWAN is a senior lecturer in social anthropology in the School of Cultural and Community Studies at the University of Sussex. Her publications include *Dance and the Body Politic in Northern Greece* (1990, Winner of the Chicago Folklore Award 1991), an edited volume, *Macedonia: The Politics of Identity and Difference* (2000) and numerous articles on gender relations, ritual, popular music, the politics of 'tradition' and the formation of complex identities in contemporary Greece.

MARIE-BENEDICTE DEMBOUR is a lecturer in law in the School of Legal Studies at the University of Sussex. Her recent publications include *Recalling the Belgian Congo: Conversations and Introspection* (2000) and a number of articles that reflect her interests in human rights, identity and migration in Europe. She is now working on a project entitled 'Problematizing Human Rights: the European Convention in Question'.

RICHARD A. WILSON is a reader in social anthropology at the University of Sussex. His books include a monograph on an ethnic revivalist movement in Guatemala, *Maya Resurgence in Guatemala* (1995), an edited collection, *Human Rights, Culture and Context: Anthropological Perspectives* (1997) and *The Politics of Truth and Reconciliation in South Africa* (2000, Cambridge University Press).

Culture and Rights

Anthropological Perspectives

Edited by

Jane K. Cowan, Marie-Bénédicte Dembour and
Richard A. Wilson

*Return to
Knadeau@csusb.edu*

CAMBRIDGE
UNIVERSITY PRESS

CAMBRIDGE UNIVERSITY PRESS
Cambridge, New York, Melbourne, Madrid, Cape Town, Singapore,
São Paulo, Delhi, Dubai, Tokyo, Mexico City

Cambridge University Press
The Edinburgh Building, Cambridge CB2 8RU, UK

Published in the United States of America by Cambridge University Press, New York

www.cambridge.org
Information on this title: www.cambridge.org/9780521797351

First published 2001
Fourth printing 2004

A catalogue record for this publication is available from the British Library

Library of Congress Cataloguing in Publication data

Culture and rights: anthropological perspectives / edited by Jane K. Cowan,
Marie-Bénédicte Dembour, and Richard A. Wilson.
      p. cm.
Includes bibliographical references and index.
ISBN 0 521 79339 4 – ISBN 0 521 79735 7 (pb)
1. Human rights – Cross-cultural studies.   2. Cultural relativism.
I. Cowan, Jane K., 1954–   .   II. Dembour, Marie-Bénédicte, 1961–   .
III. Wilson, Richard A., 1964–   .
JC571.C75   2001   306–dc21   00–045523

ISBN 978-0-521-79339-1 Hardback
ISBN 978-0-521-79735-1 Paperback

To Jacques Vanderlinden

Contents

Contributors

JANE K. COWAN is a senior lecturer in social anthropology in the School of Cultural and Community Studies at the University of Sussex. Her publications include *Dance and the Body Politic in Northern Greece* (1990, Winner of the Chicago Folklore Award 1991), an edited volume, *Macedonia: The Politics of Identity and Difference* (2000), and numerous articles on gender relations, ritual, popular music, the politics of 'tradition' and the formation of complex identities in contemporary Greece. Her current work on the League of Nations' interwar supervision of minorities treaties traces the changing ways cultural difference has been defined, contested and regulated in the southern Balkan region.

MARIE-BENEDICTE DEMBOUR is a lecturer in law in the School of Legal Studies at the University of Sussex. She also holds a doctorate in social anthropology. Her publications include *Recalling the Belgian Congo: Conversations and Introspection* (2000) and a number of articles that reflect her interests in human rights, identity and migration in Europe. She is now working on a project entitled 'Problematizing Human Rights: the European Convention in Question'.

THOMAS HYLLAND ERIKSEN is a professor of social anthropology at the University of Oslo and has carried out field research in Mauritius and Trinidad. His publications in English and Norwegian include textbooks, monographs and essays, often with a focus on identity politics and globalisation. His most recent books are *Charles Darwin* (1997), *Common Denominators* (1998), *Ambivalens og Fundamentalisme*, with Oscar Hemer (1999), and *Egoisme*, co-edited with Dag O. Hessen (1999).

DAVID N. GELLNER is a reader in social anthropology in the Department of Human Sciences at Brunel University, London. His publications include *Monk, Householder, and Tantric Priest: Newar Buddhism and Its Hierarchy of Ritual*, edited with Declan Quigley (1992), *Contested Hierarchies: A Collaborative Ethnography of Caste among the Newars of the Kathmandu Valley, Nepal* (1995) and *Nationalism and Ethnicity in a Hindu Kingdom: The Politics of Culture in Contemporary Nepal* (1997), which he edited with J. Pfaff-Czarnecka and J. Whelpton. A collection of his essays, entitled *The Anthropology of Buddhism and Hinduism: Weberian Themes*, is in press.

ANNE GRIFFITHS is a reader in law at Edinburgh University. Her specialist interests include comparative family law (Scotland, Botswana and the USA), anthropology of law, and gender and law. She has carried out fieldwork in Botswana over an eight-year period, the results of which are detailed in her book *In the Shadow of Marriage: Gender and Justice in an African Community* (1997). She is also co-author of a book on family law in Scotland. She has recently worked as a consultant on the Women and Law in Southern Africa Research Project for its research phase on 'Delivering Justice'. Her current research involves a comparative study of 'The Child's Choice in Care Proceedings', in Glasgow and a county in New York state, funded by the Annenberg Foundation in the USA.

SALLY ENGLE MERRY is a professor of anthropology at Wellesley College. Her speciality is the anthropology of law, specifically law and colonialism, conflict resolution, and gender, violence and human rights. She is the author of *Urban Danger: Life in a Neighborhood of Strangers* (1981), *Getting Justice and Getting Even: Legal Consciousness among Working Class Americans* (1990), *The Possibility of Popular Justice: A Case Study in American Community Mediation*, co-edited with Neal Milner (1993), and *Colonizing Hawai'i: The Cultural Power of Law* (in press). She is President of the Association for Political Legal Anthropology and past-president of the Law and Society Association.

HEATHER MONTGOMERY currently holds a British Academy postdoctoral fellowship at the Institute of Social and Cultural Anthropology at St Hugh's College, Oxford. She is the author of several articles on children's rights and child sexual abuse, including contributions in *Nobody's Children: Anthropological and Historical Perspectives on Child Abandonment and the Lives of Children without Families*, edited by Catherine Panter-Brick (1999), and *Global Sex Workers: Rights, Resistance and Redefinition*, edited by Kemala Kempadoo (1998). She is currently working on a book about child prostitution in Thailand.

COLIN SAMSON is a lecturer in sociology at the University of Essex, where he is a Director of the MA in Native American Studies. He has been working in the Innu communities of Sheshatshiu and Utshimassits, Labrador, since 1994. He is co-author of *Canada's Tibet: the Killing of the Innu*, a human rights report commissioned by Survival International, and has written several scholarly articles on dispossession and land claims. In the spring of 1999 he worked for the Sheshatshiu Innu Band Council and produced a report on the impact of Euro-Canadian schooling. He also maintains interests in, and has published works on, Native American literature, cultural studies and medical sociology.

RACHEL SIEDER is a senior lecturer in politics at the Institute of Latin American Studies, University of London, where she teaches courses in comparative politics and in human rights. She is also an associate fellow at FLASCO Guatemala, where she is involved in research on indigenous customary law and legal reform. Her books include *Central America: Fragile Transition* (1995), *Derecho consuetudinario y transición democrática en Guatemala* (1996), and *Guatemala After the Peace Accords* (1998). She is currently working on a historical analysis of law and citizenship in Guatemala.

RICHARD A. WILSON is a reader in social anthropology at the University of Sussex. He has studied human rights and informal justice in countries such as South Africa and Guatemala which have moved from authoritarian and repressive regimes towards more democratic political dispensations. His books include a monograph on an ethnic revivalist movement in Guatemala, *Maya Resurgence in Guatemala* (1995), and an edited collection, *Human Rights, Culture and Context: Anthropological Perspectives* (1997). His recent ESRC-funded research investigated reconciliation in South Africa, leading to the monograph *The Politics of Truth and Reconciliation in South Africa* (2000). He is the editor of the journal *Anthropological Theory*.

JESSICA WITCHELL works as a development education worker at Reading International Solidarity centre, using participatory learning and action (PLA) methodology to facilitate an understanding of global issues in a local context. She has also led a participatory research project in Nepal exploring local health practices, which culminated in the publication of a poster and booklet for use in Nepali adult education classes.

Preface

The political rhetoric of 'culture' confronts us each time we open a newspaper, or turn on the television or radio. For example, in autumn 1999 international media carried the story of a treaty successfully negotiated between the Canadian Parliament and the Nisga'a people, granting the latter land, access to natural resources and self-government. In that same period, a British Airways inflight magazine carried a colour spread on the Sorbs, 'the forgotten people', 'one of the smallest races in Europe' and survivors of '1300 years of oppression'. The Sorbs were reported to have brought a case before the European Commission of Human Rights concerning the actions of a mining company which threatened to displace them and irreversably alter their distinctive way of life. These are just two random illustrations of a rhetoric which is specific to our times and in which culture is presented as an object of rights.

In the hope of grappling with the motives and consequences of claims to culture in the language of rights, in July 1997 we organised the Sussex Workshop on Culture and Rights', in Brighton. The workshop brought together an international and interdisciplinary group of scholars (from anthropology, sociology, law, social and political theory, and feminist studies) with the aim of developing a rich and conceptually useful understanding of contemporary rights struggles. We are grateful to the participants of the workshop for their sharp but generous critical engagement and for their help in formulating meaningful questions (as much as answers) about this still underexamined conjunction. The stimulating discussions held at the workshop helped to define the agenda for the present book. Apart from the five participants whose work is included in this book, we acknowledge the participation and contributions of Peter Fitzpatrick, Vivien Hart, Jane Hindley, Neil Stammers, Ann Whitehead and Nira Yuval-Davis.

We also thank Jan Brogden, Peter Leutchford, Davide Però and Betta Zontini, who assisted in the organisation and the smooth running of the workshop. We acknowledge the financial support provided for the workshop and the editorial process by a University of Sussex Research Development Grant. Jessica Kuper's enthusiasm for the project since its inception oiled the wheels for us at Cambridge University Press, and we have appreciated her support through the publication process. We are grateful to David Sutton for comments on the introduction, and to two anonymous readers for the Press, whose penetrating comments on the whole manuscript vastly improved the final text. Lysbeth Gehrels, our editorial assistant, was highly organised and a marvellous copy-editor, and her calm efficiency considerably eased the tensions of the hectic final stages. We thank all the contributors for submitting graciously to our demands for multiple revisions. During this exciting and rewarding project, we learned much from them and from each other, not only about culture and rights, but also about cooperation and complementarity in joint intellectual labour.

JANE K. COWAN, MARIE-BENEDICTE DEMBOUR
AND RICHARD A. WILSON
April 2000

1   Introduction

Jane K. Cowan, Marie-Bénédicte Dembour and
Richard A. Wilson

Rights and culture as emergent global discourses

In the past few decades there has been a dramatic increase in negotiations between social groups of various kinds and political institutions, whether at the local, national or supra-national level, phrased in a language of 'rights'. Processes of globalization have led to rights discourses being adopted widely throughout the world, far from their original sites in the French and American revolutions. Just as importantly, they have framed new domains of political struggle, such as reproductive rights, animal rights and ecological rights. Constituting one historically specific way of conceptualizing the relations of entitlement and obligation, the model of rights is today hegemonic, and imbued with an emancipatory aura. Yet this model has had complex and contradictory implications for individuals and groups whose claims must be articulated within its terms.

The ubiquity and the diversity of both rights discourses and rights practices on the one hand, and their enormous implications for justice and peace on the other, make it more compelling than ever to widen the debate and make it more interdisciplinary. This volume adds an anthropological perspective to the debate: we argue for the need of a forum in which theoretical explorations of rights, citizenship and related concepts can engage with empirical, contextual studies of rights processes. This is important because local concerns continue to shape how universal categories of rights are implemented, resisted and transformed. However, despite the global spread of rights-based political values, the specificities of any particular struggle cannot be grasped empirically through a methodological focus on the local community alone. For in the process of seeking access to social goods (ranging from land, work and education to freedom of belief and recognition of a distinctive group identity) through a language of rights, claimants are increasingly becoming involved in legal and political processes that transcend nation-state boundaries. Our desire to explore the tensions between local and global

1

formulations of rights leads us to consider in more detail the interplay between the languages and institutions at a multiple of levels, from the local through to the transnational.

A striking feature within the contemporary efflorescence of rights discourse is the increasing deployment of a rhetoric of 'culture'. We are particularly concerned with the implications of introducing 'culture' into rights talk. Although 'rights' and 'culture' have emerged as key-words of the late twentieth century, their relationship to each other, both historically and in the present, has been conceived in quite variable ways. Nancy Fraser (1997: 2) has identified the 'shift in the grammar of political claims-making' from claims of social equality to claims of group difference to be a defining feature of 'a post-socialist condition'. Yet this condition clearly draws on forms of activism and critique developed within civil society in the past four decades, particularly in North America and Europe. These are worth summarizing briefly.

The 1960s were characterized by struggles in both North America and Europe to achieve political and economic equality for groups facing disadvantage on the basis of race and class and, with respect to Southeast Asia, Latin America and elsewhere, by struggles against neo-colonial exploitation. The failure of these movements to achieve funda-mental reforms led, for some, to disillusionment with the legislative and judicial practices of liberal democracies and their models of neutral justice and formal equality. In the absence of economic enfranchisement and greater involvement in political decision-making, attempts to change societal discrimination became focused on 'culture' at the level of discourse and representation. Some activists sought to transform the fundamental values of their society, for instance by creating a global environmental movement, while others worked to renegotiate an ex-isting group's position and status within the larger polity, as happened with the Black Power movement in the US. The latter process involved revalorizing ethnic or racial markers of a despised distinctiveness, and in some cases, creating new markers where had none previously existed.

The emphasis on 'culture' – ideas, beliefs, meanings, values – emerged in the context of the social movements of the 1960s and 1970s as part of a radical questioning of what was derisively dubbed 'the System'. To take the US, where such developments were most promi-nent, the ensuing ethnic and Native American movements followed the lead of Black activists in criticizing the melting-pot ideal and celebrating their differences from the Anglo-Saxon majority. In the identity politics which have ensued, culture holds a central place. Discourses of identity have appropriated the old anthropological sense of this term as the shared customs and worldview of a *particular* group or kind of people.

The popular conception that a group is defined by a distinctive culture and that cultures are discrete, clearly bounded and internally homogenous, with relatively fixed meanings and values – what we call an *essentialist* view of 'culture' – echoes what was until recently a dominant, if contested (see Brightman 1995), understanding of 'culture' within the discipline of anthropology. Significantly, this view reflects *both* Romantic nationalism, which conceives of diversity as a problem to be solved, and what Terence Turner (1993) has labelled 'difference multiculturalism', which conceives of diversity as a richness to be celebrated (although only as a mosaic of *separate and distinct* cultural units).[1] Intriguingly, in the 1980s, at the very moment in which anthropologists were engaged in an intense and wide-ranging critique especially of the more essentialist interpretations of the concept, to the point of querying its usefulness at all,[2] they found themselves witnessing, often during fieldwork, the increasing prevalence of 'culture' as a rhetorical object – often in a highly essentialized form – in contemporary political talk.[3]

Inspired in part by the surprise of this collision of two quite different manifestations of the concept in anthropological research, this volume examines 'culture' as an object of rights discourses, as well as examining the local and global conditions which compel and constrain such claims and the contexts in which they are articulated. But it seeks, also, to explore the extent to which the concept of 'culture' – *revised*, to be sure, in the light of the thoroughgoing critique – could be useful as an *analytical* tool to make sense of claims-making in the global context. Might it not help us, for example, to identify and think more productively about the *specificities of*, and *differences* and *relations between*, (a) local or group-specific, (b) nation-state and (c) supra-national concepts, institutions and processes concerning rights? In shifting attention from a formulation which *opposes* culture and human rights to one in which the pursuit of human rights is approached as itself *a cultural process* which impinges on human subjects and subjectivities in multiple and contradictory ways – might it not also help us transcend certain impasses and raise new kinds of questions?

Culture/rights: diverse conjunctions

In the traditional terms of political philosophy, a focus on culture expresses a Romantic political vision, while a focus on rights is characteristic of liberalism. In political struggles over the past two centuries, culture and rights have been portrayed, sometimes as natural allies, at other times as strange bedfellows. These varying positions on the compatibility of rights and culture have characterized contemporary political and academic debates as well. We see three major ways in which culture and rights have been conjoined in recent debates. The first two conjunctions – rights *versus* culture, and rights *to* culture – have preoccupied legal and political theorists, philosophers, anthropologists, lawyers, bureaucrats, non-governmental organizations (NGOs) and lay people, and compelled them to engage in conversations about the legal and political status which 'a culture' does or should have. These conversations occur more often in national and international institutions than in academia. The third conjunction – rights *as* culture – indicates a perspective that anthropologists have brought to the study of rights and legal processes generally, to delineate their structuring qualities and their connections to other aspects of social life. It is a perspective that can illuminate many aspects of rights processes. From this tradition we derive a fourth conjunction, of culture as a heuristic analytical abstraction through which to think about rights. We suggest that culture, rather than being solely an *object* of analysis, can be employed as a *means* of analysing and better understanding the particular ways that rights processes operate as situated social action.

(a)   *Rights versus culture*

Not surprisingly, perhaps, the initial formulation of the link between rights and culture was one of opposition: rights *versus* culture. Recognizing rights was seen to entail a denial, rejection or overriding of culture; conversely, recognizing culture was seen to prohibit, at least potentially and in some cases, the pursuit of universal individual rights. The figuring of culture and rights in a relationship of binary opposition is rooted in a prior politico-philosophical antagonism – that of the 'blood and soil' response of nineteenth century German Romanticism to the universalism of the French Enlightenment. This binary opposition has been a core element of most post-eighteenth-century European thinking about society and political constitutions. It has also shown a remarkable ability to transpose itself to other historical moments and places.

One of its obvious contemporary expressions is to be found in the discourse of human rights. This discourse is animated by a fundamental tension between, on the one hand, the desire to establish universal rights and, on the other, the awareness of cultural differences, which seems to negate the possibility of finding common ground on which to base such rights. Hence, the most serious and still ongoing debate about human rights invites us to *choose between* universalism and cultural relativism.[4]

The competing claims of universalism versus cultural relativism have been exhaustively debated and it is generally agreed that the debate has reached an impasse. It is not that cultural difference as such has disappeared. Different understandings of personhood, agency and bodily integrity, for example – part of what is meant by cultural difference – persist, even in a world replete with global connections, as Marie-Bénédicte Dembour's chapter on female circumcision in this volume reveals. Yet it is undoubtedly misleading to represent conflicts over such an issue as concerning *only* the competing claims of culture and human rights. It is doubtful that cultural practices of circumcision enjoy total consensual support even within the community in which they occur. This is almost certainly the case for African migrants to European urban centres, whose daughters grow up in and are influenced by a milieu generally horrified by such cutting practices, but probably also obtains in their homeland, where African feminist organizations have noisily protested them. Rather than seeing a singular culture with a set of fixed meanings that are incompatible with those of human rights, it is more illuminating to think of culture as a field of creative interchange and contestation, often around certain shared symbols, propositions or practices, and continuous transformation.

Another criticism relating to this putative opposition focuses not on the internal tensions within a cultural field and its dynamic nature, but rather on the ways that these fields – slightly more autonomous in the past, perhaps – have by now been penetrated decisively by external meanings and power relations, while the presents and futures of previously 'separate' societies have become ever more entangled through the vast and expanding regimes of global institutions. It is no use imagining a 'primitive' tribe which has not yet heard of human rights. In the present era, it is precisely some of the smaller, marginalized 'Fourth World Nation' groups that are using international fora to press their claims (Tennant 1994). In so doing, what it means to be 'indigenous' is itself transformed through interaction with human rights discourses and institutions such as the UN Working Party.[5]

Such observations are borne out and expanded in the chapters by Rachel Sieder and Jessica Witchell and David Gellner with reference to Guatemala and Nepal. Yet Colin Samson's chapter about another 'Fourth World' nation, the Innu of northeast Canada, insists that we should not assume thereby that cultural difference has been eradicated. Indeed, he emphasizes the devastating consequences for the Innu of the Canadian state's historical refusal to acknowledge difference, and its insistence on making 'cultural sameness' the price for gaining rights.

There is yet another reason why we argue that the stark either/or terms of the debate are wrongly conceived. The perceived dichotomy is not just about incompatible values, attitudes and practices – what we might call, in their entirety, worldviews – but relates to a fundamental aspect of rights as a legal process. It is located in the inherent tension between the desire to formulate general principles and the need to apply these principles within particular circumstances and contexts. The tension goes beyond the human rights discourse to pervade legal discourse in many of its conceptions, particularly Western positive law and Islamic law.[6] This is because a universal status is claimed for legal rules by legal officials. As it is usually grounded in a positivist[7] view of truth, law essentializes social categories and identities. However, it never completely eradicates the complexity of social facts, which present themselves in the courtroom, in the legislative arena and in political struggles. Legal principles are constantly being readjusted to the demands of the present, the unpredictable and the local. This explains the contradictions that exist – without necessarily being acknowledged – in case-law, the constant need for legislative reforms, and the evolution of the legal system.

This way of understanding the tension between a universal rule and a particular manifestation – reminiscent of a Sausserian system/event, or *langue/parole*, distinction – subtly alters the traditional formulation of the problem. Rather than seeing universalism and cultural relativism as alternatives which one must choose, once and for all, one should see the tension between the positions as part of the continuous process of negotiating ever-changing and interrelated global and local norms. It is inescapable as long as flux and change exist in the world. The tension is inevitably magnified in our era when there is a drive to set and to implement global standards for humanity.

Granted, such philosophical nuances are seldom noted in the cut-and-thrust of the politics of culture in international arenas, in which arguments opposing universalism to cultural relativism have been used instrumentally in the light of which 'culture' (as an abstract entity) is either criticized or championed. Yet even here, the question must be posed: is it always *really* 'culture' that is at issue?

Consider the following case. In an early and notorious manifestation of the universalism *versus* cultural relativism debate in the international forum, a few Asian states argued that it was justifiable for them to resist western-cum-universal human rights in order to preserve their own cultural values. Ironically, the elites in states most vocal in defence of 'Asian values' – Indonesia and Singapore – are highly westernized. In the economic sphere, elites have welcomed industrialization and its consequences, at least until the market crash of 1998 sent their economies spiralling downwards. This inconsistent attitude towards westernization makes their rejection of the human rights discourse in the name of 'Asian values' highly suspicious. The rejection may be more accurately read as a political tactic used to bolster state sovereignty and resist international denunciations of internal repression of political dissent.[8]

In this case, then, the rhetoric of cultural relativism appears to have been motivated by a political opportunism which has little to do with a concern for cultural values. Yet its rhetorical invocation has forced challengers of those governments' views themselves to adopt the language of culture. Dissidents and critics of state policy now frequently argue that 'traditional Asian values' are by no means incompatible with human rights. To the contrary, the core values in Western human rights discourse are easily found, they argue, in Buddhism and in the moral lessons of Indian epics (Cowan n.d.).

A second case, developed in more detail in this volume by Heather Montgomery, concerns child prostitution in Thailand. Montgomery questions whether the right of children to be free from prostitution should be implemented, considering that the children directly concerned do not want this right. At first sight this seems a classic illustration of the debate between universalism and cultural relativism. On the one hand, we have the right of the child to be protected from all forms of sexual exploitation, as inscribed in Article 34 of the UN Convention on the Rights of the Child. On the other hand, we have the right of Thai children to act as they see fit, in accordance with the demands of their cultural environment. The children with whom Montgomery has worked appear willingly to subscribe to a 'way of life', and in particular to a 'cultural value' of filial duty towards their mothers, which enjoins them to support the economic survival of the family through prostitution. However, it is possible to read the situation in a different way. Despite the long history of prostitution in Thailand, it is clear that the children only prostitute themselves because of the lack of other viable economic opportunities. If they could, they would avoid prostitution. But they have reasoned that begging and rummaging through garbage constitute poor and less lucrative alternatives. In this case, we are confronted less with a problem of culture than with one of poverty.

The tensions between the dictates of universalism and those of respect for cultural difference, and thus between 'rights' and 'culture', are in important ways real and persistent. They cannot be made to vanish through an analytical sleight of hand which appeals to the eradication of local forms of difference through global processes and to the increasing hybridity of identities and cultures, because these phenomena occur at an uneven pace. Moreover the responses generated mix local and global elements into ever new and more potent cocktails. Even

so, we believe that the debate has tended to exaggerate the irreconcil-
ability of the terms 'rights' and 'culture'. This is in part a consequence
of essentializing them and of ignoring their close historical inter-
dependencies, as Sally Engle Merry's chapter reminds us. The debate
has also exaggerated the incommensurability of different worlds at the
very moment when a new global 'culture of human rights' (see Rabossi
1990) is becoming entrenched and, as Dembour's and Montgomery's
analyses emphasize, when this very fact makes possible – and imperative
– the development of *conversations* between local worlds of meaning and
global ones. Merry goes even further, showing through the example of
Hawaiian women organizing around the problem of male violence
against women, that local appropriations of both 'culture' and 'rights'
have led to the transformation of both terms. Finally, we think that
shifting our approach to this opposition, from a focus on supposedly
irreconcilable worldviews to that of the inherent tensions between an
abstract ideal and its implementation in the real world, between
principle and practice, helps to clear a new path.

A right to culture

A second conjoining of the two terms reverses their relationship,
asserting a universal right *to* culture. The human rights discourse has
stretched to allow culture to become an object of rights claims. The
rights of an individual to 'belong to' and 'enjoy' a culture are enshrined
in several international instruments: notably, Article 2.1 of the United
Nations Declaration on the Rights of Persons Belonging to Ethnic or
National, Linguistic and Religious Minorities, and Article 27 of the
International Covenant on Civil and Political Rights. A third example,
the International Labour Organization Convention (No 169) concerning Indigenous and Tribal Persons in Independent Countries,
signed in 1989, aims at 'promoting the full realization of the . . . cultural
rights of these peoples with respect for their social and cultural identity,
their customs and traditions and their institutions' (Article 2 (2) b of the
Convention). In this formulation, cultural features are seen as intrinsic-
ally valuable and worthy of recognition and legal protection. As in the
rights *versus* culture phrasing, culture here is understood as a unified
arrangement of practices and meanings. It is yet another 'thing' that an
already formed actor is entitled to 'have' and 'enjoy'. Acknowledgement
of its ontological aspect, its role in constituting persons, is muted.

In a certain sense, a right to culture is not a new idea. Most cogently
expressed by Herder, the right to follow one's culture is one of the central
tenets of European Romantic nationalism (Berlin 2000). Yet inter-

national treaties from the late nineteenth century until the mid-twentieth century dealt in an ambivalent fashion with sub-national and transnational minorities. In the (rather enlightened, in many respects) Minorities Treaties agreed at the Paris Peace Conference after the First World War and 'guaranteed' by the League of Nations in the 1920s and 1930s, for example, the rights of members of 'racial, religious and linguistic minorities' (as it was then phrased) to pursue their distinctive ways of life were recognized and protected by law. Yet League reluctance both to challenge state sovereignty and to upset the fragile European peace constrained its efforts to enforce compliance by states. In 1948, with the establishment of the United Nations and the Declaration of Human Rights, the recognition of cultural diversity was placed on a different footing, grounded in the human rights of each individual. Protection of the 'rights of minorities', a prerogative sullied by its exploitation by the Nazis in the 1930s, was discontinued. Given the individualist philosophical assumptions of the new regime, moreover, rights could not be extended to groups.

However, attention to minority rights and more generally to cultural diversity has received a renewed impetus and reached an unprecedented scale in the last two decades. Under pressure from an ever proliferating range of supra-national institutions (now including not only UN agencies but also, for example, those of the Council of Europe, the Helsinki Convention, the Inter-American institutions and the OSCE) to accommodate with greater justice the 'others' in their midst, be they migrants, minorities or indigenous populations, nation-states have been increasingly challenged to encourage, rather than repress or even merely tolerate, diversity within their boundaries.[9] Group rights has returned to the agenda, involving re-theorizations such as 'the rights of peoples', particularly as a response to concerns about, and mobilizations by, 'indigenous' peoples. Such developments signal a significant historical shift.

Consequently, 'culturalist' claims – claims which invoke notions of culture, tradition, language, religion, ethnicity, locality, tribe or race – have become a familiar rhetorical element in contemporary rights processes. More and more, though not without exception, they are likely to carry weight in contexts of adjudication. They may, additionally, be used to ground and justify other kinds of claims, for example, to land, environmental protection, education, employment and even political autonomy or independence.[10] They may be invoked to argue for exemption from laws binding other citizens, such as the exemption for Sikh men from the requirement to wear motorcycle helmets granted by British law (Poulter 1997: 258), or for legal interpretations that take into account the claimants' particular cultural identities and beliefs. Opposition to infrastructure and economic development projects is now conducted by pointing to the threat these projects represent for cultural survival (see Samson's contribution to this volume).

Invocations of culture have seemingly become inseparable from the language of resistance. However, the political implications of such claims cannot be generalized because culture may be called upon to legitimise reactionary projects as easily as progressive ones. In June 1997 a spokesman for the loyalist Protestant Orangemen in Northern Ireland invoked their 'cultural right' to parade through Catholic neighbourhoods during the 'drumming season' in triumphalist celebration of the historical memory of William of Orange's violent routing of Catholics from the region – a 'right' that had led to riots in the recent past. Conversely, indigenous groups in the Americas that have long been marginalized within formal state institutions are invoking the language of culture and rights in national and international tribunals to further claims to land and political autonomy – a process that Rachel Sieder and Jessica Witchell's paper on the Guatemalan case explores in some detail (see also Kymlicka 1989).

Jane Cowan's chapter on the Macedonian human rights movement reveals a situation of greater ambiguity; the impulse to label this movement as 'progressive' and those resisting it as 'anti-progressive' simply obscures a complex contestation within the community over its identity and the nature of claims it might generate, as well as over tactics and goals. Considering how such conundrums are faced (or avoided) at an international level, Thomas Eriksen's chapter examines the view of culture articulated in UNESCO's 1995 report *Our Creative Diversity*. He shows this product of an international committee to be an optimistic celebration of diversity, seen in fairly essentialist terms, and an affirmation of cultural rights, which skirts round the matter of the explosions that competing claims around culture can trigger. Whether negotiated locally or in meeting-rooms in Geneva and New York, the uses to which culture can be put in relation to rights are evidently multiple.

Culturalist claims may be only slightly more sophisticated versions of ethno-nationalism, or they may represent what has been called a 'strategic essentialism'. Activists from, or working on behalf of, communities making claims are often well aware that they are essentializing something which is, in fact, much more fluid and contradictory, but they do so in order that their claims be heard. Moreover, as David Gellner's chapter illustrates, the proclivity of legal systems to demand clearly defined, context-neutral categories (including categories of identity and membership) in order to be able to classify persons and deal with them on the basis of these categories – the *essentializing proclivities of law*, in other words – contributes enormously to the strategic essentializing of culturally defined groups. According rights to collectivities may exacerbate this tendency by compelling them to define 'a unanimous, or seemingly unanimous, set of demands' (Tamir 1993: 47). This point is important, but not yet well appreciated, as analysts typically view a group's tendency to essentialize as a product solely of its own enchantment with the presuppositions of Romantic or cultural nationalism. James Clifford's (1988) famous account of the Mashpee Indians' courtroom battle – an attempt to institute a land claim which, it transpired, could only be successful if they could prove to the courts that they 'were now' and 'always had been' a 'tribe' – sharply reveals the political pitfalls of arguments deconstructing their 'culture' and emphasizing the situational nature of 'tribal identity'.

Indeed, such insights lead to a larger issue: the extent to which not only national but also international legal regimes, including the human rights regime, dictate the contours and content of claims and even of identities. There is an intriguing, and as yet mostly unexplored, dialectic between the discourse and practices – one might say, the culture – of human rights, and those of the groups that appeal to them. It is not even clear that all the 'cultures' caught up in the process exist prior to rights claims on their behalf; rights may be *constitutive* of cultures and their associated identities. Sieder and Witchell allude to such a phenomenon in Guatemala, and Cowan considers its relevance for understanding the Macedonian human rights movement in northern Greece. To the extent that claimants are compelled to use a language of rights in pursuit of what they need or want, and to portray themselves as certain kinds of persons, when these may be alien to their self-understandings, it is evident that rights discourses are not ethically unambiguous or neutral. While emanating an emancipatory aura, their consequences both for those who use them and for those asked to recognize them are more contradictory. This volume enhances our understanding of the *paradox of rights*, the ways in which rights discourses can be both enabling and constraining.

Rights as culture

A third formulation of the relationship between the terms under investigation could be phrased as: rights *as* culture. It proposes that rights constitute a kind of culture, in the sense that the rights discourse embodies certain features that anthropologists recognize as constituting culture. Rights – understood as rights talk, rights thinking, rights practices – entail certain constructions of self and sociality, and specific modes of agency. This formulation draws from and extends insights developed about law – which is analogous in certain ways to rights, though rights are also a subsidiary element in a larger framework of law – in the 'law and culture' anthropological paradigm, initiated by Clifford Geertz and carried forward by Laura Nader (1996), Laurence Rosen (1989) and non-anthropologists such as Santos (1995). In this paradigm, law is conceived as a worldview or structuring discourse which shapes how the world is apprehended. 'Facts' are not simply lying around waiting to be discovered; they are socially constructed through rules of evidence, legal conventions, and the rhetoric of legal actors. Certain things can be said; others cannot be said and thus simply disappear from view. In many societies, legal reasoning becomes one of the most important ways in which people try to make sense of their world. *Pace* Geertz (1983: 184), law is 'part of a distinctive manner of imagining the real'.

As the human rights regime becomes increasingly entrenched at a global level in international declarations, conventions and agreements which are negotiated, implemented and monitored by national, international and transnational institutions, this understanding of rights as a structuring discourse seems increasingly persuasive. Many analysts already talk about the human rights culture as a core aspect of a new global, transnational culture, a *sui generis* phenomenon of modernity.[11] A 'culture of rights' has its own possibilities and limitations, both as a set of ideas and as a realm of practices. To name a few of its structuring ideas: it is individualistic in conception; it addresses suffering through a legal/technical, rather than an ethical, framework; and it emphasizes certain aspects of human coexistence (an individual's rights) over others (an individual's duties or needs). These are foundational ideas, even though they are contested and modified in an ongoing process, as evidenced in the African Charter, for instance.

With respect to practices, the pursuit of human rights requires people to become involved in specific political and legal processes. It often entails moving between the local site of a particular 'human rights violation', national courts, and supra-national or international fora such as the European Court of Human Rights or the UN Human Rights Commission. However, it is important to understand when and why this *does not* happen, an issue that Anne Griffiths' chapter on Kwena women's use of the Botswana legal system explores. While each of these sites may have its own particular rules and practices, it is the culture of human rights itself which has intensified the ways they interpenetrate. The process may be manipulated, moreover, by claimants who may deem it strategic to have a case fail at national level in order to carry it to an international forum, in the hope of a more sympathetic hearing and an ultimately more favourable resolution. Finally, as Wilson has stressed in an analysis of human rights reporting in Guatemala (1997: 134–160) the culture of human rights dictates that certain ways (and certain ways *only*) of representing violations, motives and the subjectivity of victims be adopted by both claimants and their advocates if they are to have any chance of being heard. As he points out, this is engendered by the fact that human rights are saturated with what Habermas (1971: 112–113) refers to as a 'technocratic consciousness', which entails (again in Habermas' words) 'a repression of ethics as a category of life' (Wilson 1997: 155).

It has been argued that although human rights (as discourse and practice) is in many ways 'culture-like', it constitutes a truncated and artificial culture in relation to the 'more organic' cultures it impinges upon. It is true that this 'culture' differs from what is usually described by the term, as a product of modernity and transnational intercourse. Yet we prefer to turn this criticism on its head, and insist that thinking of human rights as a 'culture', if it is to be useful at all, is useful for precisely this reason: to unsettle the organic assumptions which the term too often carries. Moreover, the ways that this structuring discourse is not bounded in time or space or with respect to particular institutions, but interpenetrates other structuring discourses is an apt illustration of what anthropologists mean when they argue, as Eriksen has in this volume, against the metaphor of a mosaic of bounded and discrete world cultures.

Culture as analytic to rights

We think it helpful, in this context, to disaggregate two aspects of the law-as-culture project which tended either to be conflated, or to oscillate uncertainly between two meanings. The law-as-culture project applied culture to law in two subtly different ways. First, as we outlined in the previous section, it made law-as-culture an *object of analysis* (much as we have done in making rights such an object) in order to delineate the 'culture-like' qualities of law. It also reframed law in relation to culture (while shifting ambiguously between law-*in*-culture, and law-*as*-culture approaches), granting law more autonomy than traditional frameworks had and stressing its own framing capacities. Yet in seeking to reconceptualize the relation between law and culture, and more broadly, between law and society – that is, by showing how law influenced myriad dimensions of people's lives and experiences, but also how social institutions including kinship or social practices such as gossip affected how power was wielded and resisted in legal contexts – this project entailed a second application of culture, this time in its *analytic* sense, to tease out patterns and relationships of meaning and practice between different domains of social life.

It may be that culture is too implicated in the language of neo-romanticism, too laden with its ideological baggage, to be of much use as an analytical tool. It may also be just too indeterminate as a concept to offer the clarity which is so much needed. This is the position of some of the contributors to this volume. Without doubt, few words in the English language are so fetishized, and so contested – and not just by anthropologists – as 'culture'. Raymond Williams, working in the fields of literature and media, saw it as a keyword of British society, incessantly defined and redefined over the course of the last two centuries (1976; see also Kahn 1995). Yet he did not, for that reason, abandon it, but instead went on to rework the concept, helping to inspire the new academic field of cultural studies. A second position articulated in this volume, engaged in constructive dialogue with the first, holds that anthropologists, too, still need such a concept, and in any case that they would be wise not to hand culture over too quickly to those who would essentialize it, if only because the stakes in the real world are so high.

Those of us subscribing to the second position suggest that a similarly reworked anthropological notion of culture retains value as an analytical tool, as a heuristic device that can help the analyst to talk about processes, grasp connections between different domains, and abstract more general patterns and relationships from specific manifestations. This entails a sensibility, a way of seeing and of discerning the connections offered up by the particular context being investigated, rather than a prescriptive set of analytical moves. Roy Wagner's sense of culture as an 'invention' of the anthropologist, a 'foil (and a kind of false objective) to aid the anthropologist in arranging his experiences' (1975: xii), rather than a description of something which exists in the world, is therefore still provocative. Culture in this sense 'does not *cause* behaviour, but summarizes an abstraction from it, and is thus neither normative nor predictive' (Baumann 1996: 11). Culture is a sociological fiction, a shorthand referring to a disordered social field of connected practices and beliefs which are produced out of social action, and thus it is mistaken to imbue it with any independent agency or will of its own.

However, an analytical concept of culture which emphasizes process, fluidity and contestation could still elucidate rights processes, including those with a particular culture as their object, much better than one which negates or underestimates these aspects. As many of our chapters exemplify, this analytical approach to culture in the context of detailed empirical accounts of actual struggles around rights enables a better grasp of both the patterns and the contingencies, the logics and the contradictions, of these social processes.

Theories of culture and rights in political philosophy

The agitations of recent years around rights and culture have posed new challenges to political theory and philosophy. Theorists of rights have been confronted with critiques of universalism and demands that various forms of difference be taken into account when formulating and implementing rights. These critiques have emanated from diverse quarters – from new social movements such as feminism, gay and lesbian liberation, anti-racist politics, from ethnic and nationalist movements, from critical social theory and from post-structuralist deconstructionism – with often quite divergent epistemological assumptions and political goals.[12] Critics have identified both disguised particularisms in universalism (its androcentrism, heterosexism and Eurocentrism) and the exclusions and disparagement towards certain collectivities that it entails (sexism, homophobia, racism). Those theorists of rights who have not simply ignored such criticisms, viewing them presumably as the 'false consciousness' of identity politics (Fraser 1997: 5), have often responded by an axiomatic acceptance of the existence of other cultures and by exploring how their differences affect and are affected by a regime of rights. Strikingly, even though ostensibly opposed in their views on multiculturalism in education or on self-determination for minorities, prominent exponents of both liberal and communitarian positions share similar views on culture.

Thus, in the universalistic ethos of what Michael Walzer (1994) calls 'Liberalism 1', an orthodox liberalism espoused by Ronald Dworkin among others, rules defining rights are meant to be applied uniformly, regardless of the religious, linguistic or gender characteristics of the *dramatis personae*, with certain basic rights (such as freedom of speech and freedom of conscience and religion) considered as absolute. This kind of procedural liberalism was hegemonic in twentieth-century North American politics and in the democratizing countries of Eastern Europe and Latin America. It asserts no *substantive* conception of the common good but only creates mechanisms to facilitate a dialogue over what may constitute a collective good. In substantial works such as *Taking Rights Seriously* (1977), as well as in shorter, more polemical pieces (eg, 1994), Dworkin argues that freedom of speech is an absolute right on which no reservations should be placed by, for example, the need to protect minorities from hate speech. Such a position places Dworkin's model in conflict with the claims of groups which insist that the state should actively facilitate positive recognition of their particular forms of distinctiveness.

Although he supports a procedural liberalism and state neutralism which is blind to difference, Dworkin (1977:160–8), following the philosopher Quine, is an avowed constructionist and opposes grounding basic rights in a notion of natural rights. Unlike many proponents of 'Liberalism 1', he concedes that relativism is 'logically impeccable', though morally wrong. Thus, even if culture rarely figures in his discussions, existing primarily as a source of difference which must be bracketed, the conception of culture which can be abstracted from his work seems unreconstructedly nineteenth century in its bounded, whole and static nature. He sees community, community morality and cultural difference as ontologically prior to rights.

Communitarian approaches that have emerged within political philosophy attempt to address the limits of an alleged philosophical 'atomism' within liberalism, and to incorporate an acknowledgment of the community's role in relation to the subject at two quite different levels: ontological and normative.[13] Much like anthropologists, they stress the social nature of being, and the ways in which subjectivity is formed in the context of social relations. They thus point out the inadequacy of both methodological and ontological individualism for understanding human needs, desires and capacities, which are always formed within – rather than prior to, or outside of – society. It is their arguments at the normative level, however, which pose the most direct difficulties for a liberal conception of justice and rights. Communitarians insist that the community, as the social collectivity in which individual subjectivity is formed and nurtured, and as the site which makes possible the expression of that subject's selfhood, must also be taken into account in considerations of rights and justice.

Charles Taylor, who does not call himself a communitarian yet is often deemed one of its leading theorists, has participated in this debate not only as a philosopher but also as a Canadian of mixed parentage, growing up under the influence of both the English-speaking and the French-speaking Quebecois traditions. In the face of what he and others have perceived as a threat to the long-term collective survival of the 'Quebecker' community, and in the context of the debate around the implementation of the new Canadian Charter of Rights in the 1980s and early 1990s, he has supported political efforts toward Quebec's formal recognition as a distinct society within Canada, a status that would, in exceptional cases, allow the pursuit of collective goals to justify certain limited restrictions on individual freedoms. Taylor's conviction that collective goals may validly be recognized in modern constitutions contrasts with Dworkin's preference for complete state neutrality, and leads him to the position Walzer describes as 'Liberalism 2'. This position accepts the invariant defence of certain rights, such as *habeus corpus*, but encourages flexibility on others, depending on the collectively negotiated view about how distinct cultures in one society should relate, as well as about what constitutes 'the good life', and providing that such decisions are subject to democratic accountability. Taylor argues that communities are culturally distinctive, yet this does not entail, on the evidence of his other work, that he sees Quebecois or any other culture as a fixed, homogeneous and consensual entity. 'Any cultural field involves a struggle', he writes in another context. 'People with different and incompatible views contend, criticize and condemn each other' (1991: 72). More recently, he has reiterated that unity of 'the people' as an agent of decision does not require uniformity (1994: 256) . Indeed, an understanding of culture as static would ill fit his dialogical conception of the formation of subjectivity.

In his essay 'Multiculturalism and "the Politics of Recognition"', however, Taylor assumes the task of assessing the claims of those arguing for the recognition of 'distinct cultural identities'. It is problematic to take the text as representing Taylor's own view on the subject, since sometimes he appears merely to present their views in order to examine them, while at other times he seems to speak with them, extending their insights and elaborating their claims. Without attributing all the views expressed to Taylor himself, we can take his text as a sympathetic presentation of voices within the field of multiculturalism and identity politics, articulating views with which many communitarians concur. In that discussion, culture and the relationships between different cultures emerge as a primary preoccupation. Despite qualifications and although he also uses terms such as 'community', 'distinct society' and 'cultural community', Taylor often slips into a more reified rhetoric. Cultures are referred to as distinct, bounded entities, even if they are not necessarily co-terminous with a national society, but rather, are 'commingled in each individual society' (1992:72).

In both liberal and communitarian texts, 'the community' is the favoured term for a collectivity, rather than 'culture', which has made its appearance rather belatedly. Both theories treat the community as a universalized abstraction, one whose scale is usually not specified. Kymlicka (1989) argues that communitarians have underestimated the importance which liberalism attaches to the community, in the sense of acknowledging that human beings are ineluctably social and that an individual's revision of his or her projects necessarily occurs within a communal field, even if contemporary liberals such as Ronald Dworkin and John Rawls do not talk about this very much. However, both approaches, have until recently tended to take 'the community' as meaning 'the political community' (that is, the nation-state), assuming that the the political community and what Kymlicka calls 'the cultural community' coincide. The mobilization over the past few decades of marginalized groups and categories of person – the 'others' within – aimed precisely to upset this complacent assumption, both in politics and theory, by citing the multiple axes of differentiation within 'the community'. Yet it could be argued that the alternative conceptualization they were proffering, of multiple and distinct 'cultures' coexisting within a larger 'community' (or society or polity), simply transposed the problem to another level. The units are perhaps smaller, and mono-focused (around a specific 'identity'), but assumptions about, and sometimes demands for, uniformity and consensus can remain.

In both models, cultures, like communities, simply exist. They are empirically and logically prior to the question of rights. Neither Dworkin nor Taylor (or those he is representing) poses the questions: how does 'culture' come to exist and through what social and political processes? In what sense may 'culture' itself be the product of legal categories and institutional practices? The *a priori* and decontextualized view of distinctiveness exhibited by both Dworkin and Taylor ignores the cross-over, intermingling and borrowing which undermine simplistic depictions of 'distinct cultures'. In a rejoinder to Taylor's essay, Anthony Appiah (1992) remarked that the important point about cultures is not that they are *distinct*, but rather that they are *related*. 'Black culture', for instance, is in no way simply an expression of the African roots of former slaves, but something that emerges out of certain politically asymmetrical historical relationships between social groups. It is, in addition, a response to a *contemporary* politics of culture in which, as Appiah has ruefully noted, the more culturally similar Americans become, the more loudly they proclaim their cultural differences. Culture neither is, nor should be, the sole basis of identity, political or otherwise, according to Appiah. Indeed, he equates the politics of recognition with the politics of compulsion, where difference is tightly scripted and forced upon the bearer of an identity.

The multiculturalist emphasis on the equal worth of different cultures and the indignity of cultural disparagement also comes through in Taylor's answer to a famous remark attributed to Saul Bellow, that 'When the Zulus produce a Tolstoy, we will read him'. Taylor takes issue with Bellow's Eurocentric reasoning: 'The possibility that the Zulus, while having the same potential for culture formation as anyone else, might nevertheless have come up with a culture that is any less valuable than others is ruled out from the start' (1992: 42).

While we might want to be sympathetic to Taylor's puncturing of Bellow's arrogance (cultural or otherwise), we would be reticent to do so on the basis of notions of an independent and benign process of 'culture formation' which leads to 'a culture'. As any cursory perusal of the history of the articulations of white and Zulu nationalisms in South Africa would show, 'Zulu-ness' is very much the product of concrete political processes.[14] These include apartheid policies, which created a homeland on the basis of a single, fixed vision of 'Zulu culture', but also the violent, primordialist ethnonationalism pursued by Chief Mangosuthu Buthelezi and the Inkatha Freedom Party during the collapse of apartheid in 1990–4 in particular.

When legal and political philosophers make statements about culture extracted from any specific social and historical context, they are liable to ignore its shifting political meanings. Lacking a theory of the relational attributes of cultures and their capacities for transformation, both scholars and activists who support cultural recognition tend to become preoccupied with 'cultural survival', rather than seeing cultural change as potentially positive, as well as inevitable. In the stark distinction between mass or majoritarian cultures, on the one hand, and disadvantaged minority cultures, on the other, internal homogeneity is too easily assumed and taken as natural. An endangered 'culture' is perceived as a pre-existing given which must be defended, rather than as something creatively reworked during struggles to actualize rights.

Such difficulties surrounding the usages of 'culture' and 'community' in relation to 'rights' have not gone unremarked within the field of political philosophy. Kymlicka, notably, has argued that many of the concerns about culture and community presented by communitarians, including cultural survival, are best defended from *within* a liberal framework of rights (1989). This requires, however, a more differentiated understanding of the term 'culture'. For Kymlicka, 'Culture is defined, as I think it should be defined for these purposes, in terms of the existence of a viable community of individuals with a shared heritage (language, history, etc.)' (1989: 168). He then distinguishes between 'cultural membership', a phrase acknowledging a person's attachment to a 'cultural structure' seen as 'a context of individual choice', which both liberals and communitarians claim to value; and the *character* of a culture at a particular historical moment, which is *not* coterminous with 'the culture' as such, since it may represent simply the version of 'the culture' promoted by the social groups which happen to be in power.

Kymlicka further criticizes communitarian arguments which assume, rather than investigate, 'shared meanings' and 'shared projects'.

These are caveats that we endorse. They resonate with many points made within the anthropological debate, some of which we have reiterated here. Kymlicka's more differentiated approach to culture seems a promising move. Yet we note that it illuminates some cases better than others. It is significant that Kymlicka's primary political concern is with Canada's aboriginal communities. While not making them paradigmatic, he insists that their case has wrongly been seen as anomalous and of little interest, when, in fact 'far more of the world's minorities are in a similar position to American Indians (i.e. as a stable and geographically distinct historical community with separate language and culture rendered a minority by conquest or immigration or the redrawing of political boundaries)' (1989: 258). The formal similarities to which Kymlicka points are intriguing. Yet the particular features of the Canadian case, including relatively recent sustained contact, in certain cases, between aboriginal groups and the European settlers and state institutions, the geographically remote locations concerned and the consequently restricted interaction between these two groups, and the ambiguity around the rights and sovereignty of aboriginal communities (see Samson in this volume), differ substantially from cases of minority groups in Europe, for example. There, such a degree of isolation is virtually unthinkable. Even when groups proclaim cultural difference, they typically do so from a context of greater social proximity to and interaction within and across groups. As an everyday lived experience, this can produce hybridities of identity and cultural forms, as much as perceptions of difference, and one is led to ask when, why and from whom such claims arise. We are brought back to where we started, to the task of trying to account for claims to culture as a human right in an increasingly globalized, post-socialist world.

Conclusion: towards better theory and practice

The cases in which rights and culture are mutually implicated have proliferated, emerging in the context of diverse local and national regimes and stymying the international community's efforts to deal with them coherently at the level of principle. It is therefore unlikely that any single model of the relationship between culture and rights, or between minority and majority rights, is going to be adequate for all cases, either normatively or analytically. Clearly, all of us, but especially those involved in advocating or adjudicating rights such as theorists, NGOs and legal and political institutions, need to become more sceptical about claims to culture, and to examine more closely the power relations and divisions they sometimes mask. At the same time, we need to be more cognizant of the role played by the law in essentializing categories and fixing identities, as a concomitant of its task of developing general principles to include, ideally, all possible cases. But the search for a single theory that would provide definitive guidance in all cases is quixotic, not only because of the existence of irreducible difference and contingency across contexts and situations, but also because it misconstrues what actually happens when universal principles are applied in the real world.

Although there is certainly scope for refining theories of rights in relation to culture, a project to which we hope this volume will contribute, we think it is time that more attention is paid to empirical, contextual analyses of specific rights struggles. This intellectual strategy allows us to follow how individuals, groups, communities and states use a discourse of rights in the pursuit of particular ends, and how they become enmeshed in its logic. It reveals the moral ambiguities that are not always noticed in purely theoretical accounts, as well as the unavoidable messiness of social life, where competing claims and contestation over meaning are not a sign of cultural or community failure but, rather, part of the human condition. It enables us to ask: who benefits from this or that version of culture, tradition or community? Are there different versions at issue and who subscribes to each? What is the nature of the competition over these terms?

Empirical studies offer a further opportunity of exploring the ways that rights struggles no longer necessarily entail a single system of justice, but more typically, involve political and legal institutions at different levels – local, regional, national and international. Claims about rights to culture – Sikh protests against having to wear motorcycle helmets in the UK, Muslim women's insistence on wearing headscarves in European societies (Dembour forthcoming) – are among the most likely to traverse these multiple levels, as claimants appeal to higher authorities to overturn decisions of lower bodies. However, the interrelations and interpenetrations of the different levels are complex and by no means unidirectional, and speak as much to issues of the cultures of the different legal, political and judiciary systems as to the cultures which are their object.

Finally, case studies such as those presented and analyzed here by anthropologists and sociologists enable a stronger grounding of the conversation between theory and practice. This is unquestionably a concern for theorists and activists alike. Claims around culture and rights show no sign of abating. To numberless activists and their communities, they provide a powerful, universally recognized language into which to translate – and validate – local struggles. There is a pressing need to develop approaches to such claims which are principled and theoretically informed, yet also sensitive to the contingencies and ambiguities that the world never ceases to offer up.

NOTES

1 For a lucid anthropological discussion of multiculturalism, particularly in France, see Grillo 1998.
2 See, for example, Asad 1979; Clifford 1986; Kahn 1989; Marcus 1986; Ortner 1984; Yengoyam 1986.
3 For a particularly brilliant and detailed case study of this phenomenon, see Baumann 1996. There is an extensive anthropological literature on the reification of culture, particularly 'customs' and 'traditions', for strategic aims. See for example Cowan 1988; Handler 1988; Keesing and Tonkinson 1982; McDonald 1989.
4 See An-Na'im 1990; Howard 1993; *Journal of Anthropological Research* 1997; North–South Coalition 1998; Renteln 1990.
5 Thus in Africa, until recently, the notion of an 'indigenous people' was meaningless, and difference politics was instead subsumed under the category of 'race' and then 'ethnicity'. Yet by the 1990s, due to their subordinate position in Nigeria's ethnicized hierarchy and because of contact with organizations such as UNPO (Unrepresented Nations and Peoples Organization), funded in part by the Body Shop, Ogoni politicians such as Ken Saro-Wiwa came to represent the Ogoni as an 'indigenous people'.
6 On the latter, see Clifford Geertz's (1983) discussion of *haqq* in Islamic law.
7 Legal positivism sees law as a 'given', made up of data-or rules-which can be recognized and analyzed according to certain observational tests; see Hart (1961); Cotterrell (1992: 8–10).
8 The Asian Human Rights Charter of 1998 (*www.hk.super.net/~ahrchk*) opposes (p.5) 'the exhortation of spurious theories of "Asian Values" which are a thin disguise for their authoritarianism'.
9 See Thornberry 1991; Wheatley 1996.
10 See Clifford 1988; Sieder 1997; the chapters by Gellner, Sieder and Witchell in this volume.
11 For example, Hannerz 1996; Pries 1996; Rabossi 1990; Rorty 1993.
12 There is a massive literature critiquing universalistic approaches to rights and justice. See for example Kymlicka 1995, as well as the interesting overview of three dimensions of critique – post-modernist, cultural feminist and interculturalist – in chapter 2 of Tully 1995. A particularly fruitful critique has developed within feminist political and critical theory; see for example, Fraser 1989, 1997; Okin 1989; Pateman 1988; Young 1990.
13 See Bell 1993; Sandel 1982; Taylor 1979; Tuck 1994.
14 See Shula Marks 1986 and Carolyn Hamilton 1995.

REFERENCES

An-Na'im, A.A. 1992. *Human Rights in Cross-Cultural Perspectives: A Quest for Consensus*. Philadelphia: Temple University Press.

Appiah, A. 1992. Identity, Authenticity, Survival: Multicultural Societies and Social Reproduction. In *Multiculturalism and 'The Politics of Recognition'*. (Ed.) A. Gutmann. Princeton, NJ: Princeton University Press.

Asad, T. 1979. Anthropology and the Analysis of Ideology. *Man* 14, 603–627.

Baumann, G. 1996. *Contesting Culture: Discourses of Identity in Multi-Ethnic London*. Cambridge: Cambridge University Press.

Bell, D. 1993. *Communitarianism and its Critics*. Oxford: Oxford University Press.

Berlin, I. 2000. *The Roots of Romanticism*. London: Pimlico.

Bobbio, N. 1996. *The Age of Rights*. Cambridge: Polity Press.

Brightman, R. 1995. Forget Culture: Replacement, Transcendence, Relexification. *Cultural Anthropology* 10(4), 509–546.

Clifford, J. 1986. Introduction: Partial Truths. In *Writing Culture: The Poetics and Politics of Ethnography*. (Eds.) J. Clifford and G. Marcus. Berkeley: University of California Press.

Clifford, J. 1988. Identity in Mashpee. *The Predicament of Culture*. Berkeley: University of California Press.

Cotterrell, R. 1992. *The Sociology of Law*. 2nd edition. London: Butterworths.

Cowan, J. 1988. Folk Truth: When the Scholar Comes to Carnival in a 'Traditional' Community. *Journal of Modern Greek Studies* 6(2), 245–260.

Cowan, J. n.d. Personal observations at seminar on 'Culture and Human Rights' at meetings of the United Nations, Geneva, April 1998.

Dembour, M-B. Forthcoming. The Cases that were not to be: Explaining the Dearth of Case Law on Freedom of Religion at Strasbourg. In *Morals of Legitimacy. Between Agency and the System*. (Ed.) I. Pardo. Oxford: Berghahn.

Donnelly, J. 1989. *Universal Human Rights in Theory and Practice*. Ithaca, NY: Cornell University Press.

Dworkin, R. 1977. *Taking Rights Seriously*. London: Duckworth.

Dworkin, R. 1994. A New Map of Censorship. *Index on Censorship* 1(2), 9–15.

Featherstone, M. (Ed.). 1990. *Global Culture: Nationalism, Globalization and Modernity*. London: Sage.

Fraser, N. 1989. *Unruly Practices: Power, Discourse and Gender in Contemporary Social Theory*. Minneapolis: University of Minnesota Press.

Fraser, N. 1997. *Justice Interruptus: Critical Reflections on the 'Postsocialist' Condition*. London: Routledge.

Geertz, C. 1983. Local Knowledge: Fact and Law in Comparative Perspective. *Local Knowledge*. New York: Basic Books.

Grillo, R. 1998. *Pluralism and the Politics of Difference: State, Culture and Ethnicity in Comparative Perspective*. Oxford: Clarendon Press.

Habermas, J. 1971. *Towards a Rational Society*, trans. J. J. Shapiro. London: Heinemann.

Hamilton, C. (Ed.). 1995. *The Mfecane Aftermath: Reconstructive Debates in South African History*. Johannesburg: University of the Witwatersrand Press.

Handler, R. 1988. *Nationalism and the Politics of Culture in Quebec*. Madison: University of Wisconsin Press.

Hart, H.L.A. 1961. *The Concept of Law*. Oxford: Oxford University Press.

Hannerz, U. 1996. *Transnational Connections: Culture, People, Places*. London: Routledge.

Howard, R. 1993. Cultural Absolutism and the Nostalgia for Community. In *Human Rights Quarterly* 15, 315–338.

Kahn, J. 1989. Culture, Demise or Resurrection? *Critique of Anthropology* 9(2), 5–25.

Kahn, J. 1995. *Culture, Multiculture, Postculture*. London: Sage.

Keesing, R.M. and R. Tonkinson (Eds.). 1982. Reinventing Traditional Culture: The Politics of Kastom in Island Melanesia. *Mankind* (Special Issue) 13(4).

Kymlicka, W. 1989. *Liberalism, Community and Culture*. Oxford: Clarendon Press.

Kymlicka, W. 1995. *Multicultural Citizenship: A Liberal Theory of Minority Rights*. Oxford: Oxford University Press.

Marks, S. 1986. *The Ambiguities of Dependence in South Africa: Class, Nationalism and the State in Twentieth Century Natal*. Baltimore: Johns Hopkins University Press.

McDonald, M. 1989. *'We are not French!' Language, Culture and Identity in Brittany*. London: Routledge.

Messer, E. 1993. Anthropology and Human Rights. *Annual Review of Anthropology* 22, 221–249.

Nader, L. 1996. *Law in Culture and Society*. Chicago: Aldine.

North–South Coalition. 1998. *Human Rights: Universal or Culture Specific*. Information Bulletin, n. 1.

Okin, S.M. 1989. *Justice, Gender and the Family*. New York: Basic Books.

Pannikar, R. 1982. Is the Notion of Human Rights a Western Concept? *Diogenes* 120, 75–102

Pateman, C. 1988. *The Sexual Contract*. Stanford: Stanford University Press.

Pollis, A. 1996. Cultural Relativism Revisited: Through a State Prism. *Human Rights Quarterly* 18, 316–344.

Poulter, S. 1997. The Rights of Ethnic, Religious and Linguistic Minorities. *European Human Rights Law Review* 3, 254–264.

Preis, A-B.S. 1996. Human Rights as Cultural Practice: An Anthropological Critique. *Human Rights Quarterly* 18, 286–315.

Rabossi, E. 1990. La Teoria de los Derechos Humanos Naturalizada. *Revista del Centro de Estudios Constitucionales* (Madrid) 5, 159–179.

Renteln, A.D. 1985. The Unanswered Challenge of Relativism and the Consequences for Human Rights. *Human Rights Quarterly* 7, 514–540.

Renteln, A.D. 1990. *International Human Rights: Universalism versus Relativism*. London: Sage.

Robertson, R. 1992. *Globalization: Social Theory and Global Culture*. London: Sage.

Rorty, R. 1993. Human Rights, Rationality and Sentimentality. In *On Human Rights: The Oxford Amnesty Lectures 1993*. (Eds.) S. Shute and S. Hurley. New York: Basic Books.

Rosen, L. *The Anthropology of Justice: Law as Culture in Islamic Society*. Cambridge: Cambridge University Press.

Sandel, M. 1992. *Liberalism and the Limits of Justice*. Cambridge: Cambridge University Press.

Santos, B. de Sousa 1995. *Toward a New Common Sense: Law, Science and Politics in the Paradigmatic Transition*. Routledge: New York.

Street, B. 1993. Culture is a Verb: Anthropological Aspects of Language and Cultural Process. In *Language and Culture*. (Eds.) D. Graddol, L. Thompson and M. Byram. Clevedon: BAAL and Multilingual Matters.

Tamir, Y. 1993. *Liberal Nationalism*. Princeton, NJ: Princeton University Press.

Taylor, C. 1979. Atomism. In *Powers, Possessions and Freedom: Essays in Honour of G.E.M. Macpherson*. (Ed.) A. Kontos. Toronto: University of Toronto Press.

Taylor, C. 1991. *The Ethics of Authenticity*. Cambridge, MA and London: Harvard University Press.

Taylor, C. 1992. *Multiculturalism and 'The Politics of Recognition'* (with commentary by Amy Gutmann, editor, Steven C. Rockefeller, Michael Walzer and Susan Wolf). Princeton, NJ: Princeton University Press.

Taylor, C. 1994. Reply and Rearticulation: Charles Taylor Replies. In *Philosophy in an Age of Pluralism: The Philosophy of Charles Taylor in Question*. (Ed.) J. Tully. Cambridge: Cambridge University Press.

Tennant, C. 1994. Indigenous Peoples, International Institutions and the International Legal Literature. *Human Rights Quarterly* 16, 1–57.

Thornberry, P. 1991. *International Law and the Rights of Minorities*. Oxford: Clarendon Press.

Tuck, R. 1994. Rights and Pluralism. In *Philosophy in an Age of Pluralism: The Philosophy of Charles Taylor in Question*. (Ed.) J. Tully. Cambridge: Cambridge University Press.

Tully, J. 1995. *Strange Multiplicity: Constitutionalism in an Age of Diversity*. Cambridge: Cambridge University Press.

Turner, T. 1993. Anthropology and Multiculturalism: What is Anthropology that Multiculturalists Should be Mindful of? *Cultural Anthropology* 8:4, 411–429.

Turner, T. and C. Nagengast (guest eds). 1997. Universal Human Rights Versus Cultural Relativity. *Journal of Anthropological Research* (Special Issue) 53(3).

Wagner, R. 1981. *The Invention of Culture*. Chicago: University of Chicago Press.

Walzer, M. 1983. *Spheres of Justice: A Defense of Pluralism and Equality*. Oxford and Cambridge, MA: Blackwell.

Walzer, M. 1994. 'Comment' on/in Charles Taylor. *Multiculturalism and 'The Politics of Recognition'*. Princeton: Princeton University Press.

Wheatley, S. 1996. Current Topic: The Framework Convention for the Protection of National Minorities. *European Human Rights Law Review* 6, 583–591.

Williams, R. 1976. *Keywords: A Vocabulary of Culture and Society*. London: Fontana Croom Helm.

Williams, R. 1981. *Culture*. Glasgow: Fontana Paperbacks.

Wilson, R.A. (Ed.) 1997a. *Human Rights, Culture and Context: Anthropological Perspectives*. London: Pluto Press.

Wilson, R.A. 1997b. Representing Human Rights Violations: Social Contexts and Subjectivities. In *Human Rights, Culture and Context: Anthropological Perspectives*. (Ed.) R. A. Wilson. London: Pluto Press.

Young, I.M. 1990. *Justice and the Politics of Difference*. Princeton: Princeton University Press.

Part I

Setting universal rights

There was a time in anthropology when cultural relativism was advocated as a means to counteract the negative effects brought about by the imposition of universal rights. However, demanding that 'culture' be respected is misleading, since the kind of bounded culture implied in such a formulation simply does not exist. What is more, the universal rights implied in the same formulation do not exist either, in the sense that rights, including so-called universal ones, are not natural and eternal but always emergent and historically specific. What is needed, therefore, are more sophisticated views of both relativism and universalism, but also of the relationship between these two moral positions. The five chapters included in the first part of this volume call for an empirical and/or theoretical reassessment of the dichotomy traditionally posited between relativism and universalism.

The first four contributions examine the relationship between ostensibly universal rules and abhorrent, or at least discouraged, practices: domestic violence against women, female genital mutilation, child prostitution, and customary marriage. These classic cases, examined in the respective national contexts of the US state of Hawai'i, France, Thailand and Botswana, are considered by most commentators to be emblematic of the opposition between universalism and relativism. The authors, however, offer a different reading. On the one hand, they reject the idea of a stark opposition between the two poles of universalism and relativism. On the other hand, they call for attentiveness to empirical needs that are discovered through dialogue rather than posited in an abstract and essentialized way. The last contribution to this section examines the conceptual premises underlying a recent UNESCO policy document; it reassesses the debate between universalism and relativism by making clear that the document implicitly relies on an inadequate concept of culture.

In the first contribution, Sally Engle Merry stresses that the enduring debate between universalism and relativism is grounded in historical processes of colonization and decolonization. She reminds us that the

debate is premised upon a fixed and abstract conception of *both* rights
and culture. However, neither rights nor culture should be essentialized.
Both concepts are historical, fluid, and contested; they have been and
are continually changing. Merry traces the development of each concept
in the twentieth century and then looks at the ways in which they have
been linked in new ways by the Hawaiian sovereignty movement. Her
specific interest is how women activists seek to develop indigenous
concepts of women's rights at the same time as they draw on the global
framework of rights and feminism to fight domestic violence. In this
struggle, local appropriation leads to a transformation of the appropriated institution. The implication for the universalism/relativism
debate is that it is unlikely to be resolved in the abstract since its terms
take on new meanings following shifts in the political meaning of each
position.

For her part, Marie-Bénédicte Dembour argues that universalism and
relativism are positions which do not exist independently from each
other. She uses the example of the French excision trials, where judgements have oscillated between suspended condemnations, acquittal and
firm condemnation, to illustrate her argument that those adjudicating
are always caught in intermediary positions in a pendulum-like movement. It is clear to her that the perennial debate which invites us to
choose between (a potentially arrogant) universalism and (a potentially
indifferent) relativism is not confined to a North–South divide. This
distinction arises everywhere rights are being claimed, as evidenced by
the doctrine of the margin of appreciation developed by the European
Court of Human Rights. Dembour concludes that we must accept being
torn between the two extremes of universalism and relativism in making
our way through (political and moral) life.

Like female genital mutilation, child prostitution is often heralded as
a practice which should be eradicated without any need for further
discussion. Heather Montgomery invites us to rethink the apparent
unassailability of this universalist position. On the basis of fieldwork
with Thai children led by poverty to prostitution, she asks whether the
1989 UN Convention on the Rights of the Child imposes rights that the
children do not actually want. Enforcing the children's right to be free
from sexual exploitation in effect means removing them from their
family, thus infringing another right the children claim they value more.
Moreover, the children find it important to fulfil their filial duty to
support their parents – which is not to say that 'culture' *per se* requires
them to prostitute themselves. Montgomery notes that her data do not
warrant a dichotomy between cultural relativism and universal rights as
mutually exclusive moral frameworks. She argues that what is needed

are discussions which explore what is best for children, given their unique cultural and economic circumstances.

In her case-study of Kwena women's rights, Anne Griffiths looks at another international document, the 1979 UN Convention on the Elimination of All Forms of Discrimination Against Women. Focusing on the provisions dealing with marriage, Griffiths questions the adequacy of the Convention for relieving difficult local circumstances, especially for Botswanan peasant women. In the name of sexual equality, the Convention favours monogamy and registration of marriage. However, through detailed family life histories which explore how women negotiate procreative relationships, Griffiths shows that peasant women are often, in practice, precluded from entering the form of marriage envisaged by the Convention. These women benefit economically in relations with male partners by being able to demonstrate that, over the years, a customary marriage does indeed exist. Griffiths does not deny that an elite, including, most famously, the lawyer Unity Dow, has mobilized a Western-based rights discourse to promote women's interests. But she insists that international legislation must be sensitive to context in order to meet the needs of different groups within one state. She calls for a non-essentializing pluralism which, grounded in the reality of people's lives, is neither universalist nor relativist.

In the last contribution to this section, Thomas Hylland Eriksen discusses the premises and implications of the 1995 UNESCO document *Our Creative Diversity*. Eriksen highlights how the document, in a way somewhat reminiscent of Lévi-Strauss, propounds *both* a respect for cultural difference and a global ethic. He notes that the document manoeuvres between cultural relativism and moral universalism, but never makes this clear. While it includes a dynamic and plural concept of culture, its overall bias is nonetheless towards a view of the world as made up of an archipelago of diverse, loosely interconnected, bounded cultures. Eriksen stresses that respect for culture does not necessarily lead to tolerance. Failing to tackle the contradiction inherent in promoting a relativistic view of development and a universalist view of ethics is at best naïve and at worst dangerous. For him, the choice is clear. Not only can we not afford to treat issues related to cultural rights lightly, but the Boasian concept of culture is redundant anyway. This is because there is no need to refer to culture to support local values, context or history. In his opinion, so-called cultural rights (to religion, language and so on) are best viewed as special instances of individual rights.

Eriksen urges us to reject the concept of culture inherent in the idea of cultural relativism. The second part of this volume will further explore why the concept of culture, as used in contemporary rights struggles, is problematic. For the moment let us note that, in their effort to reassess the debate between universalism and relativism, the contributions included in this part of the book have tended to eschew the term 'culture'. What their authors have shown is that universalism and relativism cannot in themselves do justice to reality. The two terms are umbrella terms for a range of different and changing political, moral and legal positions. As Merry suggests, they come to encompass different political strategies as history unfolds. As Dembour shows, where one is found, so is the other. On the basis of their fieldwork, Montgomery and Griffith add that practice needs to be attentive to empirical needs, rather than being beholden to an abstract debate. These conclusions are consistent with each other.

2   Changing rights, changing culture

Sally Engle Merry

Introduction

The intense and enduring debate between universalism and relativism in the field of human rights is premised on a fixed and abstract conception of both culture and rights. The debate focuses on the relative merits of adopting a universal system of rights in comparison to protecting cultural diversity. Presented in this fashion, the debate becomes one between culture and rights, in which the natures of both appear uncontested and self-evident. But both concepts are fluid and changing, theoretically as well as empirically. Over the past decade, anthropologists have developed a far more unbounded and contested understanding of culture. The notion of rights deployed within transnational human rights talk has stretched to include a broad range of new meanings well beyond its individualistic European forebear. Meanwhile, globalization and capitalist expansion have transformed local social systems, shifting their repertoires of cultural meanings, while the explosion of the number of international non-governmental organizations (NGOs) and international dialogues and conferences under UN auspices has changed human rights. This chapter explores the changing meanings of both rights and culture and examines how local human rights activists are struggling to create a new space which incorporates both cultural differences and transnational conceptions of human rights.

I became acutely aware of the limitations of conventional thinking about the nature of culture and rights while listening to a panel discussion on violence against women at a 1998 conference in the Solomon Islands. The panelists, from the Solomon Islands, Australia and Samoa, insisted that they were not interested in importing a Western, rights-based model for understanding women's rights and protection from violence. They wanted to develop an indigenous conception of rights. One man told the panel that there in the Solomon Islands men valued women, paid a high bride price for them and protected them. He did not understand what else the women wanted. The panelists replied that this was not what they had in mind, struggling to describe an indigenous concept that was different from the one the man had proposed. One Solomon Islands woman resorted to the conception of women's rights to equality developed at the Beijing Conference in 1995 to make clear how their views differed from those of the male speaker.

This discussion revealed both the desire for an indigenous conception of women's status which includes safety from violence and the importance of the global framework of rights and feminism in developing this conception. In this panel discussion, as in countless other local events, the women were searching for a way to articulate goals of equal decision-making, respect and safety. They wanted the strength of the rights framework, without its individualizing, Western implications and alienation from their own local cultural understandings. The efforts of these women are typical of current human rights activists' endeavours to combine conceptions of rights with appreciation for local cultural difference.

Relativism in the first half of the twentieth century

The contradiction between rights and culture is typically described as an opposition between universalism, in the form of a transnational but European-derived conception of rights, and relativism, in the form of respect for local cultural differences. But posing the choices in such a dichotomous way ignores the extent to which activists, local people and scholars have negotiated these contradictions and redefined both the meanings of rights and the meanings of culture. The universalism/ relativism debate essentializes both culture and rights. Rights are understood as a uniquely Western idea, derived from Enlightenment conceptions of the Rights of Man which emerged in the late eighteenth century in Europe and devolved only on individuals. Culture, on the other hand, is understood as a homogenous, integrated system of beliefs and values attached to a relatively small and isolated group of people. It was this conception of culture which spawned relativism as a moral perspective.

In the early twentieth century, American anthropology promoted relativism in this sense. One of the major proponents of this position, Melville Herskovitz, built on the tradition of ethical relativism originated by Franz Boas and developed by Ruth Benedict (1972: 35–6). Herskovitz's cultural relativism began with a critique of evolutionary theory and the denigration of 'primitive' peoples. He argued that it is impossible to evaluate different cultures by any universal standard because even when other cultures are oppressive, they are still valued by their members as the best way of life for themselves (1972: 8–9). 'The very core of cultural relativism is the social discipline that comes of respect for differences – of mutual respect' (1972: 33). This doctrine affirmed the values of each culture and rejected notions that some were more primitive and childlike, or less sophisticated than others. Herskovitz's major enemy was ethnocentrism, 'the point of view that one's own way of life is to be preferred to all others', along with the impact of this position on programmes of action that are detrimental to other peoples (1972: 21). Writing during the colonial period, he was concerned about massive efforts to reshape peoples defined as 'primitive'.

Cultural relativism was a new idea at the turn of the century. It replaced earlier views that the West was the pinnacle of evolution with a far more equivocal and critical view of Western society (Hatch 1997). Benedict was sceptical about Western culture and its claims to moral superiority. She was not free of judgements – she condemned some societies as warlike and some for having jealous marital outbursts, for example – but she understood the individual in any society as behaving as he or she did because of cultural conditioning, which diminished his or her culpability (Hatch 1997: 375–6). Hatch argues that this Boasian perspective – that non-Western views are as valuable as those of the West – has continued to serve as a fundamental principle for contemporary human rights movements (1997: 380).

Boasian relativism was itself a product of its historical period. The early twentieth century saw the peak of colonialism in Europe and was a time of strong pressure for assimilation for the vast tide of immigrants reaching the US (Higham 1955; see Herskovitz 1972). The pressure on colonized peoples and on indigenous groups within European settler-states to adopt Euro-American cultural practices, law, and governance was strong. Indigenous peoples in a range of colonial and settler situations faced an unrelenting assault on their religions, languages, festivals, and marriage practices, often buttressed by criminal penalties for these activities.[1] Boasian relativism challenged this assault, asserting not that all cultures were equal but that one could not be evaluated according to the value system of another.

The relativism developed by the Boasians, especially Herskovitz, influenced the statement prepared by the Executive Board of the American Anthropological Association in 1947 for submission to the UN Commission on Human Rights, objecting to the proposed Universal Declaration on Human Rights (1947: 539–543). As the authors, probably including Herskovitz, asked (1947: 539): 'How can the proposed Declaration be applicable to all human beings, and not be a statement of rights conceived only in terms of the values prevalent in the countries of Western Europe and America?' The statement argued that notions such as the 'white man's burden' had justified control over the affairs of millions of people worldwide, and that 'the history of the expansion of the western world has been marked by the demoralization of human personality and the disintegration of human rights among the peoples over whom hegemony has been established' (1947: 541). Herskovitz was primarily concerned with the failure of the universal values of the Declaration to recognize the validity of different ways of life.

Those who opposed the Declaration were anthropologists who had studied colonized peoples in Africa and the US. But concerns about protecting cultural autonomy did not necessarily apply to other societies. As the anthropologist Julian Steward pointed out (1948: 351), 'If the plea that cultural values be respected means merely that the primitive peoples, who are on the receiving end of civilizing influences, be treated with greater understanding and tolerance, there can be little objection to it'. But, he continued, did that mean approval of the social caste system of India or the racial caste system of the United States? Or approval of the exploitation of primitive peoples through Euro-American economic imperialism? When the anthropological gaze shifted to modern states, there was clearly much to condemn. No one advocated tolerance towards Nazi Germany.

Clearly, this debate foreshadows contemporary arguments about universalism and relativism. At the time, the debate depended on what was meant by 'culture'. Herskovitz envisioned a small, conquered people, while Steward included contemporary state societies. Even in the 1940s the debate over universalism and relativism was premised on particular understandings of 'culture'. Moreover, these positions were grounded in the particular historical conditions of the late 1940s, especially the Holocaust and the transformative impact of colonialism on rural communities.

The emergence of human and women's rights

Human rights has continued to be a problematic category for anthropology. In the past decade, many anthropologists have tried to bridge this uneasy opposition (see Messer 1993), either by seeking to ground universal human rights principles within all human societies (Handweker 1997; Renteln 1988; 1990), or by interpreting the expansion of human rights as another global cultural process, following on the heels of capitalism, colonialism, and the nation-state, which endeavours to ameliorate the consequences of these institutions (Merry 1997; Wilson 1997). There has been a sustained effort to develop distinctive national and regional conceptions of human rights which mediate between universal concepts and more specific cultural understandings (An-Na'im 1990; 1992; Cohen, Hyden, & Nagen 1993). At the same time, many nations defend practices which may be harmful to women or other vulnerable populations in terms of 'culture' (Zechneter 1997). Others are mounting challenges to the cultural practices of other societies in the name of protecting women from violence, such as the campaign against female genital mutilation. Finally, a growing number of scholars argues that human rights itself is a neo-colonial discourse, incorporating conceptions of paternalism and infantilization and entitling large and powerful nations to intervene in the affairs of small and vulnerable countries, much as 'mother' countries did during colonialism.

The stark opposition between human rights and culture is a function of essentialized and non-historical ideas of rights and culture. Recognizing the extent to which both are fluid, contested, and changing entities remakes this opposition. It is clear that human rights as a discourse and an approach to justice developed from Western cultural roots and was promoted, in the early post-war period, largely by representatives of the Americas and Europe (Leary 1990). The 1948 Universal Declaration of Human Rights was drafted almost entirely by Westerners or Western-trained representatives from Africa and Asia, and the Covenants on economic, social, and cultural rights, and on civil and political rights, although passed in 1966, were largely drafted before decolonization and the admission of many African states into the UN (An-Na'im 1990: 348–51).

But human rights have been changing over the past fifty years. Transnational organizations such as the UN and innumerable non-governmental organizations (NGOs) whose activities constitute an international civil society have contributed to the development and expansion of human rights (Keck & Sikkink 1998; Turner 1997). They have created a new legal order through transnational processes of information gathering, conferences and discussions under the auspices of the UN and regional bodies (see Santos 1995). Conventions, treaties and implementation systems are created by international teams (see Riles 1999), then ratified by states which assume responsibility for enforcing them, with some monitoring by a global body. Even though the human rights system lacks the sanctioning power of state law, its expansion and elaboration creates a new discursive legal space within the global arena, one constructed by actors outside Europe and the US as well as by people within it. One dramatic illustration of the changing understanding of rights within the international legal system is the emergence of a conception of indigenous rights, attached to groups rather than individuals and defining international law as competent over matters formerly considered the domestic responsibility of states (Anaya 1996: 42). Anaya notes that international law is shifting back to the naturalist framework of early classical theory in its concern with an overarching normative concern for world peace, stability, and human rights, and is incorporating a discourse concerned with individuals and groups (1996: 42).

The case of gender violence dramatically demonstrates the creation of new rights – rights which depend on the state's failure to protect women rather than its active violation of rights. Although it had been an issue since the mid-1970s, gender violence emerged as a major focus for women's rights in the early 1990s. Inspired by important conceptual writing in 1990 (Bunch 1990), by 1992 the Committee on the Elimination of Discrimination against Women (CEDAW) had formulated a broad recommendation that defined gender-based violence as a form of discrimination, placing it squarely within the rubric of human rights and fundamental freedoms and making clear that states are obliged to eliminate violence perpetrated by public authorities and by private persons (Cook 1994: 165). At the 1993 UN Conference on Human Rights in Vienna this issue became even more important (see Schuler 1992). The Commission on the Status of Women recommended the formulation of an international instrument on violence against women and in 1993, working with groups of experts, developed the Declaration on the Elimination of Violence against Women. In 1994 the UN General Assembly adopted the Declaration. In the same year, the UN Commission on Human Rights condemned gender-based violence and appointed a Special Rapporteur.

The 1995 Platform for Action of the Fourth World Conference on Women in Beijing included a section on gender-based violence. It named as a violation of human rights any act of gender-based violence in the family or community, or perpetrated by the state, that results in physical, sexual, psychological harm or suffering to women in private or public life, including acts of violence and sexual abuse during armed conflict, forced sterilization and abortion, and female infanticide (UN 1995). The doctrine asserts that states are responsible for failures to protect women from violence, protection from violence being an internationally recognized human right (Bunch 1990; Cook 1994; Thomas & Beasley 1994). Although individuals are not legally liable under international human rights law, states are responsible for their failures to meet international obligations and even for acts by private persons if they fail to make an effort to eliminate or mitigate the acts (Cook 1994: 151). Within national legal systems, assault and murder are universally considered crimes (UN Report of Secretary General 1995: 137), but wife beating is shielded by its location in a legally and culturally constructed private sphere. Historically, in the US, as well as in many other parts of the world, it has been regarded as less serious than other kinds of assault. Therefore, the emergence of violence against women as a distinct human rights violation depends on redefining the family so that it is no longer a shelter from legal scrutiny.

Conceptualizing violence against women as a human rights violation contradicts the absolute protection of culture. Women's vulnerability to violence depends on entrenched sociocultural practices involving marriage, work, and religious and secular ideologies of masculinity and femininity.[2] Conventions on the rights of women typically require states which ratify them to change cultural practices that subordinate women. The 1992 Declaration on the Elimination of Violence Against Women issued by the CEDAW committee says that: 'States should condemn violence against women, and should not invoke any custom, tradition, or religion or other consideration to avoid their obligation with respect to its elimination.'[3] Discussions of violence against women in the human rights frame typically call for reforms of cultural practices such as dowry-deaths, son-preference, female infanticide, honour-killings, and female genital mutilation (Bunch 1997; Schuler 1992). The 1995 Platform for Action from the Beijing Fourth World Conference on Women states:

Violence against women throughout the life cycle derives essentially from cultural patterns, in particular the harmful effects of certain traditional or customary practices and all acts of extremism linked to race, sex, language or religion that perpetuate the lower status accorded to women in the family, the workplace, the community and society.[4]

Many states have opposed this conception of human rights on cultural or religious grounds and have refused to ratify treaties on women's rights or have done so only with substantial reservations. By 1997, 160 countries had ratified CEDAW but it has more substantive reservations against it than any other international treaty (Bunch 1997: 44). One third of the ratifying states have substantive reservations to parts of CEDAW (Progress of Nations 1997: 49). Some states; including China, claim that UN documents on women's rights such as CEDAW violate their own cultural practices and have ratified the treaty only with extensive reservations. Some Islamic states and the Vatican opposed the 1995 Platform, arguing that marriage, motherhood, and the family were the backbone of society (UN 1995: Holy See, Jordan, Egypt). In its statement on the Platform, for example, the Holy See stated (UN 1995: Holy See): 'To affirm the dignity and rights of all women requires respect for the roles of women whose quest for personal fulfillment and the construction of a stable society is inseparably linked to their commitment to God, family, neighbour and especially to their children.'

Thus, women's right to protection from violence appear diametrically opposed to protection of culture. But this new category of human rights violation merges a wide variety of behaviours, including rape in wartime, wife battering, and female genital mutilation (Keck and Sikkink 1998). Local cultural support for these activities varies significantly. Some, such as rape in wartime are clearly illegal; others, such as wife battering, are tolerated within the private space of the family; and others are local cultural practices supported within local communities. Of this last group, many are currently being contested and some have been outlawed; such female genital cutting is now illegal in several African states. To see violence against women as an opposition between culture and rights fails to acknowledge the contested and variable cultural support this variety of behaviour receives in different social groups. It assumes that all of these actions are 'cultural' and that there are no debates within any society about the acceptability of each one.

Any simple opposition between culture and rights misunderstands the nature of both. Rights are a cultural phenomenon, developing and changing over time in response to a variety of social, economic, political, and cultural influences. The notion of violence against women as a human rights violation was created only in the 1990s and has continued to develop (see Bunch 1990; Keck and Sikkink 1998). Over the past fifty years, the concept of human rights has shifted from its original meaning, rooted in liberal theory, of civil and political rights to an expanded notion of collective, cultural, and social and economic rights. The present system was born in radical French revolutionary thought at the end of the eighteenth century, but by the end of the twentieth, the new human rights system had become the preeminent global language of social justice. As human rights has gradually displaced socialism and communism it has incorporated some of the features of these ideologies, including economic and social rights to work and healthcare. In response to the demands of indigenous peoples, among others, human rights now include rights to culture.

The position of the American Anthropological Association reflects these changes. In 1998 the Association's committee for human rights proposed a new declaration on human rights, which asserted that:

People and groups have a generic right to realize their capacity for culture, and to produce, reproduce and change the conditions and forms of their physical, personal and social existence, so long as such activities do not diminish the same capacities of others. Anthropology as an academic discipline studies the bases and the forms of human diversity and unity; anthropology as a practice seeks to apply this knowledge to the solution of human problems.

As a professional organization of anthropologists, the AAA has long been, and should continue to be, concerned whenever human difference is made the basis for a denial of basic human rights, where 'human' is understood in its full range of cultural, social, linguistic, psychological and biological senses[5]

Clearly, this is a far cry from the way in which culture and human rights were understood by the American Anthropological Association in 1947. Both the concept of rights and the concept of culture have changed dramatically. Rights claims now incorporate group rights and rights to culture. Further, the committee that produced this statement argued that all individual rights have a collective dimension (Turner 1997: 287) and that the right to difference can be a positive, transcultural basis for human rights. Culture is now understood as a process, developing and changing through actions and struggles over meaning, rather than as a static shared system of beliefs and values – the dominant view in 1947. Thus, the statement focuses on the protection of a 'capacity for culture' rather than the protection of any particular 'culture'. Unfortunately, this more flexible concept of culture has not changed the way the law defines culture in the case of indigenous peoples, which are still forced to make claims for land, resources, and cultural autonomy in terms of the outmoded concept of culture developed by anthropologists early in the twentieth century. Although this is now repudiated within the discipline, it continues to determine the course of indigenous rights litigation, forcing litigants to adopt a notion of culture as static and inflexible (see Jackson 1995; Povinelli 1998). Therefore, the important contemporary questions are not how to resolve the opposition between culture and rights, but how claims to rights and to culture are articulated in global debates about social justice.

Changing rights

The expansion of the concept of rights is an historical and social process based on the interaction of representatives from a wide variety of cultural traditions working through the UN and transnational NGOs. The original creation of the human rights system was in part a response to particular historical circumstances. Although it had beginnings in the early twentieth century, the modern human rights system developed after the Second World War out of the conviction that the protection of the human rights of individuals was no longer only a domestic concern, i.e. the sovereign prerogative of states. Instead, human rights advocates felt that individuals needed more protection against abuses suffered at the hands of the state, and created the UN and the new international legal regime of human rights on the assumption that no state can be entrusted with absolute power over its own citizens. The international regime of human rights, framed in the aftermath of the Holocaust, argued that all individuals are entitled by virtue of their humanity to a basic modicum of human dignity, and that certain human rights are universal, fundamental, and inalienable and thus cannot and should not be overridden by cultural and religious traditions. The accident of birth into a particular social group or culture has no bearing on the individual's intrinsic worth or right to be treated as a human being (Zechenter 1997: 319–20). The original creation of human rights was inspired not only by the French Enlightenment but also by Nazism, by a historical situation in which a global check on state power was deemed essential to avoid the repetition of horrors such as the Holocaust. Similarly, doctrines of self-determination emerged in the 1950s and 1960s, along with critiques of colonialism.

The UN human rights framework has evolved and changed dramatically over the past fifty years (Messer 1997). It has shifted from protecting individuals within states and protecting emerging states from colonial abuses to protecting emerging nations (peoples) from the effects of the international political economy and indigenous peoples from violations by states, including legal acceptance of collective or group rights (Messer 1997: 299). It is a pluralized, flexible, and responsive system which develops and changes over time (Messer 1997: 295). The modern human rights concept is more egalitarian than its liberal precedents and less individualistic. To civil and political rights it has added essential human welfare guarantees to employment and fair working conditions; healthcare, food, and social security; and education and participation in cultural life of the community. These so-called positive rights came from socialist and welfare concepts which emphasize economic, social and cultural rights over political rights. The US has accepted civil and political rights more enthusiastically than economic, social and cultural ones; the opposite is the case in African states; populous Asian states such as China and Indonesia argue that individual political rights are foreign to their Asian communal cultural traditions and focus on subsistence needs (1997: 297).

Collective rights, especially those which refer to rights of indigenous peoples, are among the most recent rights, although there are precedents in the minority rights, language rights, and rights to self-determination developed early in the twentieth century.[6] This distinction is not as sharp as it appears, since even individual rights exist only within social contexts defined by collectivities such as nations. Indigenous peoples in particular have sought rights which are collective and whose beneficiaries are historically-formed communities rather than individuals or states (Anaya 1996: 48). As Anaya notes, these rights not only conflict with the dominant individual/state dichotomy that underlies the creation of international standards, but also challenge state sovereignty. To some extent claims to cultural rights demand assertions of cultural authenticity that resonate with earlier anthropological conceptions of culture. The authentic and culturally distinct self-representations which this discourse sometimes requires may even constitute constructed misrepresentations or misunderstandings of shared histories (Beckett 1996; Friedman 1996; Rogers 1996; Povinelli 1998). In other words, making claims to cultural rights sometimes requires framing these claims in terms of an essentialized, homogeneous, 'traditional' culture.

Thus, the human rights system is constantly changing in response to new global circumstances. It is the product of negotiation and discussion rather than imposition. As the concept has expanded from its original meaning within liberalism – the protection of the individual from the state – to a series of obligations by states to its members, the nature, content and diversity of rights has changed.

Changing culture

The concept of culture, like the concept of rights, has also undergone a transformation. Anthropological theory now rejects the concept of culture as integrated, harmonious, consensual, and bounded in favour of an understanding of culture as historically produced, globally interconnected, internally contested, and marked with ambiguous boundaries of identity and practice. Historically, culture as an analytic concept in anthropology developed when there were understood by Europeans to be civilized people and 'primitives' who lived unchanging and utterly different, although internally coherent, lives which had to be tolerated not because they conformed to the values of the observer but because they were, in a sense, off the edge of his or her moral universe (see Vincent 1990). But in the last two decades, world system theory has criticized the model of society as an isolated 'billiard ball' within global economic and cultural processes (Wolf 1982), while the analysis of globalization, the expansion of cultural studies, and the emphasis on discourse and power in Foucauldian work have all challenged understandings of culture as based on shared norms and values and bounded or homogeneous social groups. Culture is now understood as historically produced rather than static; unbounded rather than bounded and integrated; contested rather than consensual; incorporated within structures of power such as the construction of hegemony; rooted in practices, symbols, habits, patterns of practical mastery and practical rationality within cultural categories of meaning rather than any simple dichotomy between ideas and behaviour; and negotiated and constructed through human action rather than superorganic forces.

The combined impact of technology, tourism, global capitalism, deterritorialized communities and migration are blurring and redrawing cultural boundaries at a rapid rate. Contact zones, colonial projects and borderlands, rather than 'cultures', describe contemporary social processes. Globalization has produced what Appadurai refers to as the expansion of imagination (1996). The twin phenomena of mass migration and the spread of mass media, detached from the need for literacy, have created unprecedented new arenas for imagination, at the same time as they have enabled migrants to form deterritorialized communities through media and migration connections. Although he sees these changes as the product of the past twenty years, there are many similarities in the global flow of persons, ideas and projects of nineteenth-century colonialism. It is the pace, rather than the kind, of cultural flows that has changed in recent decades.

Ironically, just as the older concept of culture seems less appropriate for contemporary society, it is being vigorously reappropriated by indigenous peoples in a search for sovereignty and self-determination. Indian movements in Colombia, as well as other indigenous societies, use this concept of culture to make claims in the modern world (Jackson 1995). Jackson observes that the concept they appropriate is based on a quasi-biological analogy by which a group of people 'has' a culture in the way that animals have fur, inherited as genes are inherited, rather than as a repertoire people create or use to adapt to changing social conditions (Jackson 1995: 19). Ethno-national groups also make claims to culture in these terms (Comaroff 1995). Many of these claims rely upon earlier views of culture, probably because these resonate with the legal audience to which they are addressed. As Clifford's account of the Mashpee trial showed, Native Americans are often required to make claims to culture in these terms in order to assert rights to land or recognition as a tribe (1988). Groups such as the Hawaiian Sovereignty Movement make claims on the basis of their 'traditional' culture, joining an interest in cultural renaissance with the political constraints of a society willing to recognize claims on the basis of cultural authenticity and tradition but not reparations based on acts of conquest and violation in the past (see Merry 1996).

Claims to protecting 'culture' in these terms may be politically effective in an environment in which the audience to these claims understands culture in these terms. But understanding culture as fixed, uniform and unchanging ignores the impacts of globalization in the present and historical transfers of cultural beliefs and practices in the past. Considering cultures as changing and interconnected, and rights as historically created and transnationally redefined by national and local actors, better describes the contemporary situation. It also reveals the impossibility of drawing sharp distinctions between culture and rights or seeing relativism and universalism as diametrically opposed and incompatible positions.

A case study: changing Hawai'i

My dissatisfaction with existing models of culture intensified as I worked on understanding the role of law in the American colonization of Hawai'i in the nineteenth and early twentieth centuries (see Merry 2000). It quickly emerged that the Hawaiian Islands during the nineteenth century were not on the periphery of an expanding capitalist system in the US and Europe but were in fact at the crossroads of a dizzying array of peoples and at the centre of a set of competing cultural logics. After Cook's 'discovery' of the islands in 1778, the islands were visited by merchants from Britain, France, the Netherlands, and the US; goods were traded in Spanish dollars brought from Chile and Peru; and Chinese merchants and sugar masters settled in Honolulu to trade or moved into the wet valleys to grow rice or sugar. The New England missionaries arriving from upstate New York, western Massachusetts, and western Connecticut in 1820 came from more isolated communities than many in Hawai'i at the time.

Between 1825 and 1852, an extensive legal transplantation drastically transformed Hawaiian society. The sovereign Kingdom of Hawai'i adopted an Anglo-American system of law, courts, and prisons, replacing the former Hawaiian system of *kapu* (tabu, restriction) and chiefship. In this period, the sovereign Kingdom of Hawai'i adopted a new constitution and Bill of Rights, a judiciary independent of the *mo'i* (king) and *ali'i* (chiefs) who had previously handled conflicts, and an array of laws borrowed from a variety of sources. Harbour regulations and a law relating to masters and servants were adopted whole, the latter probably from New York state. A new system of regulation of marriage and divorce came from New England. By 1850, gender was dramatically redefined with the introduction of coverture, the redefinition of wives as civilly dead, and the elimination of the franchise for women, which excluded them from public participation, service on juries, and running for most offices. In a kingdom where high-ranking women had exercised enormous power in the 1820s, this was a dramatic shift.

The cultural appropriation of Anglo-American law took place in two incremental steps, each of which was rooted in similar cultural logics but contained unanticipated trajectories. The first, from 1820 to 1844 was the adoption of a Christianized Hawaiian law. The second, from 1845–1852, was the adoption of a secularized Western law. By the end of the period a new code of laws imported from the US enshrined such unfamiliar ideas as private ownership of land, contract labour with penal sanctions, and an almost complete prohibition on divorce. These innovations were appropriated in order to construct the civilized nation, but brought with them new demands for discipline and punishment in prisons, a new gender order with women subordinated to husbands, and a system of hierarchy based on the market rather than relations between *ali'i* and *maka'ainana* (commoners) based on *aloha* (love) and loyalty (Merry 2000).

Thus, small steps often initiated broader, frequently unanticipated changes, shifting the landscape for future steps. Conceiving this situation as the juxtaposition of two 'cultures' and their embedded legal systems is not a useful way to make sense of it. Nor do notions of borrowing and blending of parts through processes such as syncretism and acculturation deal adequately with the power relations of the situation. On the other hand, the concept of 'imposition' also fails to recognize the collaboration of the Hawaiian *ali'i* and *mo'i* in the process of transformation and the complexities of the situation they confronted.

The Hawaiian social field was constituted by several competing cultural logics rooted in particular structures of power – a situation typical of colonial contexts. In nineteenth-century Hawai'i, the distinctive cultural worlds of Hawaiian *ali'i* and *maka'ainana*, British and American whaleship owners and crews, European sugar planters, Chinese sugar masters and rice farmers, Spanish and Peruvian merchants, American Protestant missionaries, Russian fur traders, French Catholic priests, resident American and British merchants, deserting and abandoned seamen from New England and the South Pacific, and roving fortune seekers from around the globe jostled together in a rapidly evolving social milieu. After mid-century, the importation of large numbers of sugar plantation workers from China, Portugal, Japan, Korea, Puerto Rico, the Philippines and the South Pacific further complicated the variety of cultural logics at play.

Pratt describes such fields as contact zones, 'social spaces where disparate cultures meet, clash, and grapple with each other, often in highly asymmetrical relations of domination and subordination – like colonialism, slavery, or their aftermaths as they are lived out across the globe today' (1992: 4). Unlike the term 'frontier', which privileges a centre and an edge, the term 'contact zone' focuses on intersections among equally centred entities. Pratt suggests the term 'transculturation' to describe the way subjugated peoples receive and appropriate metropolitan modes of representation and peripheral groups constitute the metropolis, creating its need to continually create and recreate itself in opposition to those peripheries (1992: 6).

Many anthropologists have worked toward developing a more dynamic and situated concept of culture to analyze contact zones. Comaroff and Comaroff (1992: 27) take culture to be 'the semantic space, the field of signs and practices, in which human beings construct and represent themselves and others, and hence their societies and histories. It is not merely an abstract order of signs, or relations among signs. Nor is it just the sum of habitual practices'. This is never a closed, entirely coherent system but contains within it polyvalent, contestable messages, images and actions.

It is, in short, a historically situated, historically unfolding ensemble of signifiers-in-action, signifiers at once material and symbolic, social and aesthetic. Some of these, at any moment in time, will be woven into more or less tightly integrated, relatively explicit worldviews; others may be heavily contested, the stuff of counterideologies and 'subcultures'; yet others may become more or less unfixed, relatively free floating, and indeterminate in their value and meaning. (ibid.)

This is a concept of culture that allows for agency and contestation in situations with multiple and contradictory cultural logics and systems of meaning.

These conceptions move us away from seeing cultures as homogeneous entities to imagining them as arenas of contest among competing cultural logics, in which variously situated actors seize and appropriate particular cultural practices. The location of culture is no longer a fixed geographical space, but is constituted in multiple locations reflecting the movement of peoples, capital and symbolic systems. Many of the struggles in the colonies to transform the social order, to expand the knowability and visibility of the population, and to implement the disciplinary systems of the modern state paralleled similar efforts to refashion the rural peasantry and the urban poor at home. In Hawai'i, for example, New England missionaries attempted to control the sex trade between sailors and the Hawaiian *maka'ainana* women during the 1820s and 1830s. This project paralleled struggles to control prostitution in the northeast United States but took on a new spin in the Hawaiian context. Christian virtue and class difference marked out seamen as sites for reforming projects in both locations. Although the Hawaiian context at first appears to be one framed by culture rather than class and morality, as European and American men converted Hawaiian women into prostitutes, class was fundamental, as lower-status Hawaiian women engaged in the sex trade while higher-status Hawaiian women married higher-status white men. This interaction assumed the cultural and ethnic features of the colonial encounter, in which women of colour were appropriated by visiting white men, while also partaking of the class and religious dimensions of the New England concern with the moral character of working-class men.

Newer understandings of culture emphasize the agentive aspects of culture and its interactive co-construction over time. Particular institutions, discourses, or practices may be appropriated, as a whole or in part, from one group by another, then reinterpreted according to local meanings and relationships. For example, the leaders of the Hawaiian Sovereignty Movement staged a tribunal in 1993 to mark the centenary of the American-backed coup against the Hawaiian Queen Lili'uokalani (see Merry 1996; Hasager and Friedman 1994). The tribunal accused the US of a series of acts of destruction of culture and appropriation of land and sovereignty using the form of a criminal trial. The seat labeled 'US representative' was vacant, but it became a prominent symbolic site as witnesses testified about the overthrow and about their cultural and economic losses to a panel of judges, eminent activists and human rights lawyers from around the world. The organizing committee issued a formal complaint before the tribunal, accusing the US of violating a series of national and international laws. Thus, this tribunal appropriated the form of American law and its language in its complaint against the US government (Merry 1996).

The important question about culture is, therefore, how cultural practices are introduced, appropriated, deployed, reintroduced and redefined in a social field of power over a historical period. Through historical processes, particular cultural conceptions and practices become embedded in politically and economically powerful institutions such as legal systems. Appropriation replaces ideas of imposition with an analysis of the negotiated and partial nature of transformation, but any appropriation is constrained by political and economic factors embedded in world historical changes.

Moreover, the trajectory of change is inevitably unpredictable. Those introducing new forms, institutions, discourses, or practices are continually confronted by frustration and failure, with the inability to impose the new system in whole cloth rather than in shreds. Those who take it on and carry it out constantly redefine its forms and practices in terms of other meanings and practices. Uncertainty plagues the process. For example, the Hawaiian kings passed laws criminalizing sexual relations outside marriage in nineteenth-century Hawai'i, then confronted repeated demands by their American lawyer and missionary advisers that they build prisons to punish offenders (Merry 2000). As Hawaiians created places of confinement that allowed men and women to socialize with one another, these advisers again intervened to emphasize the importance of chastity during punishment, of providing separate spaces for male and female prisoners and matrons or masters to supervise their charges and keep them apart. The Hawaiian monarchy was more interested in the textual and institutional creation of the governmental apparatus of modernity than in the disciplinary practices of imprisonment that this entailed.

Cultural appropriation is an uncertain process, governed in part by similarities in underlying cultural logics and characterized by the incremental nature of change. As in this example, changes take place over a period of time, with constant readjustments to changing circumstances. The contemporary appropriation of human rights follows a similar process. Although produced in the West, it is now being appropriated around the globe by other peoples and transformed in various ways in different locations. To return to my opening example, women activists in the Solomon Islands have appropriated the concept of women's rights to deal with domestic violence, but are seeking to tailor it to indigenous conditions, even though the name of the problem itself comes from outside. The long-term consequences of adopting rights talk as a way of thinking about social justice is clearly uncertain, as ideas of civilization and the rule of law were for nineteenth-century Hawaiians. But questions such as these, rather than the logical incompatibility of culture and rights, provide a way of understanding the implications of the global spread of human rights discourse.

Cultural appropriation and gender violence

The adoption of rights-based approaches in a multicultural town in Hawai'i today provides a fruitful place to address questions of gender violence. I have spent ten years studying a feminist programme which endeavours to support women victims of violence and retrain male batterers to control their violence in the town of Hilo, Hawai'i. This programme works closely with the courts, taking referrals from family courts as well as from criminal courts. Its core mission is to protect women and to redefine battering as a crime. A law passed in 1985 requires two days' imprisonment for convicted batterers and mandates a treatment programme.[7] Thus, this programme adopted the language of rights, specifying the problem as one of violation of rights and the solution as punishment for the man and separation of the couple. One of the conflicts with cultural beliefs occurs because this also means the end of the marriage and is premised on a notion of gender equality. Both ideas run counter to some of the cultural understandings of religious groups in the town, which emphasize the primacy of marriage and the complementary but unequal roles of men and women. Conservative Christian churches, for example, teach that men exercise headship over their wives (Crabb 1991). Ideas of gender equality and women's safety at the expense of marriage may also run counter to nationalist ideas that the strength of the nation lies in the unity of its families, an idea prominent in the 1980s family-values political debate in the United States. As gender violence becomes defined as a violation of human rights, it raises a contradiction for groups which view marriage as indissoluble. Will the pressures of nationalism, and the ways an increasingly fragile national identity depends on definitions of gender and the sanctity of the family, shape the local appropriation of this global project?

My ethnography of legal interventions into gender violence in Hilo, Hawai'i, suggests that local adaptations of the rights model do take place. A women's support group and batterer's treatment programme, modelled after one in Duluth, Minnesota, has been operating in this town since 1986. It emphasizes the protection of women by the law, treating men who batter through discussion and retraining, and separating women from men who batter them. But in the past two years, there have been important local adaptations. One is the development of a more 'local' curriculum, incorporating Hawaiian cultural examples and images. A second is an emphasis on positive support for men who batter, based on the assumption that battering is in part a response to insecurity, fear, and low self-esteem. Other initiatives against domestic violence in the town are even more locally adapted. For example, one anger management programme to which men are mandated by the courts is a Christian-based programme with a strong element of Hawaiian activism. In one visit to this programme, I heard the leader talk about the anger Native Hawaiians feel about the loss of land and autonomy they have suffered and their sense of displacement in contemporary society. Intriguingly, I visited another Duluth-inspired programme in New Zealand that uses a very similar curriculum and format for white men but has adopted a Maori programme, which (the director says, although I did not attend it) situates male battering of women in the context of Maori experiences of racism and degradation.

In this curriculum, facilitators talk about Maori men's experiences in New Zealand and their anger and pain, then link this to the way men treat their women. Although all of these programmes share a similar commitment to a rights-based approach that works in conjunction with the criminal justice system, each has developed a local accommodation of the curriculum, a reframing which takes into account local problems and cultural practices.

Of course, the distinction between local and global is not a simple one. The locally adapted programmes in Hilo, Hawai'i and Hamilton, New Zealand came from Minnesota and bring with them a certain language, conception of rights, and vision of gender equality between spouses. There are clearly underlying assumptions about the rights-bearing subject, about the responsibility to take charge of one's life, and about the role of the state in protecting these rights even against spouses, which are linked to a particular Western notion of individualism and legality. There is an underlying cultural vision of marriage as a bond that can be ended if there is violence and an ideal of a marriage relationship in which equal partners negotiate their differences and reach decisions together, treating each other with respect and acknowledging each other's wishes. The programme encourages battered women to seek the help of the law, even if this means antagonizing their relatives or their partner's relatives. It is not only batterers' treatment programmes which incorporate these definitions of the person and the family, of course, but the entire Anglo-American legal system adopted by the Hawaiian Kingdom in the nineteenth century. Hawai'i is also, of course, incorporated within the larger American cultural system founded on capitalist economic relations and individual rights. Nevertheless, these appropriations are not uncontested and are subject to local redefinition over time.

Conclusion

The local appropriation of a transnational institution such as a feminist rights-based batterers' treatment programme or Anglo-American law transforms underlying cultural categories and practices. However, at the same time, the appropriated institution is itself adapted and transformed. As the women in the Solomon Islands search for a way to combine their conceptions of gender and family with global human rights views, they both redefine their local cultural practices and affect the global human rights system itself. This dynamic negotiation has pushed the global human rights system towards change. Although there are individualistic aspects to notions of rights, they are being collectivized, while concepts of culture are becoming more fluid. Human rights laws change through processes of cultural appropriation which take place as NGOs, UN representatives and rights-claiming groups such as indigenous peoples negotiate new intersections between rights and culture. Even indigenous peoples such as Native Hawaiians, when making claims to cultural rights, do not view their own culture as an integrated whole but see it as rooted in identity, language and particular cultural practices. It is unfortunate, however, that indigenous peoples are often forced to ground their legal claims in outmoded concepts of culture that have proved very resistant to this reformulation.

In order to analyze these processes, it is important to avoid essentializing either culture or rights. Retaining the historically produced, changing and interconnected understandings of the way these concepts operate in social situations is critically important. Rights concepts change in response to historical conditions and appropriation is a widespread aspect of cultural processes. Material considerations, which determine where governments decide to invest resources and who is able to attend international conferences, are also critically important. Human rights offer local communities new ways of defining problems and seeing solutions through various kinds of cultural appropriation.

Finally, this overview of the universalism/relativism debate indicates how historically grounded the positions have been. The 1940s debate took place in a context of World War II and its aftermath and colonialism; the 1990s debates are shaped by the global expansion of capitalism, the demise of socialist ideologies of social justice, the end of conceptions of cultures as isolated ways of life, and the emergence of new and more dialogic processes for rights creation at the UN, with broader national participation and an expanding NGO community. Given this historicity, it is unlikely that the debate will ever be resolved in the abstract; instead, the terms will take on new meanings as the world changes and the political meaning of each position shifts.

ACKNOWLEDGEMENTS

This research was generously supported by a grants from the Law and Social Sciences Programme of the National Science Foundation, #SBR-9320009, the Cultural Anthropology Programme of the National Science Foundation, #SES-9023397, the National Endowment for the Humanities, and the Canadian Institute for Advanced Research. The American Bar Foundation provided a congenial atmosphere for research and writing.

The paper was first presented in 1997 at a conference on Culture and Rights at the University of Sussex, and benefitted from the stimulating discussions at the conference.

NOTES

1 The attack on the potlatch of the northwest coast of the US and Canada is one of the most vivid examples of this widespread practice (Cole & Chaiken 1990; see also Merry 1998).
2 See Bunch 1997; Cook 1994; Kerr 1993 and Schuler 1992.
3 Cook 1994: 167, citing CEDAW General Recommendation 19 at 1, UN Doc., CEDAW/C/1992/L.1/Add.15 (1992).
4 United Nations 1995: Platform 3 1995 D(sec.119).
5 In *Anthropology Newsletter*, Sept 1998: 9.
6 See for example Asch 1988; Coulter 1994; Sierra 1995; Tennant 1994; Trask 1993; Wilmsen 1989; Anaya 1996.
7 Legislation during the 1980s and 1990s gradually increased the severity of the punishment and decreased the severity of the injury required to initiate arrest or removal from the premises. A 1983 amendment removed the word 'substantial' in the description of injuries and added 'abuse' to 'harm' (H.R.S. 709–906: Sec 1, 1983). In 1985, the law was expanded to cover family and household members as well as spouses and to allow the police to take further action 'where the officer has reasonable grounds to believe that there was recent physical abuse or harm inflicted by one person upon a family or household member, whether or not such physical abuse or harm occurred in the officer's presence'. (H.R.S. 709–906, Sec 1.). The officer can order the person to leave for a twelve-hour cooling-off period and arrest for failure to comply. Conviction requires a mandatory forty-eight-hour prison sentence and participation in a domestic violence treatment and counselling programme (H.R.S. 709–906, Sec. 1).

REFERENCES

Anaya S.J. 1996. *Indigenous Peoples in International Law*. New York: Oxford University Press.
An-Na'im, A.A. 1990. Problems of Universal Cultural Legitimacy for Human Rights. In *Human Rights in Africa: Cross-Cultural Perspectives*. (Eds.) A.A. An-Na'im and F. Deng. Washington DC: Brookings Institution.
An-Na'im, A.A. 1992. *Human Rights in Cross-cultural Perspectives: A Quest for Consensus*. Philadelphia, PA: University of Pennsylvania Press.
Appadurai, A. 1996. *Modernity at Large: Cultural Dimensions of Globalization.*. Minneapolis: University of Minnesota Press.
Asch, M. 1988 (1984). *Home and Native Land: Aboriginal Rights and the Canadian Constitution*. Canada: Metheun.
Basu, A. 1995. Introduction. In *The Challenge of Local Feminisms: Women's Movements in Global Perspective*. (Ed.) A. Basu. Boulder: Westview Press.
Beckett, J. 1996. Contested Images: Perspectives on the Indigenous Terrain in

the Late 20th Century. *Identities: Global Studies in Culture and Power* 3, 1–15.

Bunch, C. 1990. Women's Rights as Human Rights: Toward a Re-Vision of Human Rights. *Human Rights Quarterly* 12, 489–498.

Bunch, C. 1997. The Intolerable Status Quo: Violence Against Women and Girls. In *The Progress of Nations 1997*. New York: UNICEF.

Clifford, J. 1988. Identity in Mashpee. In *The Predicament of Culture: Twentieth Century Ethnography, Literature, and Art*. Cambridge, MA: Harvard University Press.

Cohen, R., G. Hyden and W. Nagan (Eds.). 1993. *Human Rights and Governance in Africa*. Gainesville, FL: University Press of Florida.

Cole, D. and I. Chaikin. 1990. *An Iron Hand Upon the People: The Law against the Potlatch on the Northwest Coast*. Vancouver/Toronto: Douglas & McIntyre; Seattle: University of Washington Press.

Comaroff, J. and J.L. Comaroff. 1992. *Ethnography and the Historical Imagination*. Boulder: Westview.

Comaroff, J.L. 1995. Ethnicity, Nationalism, and the Politics of Difference in an Age of Revolution. In *Perspectives on Nationalism and War*. (Eds.) J. L. Comaroff & P.C. Stern. Australia: Gordon and Breach. pp. 243–276.

Cook, R.J. 1994. State Responsibility for Violations of Women's Human Rights. *Harvard Human Rights Journal* 7, 125–175.

Coulter, R.T. 1994. Commentary on the UN Draft Declaration on the Rights of Indigenous Peoples. *Cultural Survival Quarterly* 18(2), 37–41.

Crabb, L. 1991. *Men and Women: Enjoying the Difference*. Grand Rapids, MI: Zondervan.

Davies, M. (Ed.). 1994. *Women and Violence: Realities and Responses Worldwide*. London: Zed Books.

Donnelly, J. 1982. Human Rights and Human Dignity: An Analytical Critique of Non-Western Conceptions of Human Rights. *American Political Science Review* 76, 303.

Donnelly, J. 1990. Human Rights and Western Liberalism. In *Human Rights in Africa: Cross-Cultural Perspectives*. (Eds.) A.A. An-Na'im & F. Deng. Washington DC: Brookings Institution.

Elias, N. 1994 (1939). *The Civilizing Process: The History of Manners and State Formation and Civilization*, trans. by E. Jephcott. Oxford: Blackwell.

Executive Board, American Anthropological Association. 1947. Statement on Human Rights. *American Anthropologist* 49, 539–543.

Fernyhough, T. 1993. Human Rights in Precolonial Africa. In *Human Rights and Governance in Africa*. (Eds.) R. Cohen, G. Hyden and W. Nagan. Gainesville, FL: University Press of Florida.

Freeman, M.A. 1994. Women, Law and Land at the Local Level: Claiming Women's Human Rights in Domestic Legal Systems. *Human Rights Quarterly* 16, 559–75.

Friedman, J. 1996. The Politics of De-authentification: Escaping from Identity: A Commentary on 'Beyond Authenticity' by Mark Rogers. *Identities: Global Studies in Culture and Power* 3, 127–37.

Handwerker, W.P. 1997. Universal Human Rights and the Problem of Unbounded Cultural Meanings. *American Anthropologist* 99, 799–810.

Hasager, U. and J. Friedman (Eds.). 1994. *Hawai'i: Return to Nationhood.* Copenhagen: International Work Group for Indigenous Affairs, Document No. 75.

Hatch, E. 1997. The Good Side of Relativism. *Journal of Anthropological Research* 53, 371–81.

Herskovitz, M.J. 1972. *Cultural Relativism: Perspectives in Cultural Pluralism.* (Ed.) F. Herskovitz. New York: Random House.

Higham, J. 1970 (1955). *Strangers in the Land: Patterns of American Nativism, 1860–1925.* New York: Atheneum.

Jackson, J. 1995. Culture, Genuine and Spurious: The Politics of Indianness in the Vaupes, Columbia. *American Ethnologist* 22, 3–28.

Keck, M.E. and K. Sikkink. 1998. *Activists Beyond Borders: Advocacy Networks in International Politics.* Ithaca, NY: Cornell University Press.

Kerr, J. (Ed.). 1993. *Ours By Right: Women's Rights as Human Rights.* London: Zed Books.

Leary, V. 1990. The Effect of Western Perspectives on International Human Rights. In *Human Rights in Africa: Cross-Cultural Perspectives.* (Eds.) A.A. An-Na'im and F. Deng. Washington DC: Brookings Institution.

Merry, S.E. 1997. Legal Pluralism and Transnational Culture: The Ka Ho'oko-lokolonui Kanaka Maoli Tribunal, Hawai'i 1993. In *Human Rights, Culture and Context: Anthropological Perspectives.* (Ed.) R.A. Wilson. London: Pluto Press.

Merry, S.E. 1998. The Criminalization of Everyday Life. In *Everyday Practices and Trouble Cases.* (Ed.) A. Sarat. Chicago: Northwestern University Press.

Merry, S.E. 2000. *Colonizing Hawai'i: The Cultural Power of Law.* Princeton: Princeton University Press.

Messer, E. 1993. Anthropology and Human Rights. *Annual Review of Anthropology* 22: 221–249.

Messer, E. 1997. Pluralist Approaches to Human Rights. *Journal of Anthropological Research* 53, 293–317.

Nagengast, C. & T. Turner. 1997. Introduction: Universal Human Rights Versus Cultural Relativity. *Journal of Anthropological Research* 53, 269–272.

Onuma, Y. 1995. *In Quest of Intercivilizational Human Rights: 'Universal vs. Relative' Human Rights Viewed from an Asian Perspective.* Paper presented at the Conference of the Research Committee on the Sociology of Law, Tokyo, Japan.

Peters, J. and A. Wolper (Eds.). 1995. *Women's Rights, Human Rights.* New York: Routledge.

Pollis, A. 1996. Cultural Relativism Revisited: Through a State Prism. *Human Rights Quarterly* 18, 316–344.

Pratt, M.L. 1992. *Imperial Eyes: Travel Writing and Transculturation.* New York: Routledge.

Preis, A-B.S. 1996. Human Rights as Cultural Practice: An Anthropological Critique. *Human Rights Quarterly* 18, 286–315.

Renteln, A.D. 1988. Relativism and the Search for Human Rights. *American Anthropologist* 90, 56–72.

Renteln, A.D. 1990. *International Human Rights: Universalism Versus Relativism.* Newbury Park, CA: Sage Publications.

Report of the Secretary-General. 1995. *From Nairobi to Beijing: Second Review and Appraisal of the Implementation of the Nairobi Forward-looking Strategies for the Advancement of Women.* New York: UN.

Riles, A. 1998. Infinity within the Brackets. *American Ethnologist* 25: 378–399.

Rogers, M. 1996. Beyond Authenticity: Conservation, Tourism, and the Politics of Representation in the Ecuadorian Amazon. *Identities: Global Studies in Culture and Power* 3, 73–127.

Santos, B. De Sousa. 1995. *Toward a New Common Sense: Law, Science, and Politics in the Paradigmatic Transition.* New York: Routledge.

Schuler, M. (Ed.). 1992. *Freedom from Violence: Women's Strategies from Around the World.* New York: UNIFEM.

Sierra, M.T. 1995. Indian Rights and Customary Law in Mexico: A Study of the Nahuas in the Sierra de Puebla. *Law and Society Review* 29, 227–255.

Steward, J. 1948. Comments on the Statement on Human Rights. *American Anthropologist* 50: 351–352.

Tennant, C. 1994. Indigenous Peoples, International Institutions, and the International Legal Literature from 1945–1993. *Human Rights Quarterly* 16, 1–57.

Thomas, D. and M. Beaseley. 1993. Domestic Violence as a Human Rights Issue. *Human Rights Quarterly* 15, 36–62.

Trask, H-K. 1993. *From a Native Daughter: Colonialism and Sovereignty in Hawai'i.* Monroe, ME: Common Courage Press.

Turner, T. 1997. Human Rights, Human Difference: Anthropology's Contribution to an Emancipatory Cultural Politics. *Journal of Anthropological Research* 53, 273–291.

UN Commission on Human Rights. 1996. Report of the Special Rapporteur on Violence Against Women, its Causes and Consequences, Ms. Radhika Coomaraswamy.   http://193.135.156.15/html/menu4/chrrep/9653/HTM (10 December, 1997).

United Nations. 1996. Statement by the Holy See. The Fourth World Conference on Women, 1995, Beijing, China: Official Documents. gopher:// gopher.undp.org:70/00/unconfs/women/conf/gov/950905214652 (1 February 1966).

United Nations. 1996. Statement by Egypt. The Fourth World Conference on Women, 1995, Beijing, China: Official Documents. gopher://gopher.undp. org:70/00/unconfs/women/conf/gov/950906150823 (February 1, 1966).

United Nations. 1996. Address to the Fourth World Conference on Women, Secretary General. The Fourth World Conference on Women, 1995, Beijing, China: Official Documents. gopher://gopher.undp.org: 70/00/ unconfs/women/conf/gov/950904223634 (1 February 1966).

United Nations. 1995. Beijing Declaration and Platform for Action: Platform 3. The IV World Conference on Women, 1995, Beijing, China: Official Documents.   gopher://gopher.undp.org: 70/00/uncofns/women/off/plat-form.3 (25 October 1995).

United Nations. 1996. Statement by Jordan. The Fourth World Conference on Women, 1995, Beijing, China: Official Documents. gopher://gopher.undp. org: 70/00/unconfs/women/conf/gov/950905211139 (1 February 1966).

United Nations. 1997. *The Progress of Nations 1997.* UNICEF Annual Publication.

Vincent, J. 1990. *Anthropology and Politics: Visions, Traditions, and Trends.* Tucson, AZ: University of Arizona Press.

Wilmsen, E. (Ed.). 1989. *We Are Here: Politics of Aboriginal Land Tenure.* Berkeley: University of California Press.

Wilson, R.A. 1997. Introduction: Human Rights, Culture and Context. In *Human Rights, Culture and Context: Anthropological Perspectives.* (Ed.) R.A. Wilson. London: Pluto Press.

Wolf, E. 1992. *Europe and the People without History.* Berkeley: University of California Press.

Zechenter, E.M. 1997. In the Name of Culture: Cultural Relativism and the Abuse of the Individual. *Journal of Anthropological Research* 53, 319–347.

3   Following the movement of a pendulum: between universalism and relativism

Marie-Bénédicte Dembour

Universalism and relativism are often presented as two opposite and irreconcilable moral (or epistemological) positions as regards human rights. Most often, the debate is phrased as if one should embrace either one or the other position. This chapter argues that these two positions cannot be considered independently of each other. Each is untenable by itself and needs to accommodate the other to be sustainable. The position I advocate, which encompasses both the universalist and the relativist stances, is not a middle position that would constitute a happy compromise, putting at rest, once and for all, the debate concerning the respective strengths of universalism and relativism. Rather it is a position which makes sense of the fact that a moral agent is inevitably drawn into a pendulum motion. Thus, as one accepts being drawn towards relativism, there is a moment when, getting as it were too close to it, one is compelled to revert towards universalism – and vice versa. My image of the pendulum indicates that the in-between position I advocate is unstable. That my position is characterized by instability does not imply that one should abandon striving to 'get things right', for example by drafting human rights legislation, but that one should pursue political struggles in awareness of the limitations that any achievement in this field, however remarkable, entail.

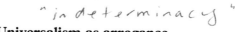

Universalism as arrogance

Exclusive claims to rationality and the ambition to attain a universal and uniform knowledge of the world characterized the eighteenth-century Enlightenment project if not always, at least in its French variant (Fitzpatrick 1992: 65). These enduring features are still noticeable in the way human rights are conceived today. This is confirmed to me each year I teach human rights courses to undergraduates. With a few exceptions, students take the existence of human rights international documents, agreed on by governments supposedly representing the whole world, as evidence that the human rights discourse sets universal standards which form a good basis on which to assess government action and, by extension, the way people behave towards each other. Such an attitude is consonant with a faith in natural law, which can be traced back in Western history to the very first manifestations of philosophical thought.

Through the centuries, at certain times more forcefully than at others, Western philosophers have put forward the idea that there exists a natural law. Despite significant variations, natural law philosophies share the following core characteristics: they rely on an absolute source (be it God, nature or the universe); they posit immutable and eternally valid principles (although the idea of a natural law with a changing content has been developed in the twentieth century); they assert that the content of natural law can be discovered through reason; and they conceive of natural law as taking precedence over positive law (Curzon 1979: 49).

For a good illustration of this position, we can turn to the following statement by Cicero (quoted in Harris 1980: 7):

True law is right reason on agreement with Nature; it is of universal application, unchanging and everlasting . . . It is a sin to try to alter this law, nor is it allowable to repeal any part of it, and it is impossible to abolish it entirely . . . And there will not be different laws at Rome and Athens . . . but one eternal and unchangeable law will be valid for all nations and for all times, and there will be one master and one ruler, that is God, over us all, for us all, for he is the author of this law, its promulgator and its enforcing judge.

This passage was written around two thousand years ago. Modern manifestations of a belief in natural law include the American Constitution, which speaks of men endowed with rights 'by their Creator' and of 'self-evident truths', and the dominant contemporary concept of human rights, which conceives of these rights as being inherent to the human person.

Natural law is a problematic idea, however, in that it assumes that everyone will arrive at the same conclusion as to what is natural/natural law through an adequate exercise of reason. However, as anthropologists are aware, what appears natural to one person may not appear so natural to another. Not surprisingly, natural law theories have often, and rightly, been criticized for justifying the status quo by mistaking what is at the moment and therefore what we know, for what ought to be (Lloyds 1985: 92). Resort to reason in order to ground rights must always be treated with suspicion and its outcomes opened to review, because there is no guarantee that the reasoning of those resorting to reason is not faulty.

To turn again to my experience in the classroom, I asked my students one year, during our very first seminar, how they knew that universal human rights standards were good. One student answered: 'I just know it'. This, of course, is a reflection of how human rights are discovered and thus a perfectly adequate answer. But a second student immediately intervened: 'Yes, but what you find good may not be what other people find good'. She added by way of illustration: 'I feel strongly about the need not to discriminate against homosexuals, but my grandmother does not see it that way'. The second student would easily understand that what a society conceives as 'natural' is often nothing else than what happens to be 'mainstream'.

It is also important to realize that human rights do not make sense outside the specific political and social history from which they have evolved, which can be summarized as the struggle to check the arbitrariness of the modern state. Tore Lindholm (1998) suggests that speaking of human rights before 1948, the year the UN Universal Declaration was signed, is an anachronism. I could not agree more with him, even if we recognize that the tradition from which the human rights discourse has evolved is a long and enduring one.

The core reason for my resistance to a universal position, however, lies elsewhere. By positing the existence of universal values which can be discovered through reason, the human rights discourse can too easily engender arrogance. One definition the *Shorter Oxford English Dictionary* provides for the latter term is 'undue assumption of knowledge'. An approach convinced of the righteousness of human rights standards must ultimately lead to arrogance because it excludes the experience of the 'other'. This is why I always try to shake the righteous beliefs of those students who readily embrace the view that human rights are universal and encourage them to remain sceptical of what they think they know. In other words, I try to instil in them an awareness of cultural relativism. If I speak of 'awareness' in the last sentence, it is because both the concept of culture and the idea of relativism underlying 'cultural relativism' are problematic, as I shall now explain.

Relativism as indifference

I have made clear that I am wary of universalism. This does not entice me to its supposed opposite, which rejects the idea of the universality of human rights to embrace a cultural relativist position. The thrust of this latter position is to argue that human rights entail negative comments upon other cultures – unjustifiably, since each culture has its own moral values. This argument is problematic on more than one count.

First, what concept of 'culture' underlies a cultural relativist position?

As pointed out in the introduction and by various contributors to this volume, cultures and societies are never as homogeneous as they appear. Quite commonly, the term culture is used to refer to a traditional mode of living shared by a group, in a way that fails to take into account historical change and the absence of completely fixed boundaries around any human group. Cultural relativism tends to assume that people are more determined by their culture than they in fact are. This is problematic because individuals are boxed in a mode which is presumed to suit them, closing them off from avenues they may have preferred to embrace.

A second problem with cultural relativism is that it often posits a stark ideological divide between the collectivism of would-be 'traditional' societies and the individualism of the West. The argument runs that the individual logic of the human rights ideology does not suit the more communatarian logic of non-Western societies (see Pollis & Schwabb 1980). This is to forget that even these societies recognize the purposeful agent (a term possibly more adequate than the 'individual', which tends to connote a Western subject endowed with rights and duties) and the need for his or her protection.[1] The stark divide posited between the West and the rest of the world just does not exist.

Following from this, cultural relativism obscures the fact that the spread of the modern state makes human rights relevant throughout the world.[2] I ask the few students who fiercely contest the value of universal human rights in my classroom whether they think that opponents who face execution in a dictatorial state would accept that the fact that they are from a non-Western culture invalidates their claims for human rights protection. I try to tell them: 'Feel something, and say something!' In other words, I ask them to resist a cultural relativist position which can make moral agents indifferent to immoral situations. As Elvin Hatch has recently observed, 'this position may lead to moral neutrality and inaction in situations that are intolerable' (Hatch 1997: 372). From a relativist perspective, culture easily becomes an excuse for abuse.

Of course all that I have said so far means that we are in a conundrum. On the one hand, I have suggested that the adoption of a cultural relativist position can foster unjustifiable indifference. This directs us back to the idea that some values must be universal. On the other hand, I have observed in the previous section that for anyone to believe that the values he or she holds are universal is dangerous, because it leads easily to arrogance. I shall argue that the one way out of this conundrum is to err uncomfortably between the two poles represented by universalism and relativism.

Before examining how to do this, it is worth asking whether some situations are so obviously clear-cut that we should not err in between but should adopt a universalist position. Hatch asserts that 'political executions, genocide, genital mutilations, honour killings, and the like' are 'situations in which ethical relativism is untenable' (ibid). This may well appear so. However, in respect to female genital mutilation, which happens to be the one area on Hatch's list in which I have done some research,[3] I would dispute his claim. This makes me think that a universalist position must *always* be approached with caution. I shall indeed argue that a cultural relativist position often creeps, unrecognized, into universalist discourses. Before making this point, let me first explain in what sense female genital mutilation is not a clear-cut case which allows us to choose firmly between universalism and relativism.[4]

Erring uncomfortably in-between: female circumcision as an unlikely illustration

Through activists' writings, the Western world has become increasingly aware since the 1970s that women inhabiting some parts of Africa have had for centuries, and continue to have, their daughters circumcised as a matter of course (Thomas 1996: 339 and references cited). Speaking of circumcision in this context is most often an euphemism. The term designates an array of practices which range from – rarely – the removal of the prepuce (circumcision in the proper sense of the term), to the ablation of the clitoris (excision), to the cutting of the labia, which are left to heal through scarring while a small hole is maintained for the passage of urine and menstruation (infibulation). To a Western sensitivity, the very idea that such operations are performed on young women and even infants sends shivers down the spine and fills one with horror. How can this be possible?

Those who practice female circumcision generally invoke tradition to justify the practice. They say they do it because 'it has always been done'. Pressed to elaborate, they cite religious, health and sexual reasons. Some groups, for example, believe that circumcision makes the woman clean, or that it enhances her fertility, or that it protects her future babies against a perceived lethal danger of the baby coming into contact with female genitals.[5] All these justifications do not stand up to Western rationality and sensibility, which see these operations as maintaining the subordination of women to men in an appalling and health-damaging way. Outright condemnations of these practices abound in the West.[6]

However, for the great majority of women born into the societies

some enlightened
me-go along. —
key

concerned, circumcision is what makes a woman a woman. These women cannot envisage not circumcising their daughters, despite the pain they thereby inflict upon them, because they know that otherwise their daughters would never become proper women, and would fail to find husbands later in life. Of course, we can dispute this knowledge from a Western perspective. But if we accept the idea of looking at the world from the perspective of these women, we can see why the practice is so resilient to efforts undertaken to eradicate it. We can also understand why migrant populations from the societies concerned continue to have their daughters circumcised even when they are living in a completely different environment (Touré 1994). In what follows I shall concentrate on what has happened in France, for the way things have developed there illustrates particularly well how one cannot squarely side with either a universalist or a relativist position.

France presents itself as *le pays des droits de l'homme* – the land of human rights.[7] The French Revolution marked a shift from a political system based on status and privilege to one which declared liberty and equality as its founding principles. The French political system was and continues to be seen by the French as embodying universal values. In this view, what makes someone French is her or his adherence to the values of the Republic, conceived as universal. Anyone can become French as long as he or she recognizes these values, but those who embrace different values cannot be truly French. Hence there is an overall tendency in contemporary migrant French policies towards integration (some would say assimilation), rather than towards recognition of difference (through 'multiculturalism') (Hargreaves 1995: 160–164; Favell 1998, ch. 3).

Considering this background, it is not surprising that France finds it difficult to accommodate, or even to ignore, the practice of female circumcision on its territory by migrant populations. In France, criminal cases have been brought against mothers and fathers who have had their daughters circumcised, as well as against women thought to have performed the operation (*exciseuses*). No other country in Europe has followed this route of instigating lawsuits, even though female circumcision is practised wherever there are migrant populations from regions where the practice is prevalent. The fact that such practices occur is well-known, and explains why Britain and Sweden, among others, have adopted laws which specifically criminalize female circumcision (Toubia & Rahman 2000). While in France no specific law has been passed, a number of prosecutions based upon general laws on assault have occurred. They have met with mixed results.

The cases have been directed mainly against Soninke and Bambara women, many of whom arrived in France around 1980. The story of Bobo Traoré made the headlines in July 1982. Bobo died, aged three months, in Créteil, near Paris. The autopsy revealed that there was no blood left in her body. The explanation was that she had been excised two days before. Despite the obvious complications, her father had decided not to take her to hospital, fearing that what he had done would be considered illegal in France. Following the media outcry, public prosecutors begun to bring out similar cases upon which they had not acted.

A number of prosecutions ensued. Five cases were brought up before correctional tribunals between 1982 and 1987.[8] The fact that the French correctional tribunal is competent to hear cases that can result in a sentence of up to five years' imprisonment indicates that an excision was not originally conceived as an offence likely to lead to a very severe sentence. The conviction of the father of Bintou Doukara, who suffered a relatively minor haemorrhage, is typical of this first wave of prosecutions. Mr Doukara was tried for voluntary assault on a child under fifteen years of age and received a one-year suspended sentence.[9] Interestingly, the Prosecutor himself had requested the suspension of the sentence. This suggests some discomfort on his part at handling the prosecution – a fact to which I shall return.

A shift in the history of the excision trials occurred in May 1986 when the correctional tribunal declared itself non-competent to hear the Coulibaly/Keita case, brought against the parents of six daughters, as well as the *exciseuse*. In July 1987 the Court of Appeal confirmed the decision of non-competence by the correctional tribunal, accepting the argument put forward by the *parties civiles*,[10] but rejected by the Prosecution, that proceedings related to the cutting of the clitoris were within the jurisdiction of the *assise* court (competent for the most serious crimes), as opposed to that of the correctional tribunal (competent for less serious crimes). To understand this development, it is necessary to mention a case which concerned an excision in the technical sense of the term but which had nothing to do with custom and culture.

In August 1983, a French woman, Danièle Richer, who had no African connection, was convicted by an *assise* Court in Britanny for having sadistically cut the clitoris of her daughter. The Court had applied Article 312 of the penal code, which provided that any voluntary violence upon a child of under fifteen years of age was to be punished by imprisonment of between ten and twenty years if mutilation, permanent disability or unintentional death resulted. The *parties civiles* in the migrant cases argued that an excision being always an excision, the Richer case constituted a precedent to be followed in the subsequent

Table 3.1 Basic information on the French excision trials[a]

Date Tribunal location	Defendant's name (status)	Incriminated excision	Sentence or other outcome
11.1979 Correctionel Paris	Unknown (exciseuse)	Performed in June 1978 on a 3-year-old who dies as a result	1 year suspended
10.1982/4? Correctionel Paris	F. Doukara (father)	Performed on 3 month-old Bintou who goes for two weeks to hospital	1 year suspended
08.1983 Cassation Court	D. Richer (mother)	Performed by the accused who was French and insane	Unknown
1984 Correctionel Paris	Unknown	Resulted in death	1 year suspended
1984 Correctionel Paris	Traoré (father)	Performed in July 1982 on 3-month-old Bobo who died as a result. Media outcry	Declaration of incompetence (upheld in appeal)[b]
05.1986 Correctionel Paris	Coulibaly (parents) / A. Keita (exciseuse)	Performed in 1982 and 1983 on six sisters aged 15 months to 8 yrs	Declaration of incompetence (upheld in appeal in July 1987)
1987 Correctionel ?	Unknown	Resulted in death	2 years suspended
05.1988 Assise Pontoise	Baradji (father and two wives)	Performed in April 1983 on Mantessa a few weeks-old, who died as a result	3 years suspended
10.1989 Assise Pontoise	D. Fofana (mother)	Performed in June 1984 on week-old Assa who suffers a minor infection as a result	3 years suspended
06.1990 Assise Bobigny	Soumaré (father)	Objected to by French mother afterwards	3 years suspended
03.1991 Assise Paris	Coulibaly (parents) / A. Keita (exciseuse)	(See above)	Parents: 5 years suspended Exciseuse: 5 years
06.1991 Assise Bobigny (closed trial)[c]	Unknown (high number of parents) / A. Keita (exciseuse)	16 excisions, one leading to death	3 fathers: acquitted mothers: 1 year suspended Exciseuse: 4 years, 1 of which suspended[d]
01.1993 Assise Paris	T. Jahate (mother)	Performed on two sisters	5 years, 4 of which suspended
01.1993 Assise Bobigny	K. Diane (mother)	(Contested) infibulation on a month-old baby	5 years suspended

Table 3.1 contd.

Date Tribunal location	Defendant's name (status)	Incriminated excision	Sentence or other outcome
02.1993 Assise Paris	Camara (father and two wives)		Father: 4 years suspended except for 1 month. His wives: 3 years suspended
02.1993 Assise Paris	T. Traoré and K. Doukoré (2 mothers and friends)	Performed on two girls, one 2-year-old and one 3-year-old, one of whom requires hospital treatment	5 years suspended
04.1993 Assise Bobigny	Abd. Keita (husband and accomplice of exciseuse)	Involved in 4 excisions	4 years, one of which suspended
06.1993 Assise Paris	A. Tandian (mother)	1989 excision, denounced through anonymous call to PMI (medical centre)	3 years, 2.5 of which suspended
09/10.1993 Assise Paris	B. Fofana (mother)		5 years suspended
09.1993 Assise Paris	Unknown (mother and father)		1 year suspended
01.1994 Assise Bobigny	Unknown (mother and father)	Performed in 1989 and signalled by a doctor	Mother: 2 years suspended Father: 1 year suspended
09.1994 Assise Paris	A. Traoré (mother), S. Diarra (father) / H. Gréou (exciseuse)	Performed ten years before	Parents: acquitted Exciseuse: 1 year suspended
		HISTORY UNKNOWN BY AUTHOR	
02.1999 Assise Paris	Koita (mother), 32 other mothers and 3 fathers / H. Gréou (exciseuse)	Some 50 excisions, one of which denounced by the grown-up daughter of Mrs. Koita	Mrs Koita: 2 years. The other parents: suspended. Exciseuse: 8 years

[a] The sources consulted are not always consistent regarding dates, spelling of names, and the kind of information provided.
[b] In 1986 the father was sentenced to a two-year sentence. He later went insane.
[c] Due to a defendant having been a minor at the time of the excision.
[d] However, the conviction was not to appear on Mrs. Keita's *casier*.

Sources: Weil-Curiel (interviews), Winter 1994, Lefeuvre-Déotte 1997 and *Le Monde* (1989–1993).

cases of excision involving Africans. Their reasoning was that any discrimination between different types of excision would be racist because it would leave girls of African origin unprotected from mutilation. This is the argument that prevailed before the correctional tribunal in 1986 and before the Court of Appeal in 1987. Since then, excision cases have always been brought under Article 312 of the penal code. As a result, they have been heard by *assise* courts from 1988 onwards. To this day, the two *assise* courts before which most excision cases have been brought are those of Paris and Bobigny.

The French *assise* court is constituted by three professional judges and a jury of nine citizens. The procedure is entirely oral. A verdict of condemnation is reached when at least eight of the twelve persons constituting the bench vote in this direction. In the case of the excision trials, commentators have remarked that the atmosphere in the courtroom was less reminiscent of a legal trial than of an academic colloquium or a political debate. This was because it is not so much the details of a particular case which are debated as the general issue of the practice of excision. In excision trials the same arguments are repeated from one trial to the next, although obviously before a different jury; the same experts (including Michel Erlich and Claude Meillassoux) say basically the same thing. Linda Weil-Curiel, who has represented a *partie civile* in more than twenty of these cases told me she found these audiences tedious. For her, what is being said in the one or two days of the trial has become highly predictable.

Three main arguments can be identified on the side of the Prosecution and the *parties civiles*. First, given that the facts are generally not disputed, the main question is whether the accused knew they were acting against the law. The answer is that they did. Second, all sane citizens are legally responsible for their acts. The force of custom must give way before the law and the act of excision can therefore not be condoned. Third, France has a duty to protect all its children, irrespective of their colour. Failing adequately to react would be both immoral and racist.

The defence also puts forward three main arguments. First, the parents are not criminals. Not only did they not intend to hurt their child, from their perspective, having the excision performed is an act of love. While the act is criminal, the criminal intention – the moral element of the infraction – is absent. Second, the accused were acting under the constraint of a powerful custom. Even if they were aware that what they were doing was illegal in France, they could not take in and act upon this information. Third, imprisoning a mother – the most likely defendant – only makes the situation worse for the children.

There is insufficient space here to show how these arguments are elaborated in the courtroom.[11] However, the argument that the mother regards excision as an act of love deserves more attention. As we have seen, female genital mutilation is commonly considered as marking one of the limits of cultural relativism. This is so even for an anthropologist such as Hatch, whose general argument is in defence of relativism. Interestingly, Hatch does not explain his position, as if it goes without saying that female genital mutilation offends universal principles. If this is so, it is presumably because, from a Western perspective, female circumcision brings about gratuitous suffering, affecting children for the rest of their life, in an irreversible way.

In this light, the argument that excision is an act of *love* appears aberrant. Indeed, female circumcision is generally regarded by outsiders to the societies concerned (and, rarely, by insiders, too) as an act of *cruelty* – hence its other, and many would argue more proper, denomination as female genital mutilation. Witness an article in *The Big Issue* (September 29 – October 5 1997) entitled 'The Unkindest Cut'. Its point was precisely to protest against the use of the term 'circumcision' to designate mutilatory practices. Cruelty runs as a leit-motif in the relevant literature.[12] However, a different image emerges from accounts which attempt to give a voice to the mothers directly concerned, and in which it becomes clear that mothers have their daughters circumcised, in perfect awareness of the pain inflicted, not out of cruelty but to enable their daughters to have a future as women. A striking illustration of this reasoning is provided by the mother who decides not to have her youngest daughter circumcised because the girl has Down's Syndrome and would not be marriageable anyway (reported in Lightfoot-Klein 1989: 264).[13]

This aspect is often lost on Western audiences. As I was waiting to interview Linda Weil-Curiel in the Paris Court of Justice, one of her clients, a French middle-aged man accused of some business misdemeanour, hearing I was doing some research on the excision trials, exclaimed: 'These things are awful. How can anyone do that to little girls – and one's own at that? These people must be jailed'. The horror he expressed not only towards the act of circumcision but also towards the persons apparently directly responsible for it, is one that I expect is widely shared in French society (and beyond). My feeling is that the nine members of the jury selected to decide each excision trial often think at the outset that the issue is straightforward. If I am right, the outcomes of the trials indicate that their views change in the course of the judicial debates.[14]

Trials have generally been directed against the mothers of the excised girls because fathers can often demonstrate that they were not physically present at the excision and therefore argue they had nothing to do with it (which, *strictly speaking*, is often true as the operation is typically arranged and performed by women). As for the *exciseuses*, their identity is rarely revealed, which allows them to escape the judicial process altogether. Major exceptions concern Aramata Keita and Hawa Gréou, who have each been tried more than once and have consistently been dealt with more severely than parents.

The first trials ended with suspended sentences, slightly increasing through time, for the parents (usually mothers) concerned. The suspended sentences were initially of one year (up to 1984), then of two years (1987) then three years (from 1988 to 1990), and subsequently again (in March 1991) five years' imprisonment. In January 1993 a mother was sentenced for the first time to serve part of her sentence (one year of a five-year sentence).[15] By that time, two sentences of imprisonment had already been pronounced against an *exciseuse*, A. Keita. The pattern of steadily increasing severity then stopped. The other trials which took place in 1993 and early 1994 resulted in sentences of various lengths, which were suspended, although not always in their entirety. A striking development in the history of the excision trials occurred in September 1994 when the parents were acquitted. In this same trial, which dealt with an excision performed ten years earlier, the *exciseuse*, H. Gréou, received a one-year suspended sentence. While I do not know the outcomes of the following trials, it is clear that this lenient trend was fiercely reversed in February 1999 when a mother, indirectly denounced to the police in 1994 by her then grown-up daughter who had brought a complaint against her *exciseuse*, was condemned to serve two years in prison. In this last trial, the *exciseuse*, Mrs Gréou, was condemned to eight years in prison for performing some fifty circumcisions on young girls belonging to a large number of families. The other parents – twenty-three mothers and three fathers – received suspended sentences.

If the debates taking place in the courtroom are predictable for those accustomed to them, the verdicts are not. The wide spectrum of verdicts includes one acquittal, but also firm sentences of imprisonment. In the great majority of cases, however, the trials have led to suspended sentences, as if the courts could condone neither the consequences of an acquittal nor those of an imprisonment. Expressing a conundrum, these suspended sentences can be seen as reflecting the adoption of a mid-way position between the relativism and the universalism respectively entailed by an acquittal and a firm condemnation. Contrary to what this last proposition suggests, however, the adoption of a universalist position need not necessarily lead to a sentence of imprisonment.

Conversely, an acquittal does not necessarily mean the adoption of a cultural relativist position.

It is possible to be against excision as a practice and to identify it as a human rights violation without calling for its criminalization. Thus, when the Inter-African Committee on Traditional Practices Affecting the Health of Women and Children, which strives to eradicate female genital mutilation in Africa, heard about the sentencing of Teneng Jahate in the January 1993 trial, it expressed its 'alarm and concern' in a letter addressed to the French Ministry of Health, Social Affairs and Integration.[16] The Committee appealed for the case to be handled with compassion, arguing that the last thing children needed was the 'double punishment of first being mutilated and then separated from their mother'. This reaction indicates that a criminal conviction was not regarded as an option by an organization whose antipathy for the criminalized practice (as opposed to its practitioners) is not in doubt.

In the same way that universalism and imprisonment need not go together, an acquittal does not necessarily represent an expression of cultural relativism. The motivation for the acquittal may lay in an awareness of the plight of the women concerned, in a refusal to treat them as criminals. In this case, the acquittal does not entail any respect for the values embodied by excision. Nonetheless, it may not be the impression which emerges from an acquittal verdict. When I met Linda Weil-Curiel in March 1997, she still regarded the acquittal of the couple Traoré-Diarra in September 1994 as a major setback in her fight against female genital mutilation.[17] She worried that it sent the wrong message to migrant African populations who would think that it was now acceptable to circumcise their daughters in France.

While not dismissing her reading of the 1994 acquittal, I tend to see it in a different light. To me, the acquittal shows that the French judiciary, which had adopted an increasingly severe stance in the late 1980s and early 1990s, felt uncomfortable with the consequences of its stance. Applying my image of the pendulum, one can speculate that, having gone too far in one direction, it was driven to revert back towards leniency. It is as if the French, renowned for believing in the values of their Republic and France, the first country in Europe to have instigated criminal proceedings over female circumcision, were unable to draw the logic of their reasoning to its conclusion. However, one senses that a judgement of acquittal is unsatisfactory. As Linda Weil-Curiel remarks, it sends the wrong message. This in turn can explain the strict condemnations of 1999, which would signal an opposite movement of the pendulum.

Interestingly, when I met her, Weil-Curiel reflected that, when they grew up, the girls who had been excised in France would ask why the country in which they were born had done nothing to protect them. In fact, as I have already stated, the February 1999 trial was initiated by Mariatou Koita, who reported her excision to the police when she reached adulthood. Mariatou's action, arguably to be understood by reference to the fact that she spent some years in a French family, nevertheless indicates that culture should never be seen as set in stone. In the light of culture's flexibility, the recent return of the French judiciary to severe sentencing can be welcomed as offering, if not actual protection, at least some recognition of the girls' plight. But the judicial reversal is not wholly satisfactory either, as it sends to jail women whose predicament, not only in the cultural sphere but also from a social and economic point of view, should attract sympathy rather than blame. This is why I expect the recent condemnations not to constitute the end of the story. There will probably be further trials, whose outcomes will continue to follow the movement of a pendulum.

Judges and jurors do not speak with one voice, as the variety of verdicts pronounced from one trial to the next indicates. This, I would suggest, must be because uncertainties creep in as they begin to hear the other side of the issue. This is so even though they cannot hear the latter very clearly. The accused must feel at a loss in the grand surroundings of the courtroom where their fate is being decided, but where they often cannot follow the debates closely, French being a language in which they generally lack fluency even though it may be the official language of their country of origin. However, their answers to the court's questions, relayed by translation, as well as the testimonies of anthropologists and other experts, start to shake the assumptions with which the jury entered – or so I suspect – the courtroom. Jurors hear that the women concerned love their children and that excision does not always mean the absence of sexual pleasure, even orgasm in some cases. Perhaps they start to reflect that the position of Western women is not always enviable either, even if constituting a different predicament. They are asked to condemn women whose cultural assumptions are different from their own, but they are no longer sure what entitles them to do so.

This explains the suspended sentences and the acquittal. But these decisions do not represent the triumph of cultural relativism. What lies behind them is the awareness that general principles (whether phrased in legal language or in terms of human rights) do not do justice to the complex reality, and need to be 'relativized' in view of the circumstances of particular cases. What these decisions also signal is the demise of the arrogance – or undue assumption of knowledge – of the universalist position.

An in-between position, not a via media

The French material shows that an apparent simple truth – that female genital mutilation is horrific and must be punished – turns out not to be so simple. The problem with the truth is that if I believe in the truth, of course I believe that it is *the* truth; I believe that I am right, full stop. In other words, believing in the truth can all too easily lead one unduly to assume one knows best, i.e. to arrogance. To quote Raimundo Panikkar (1982: 93–94):

Truth has the inbuilt claim to be universally valid, here and there, yesterday and tomorrow, for you and for me. Yet my grasping and formulating it cannot sustain the same claim without charging all the others who do not agree with me with stupidity or wickedness. Hence the necessary *via media* between agnostic relativism and dogmatic absolutism.

Panikkar wishes to relativize the truth – what I have called the arrogance – of human rights, without rejecting altogether the ideal they represent and adopting a nihilist position (what I have called indifference). He recommends finding a *via media*. Initially, I agreed with him. After further reflection, I now think that the in-between position I recommend has little to do with Panikkar's *via media*. However, it is worth reviewing what he has to say because his essay is one of the most illuminating in the existing literature on the implications of the Western origin of the human rights concept.

Panikkar conceives of human rights as one window on the world, i.e. one vision, one way of trying to install justice. His point is that there can be other windows, visions, ways of trying to achieve the same ideal. He thus recommends that we look for functional equivalents to human rights in non-Western societies (ibid.: 77–79),[18] through 'good manners' or *li* in Confucian culture, for example (ibid.: 78), or *Svadharma* in India (ibid.: 95–100).[19]

We must accept that there are a *number* of worthwhile visions of how to achieve human dignity. The problem is that the human rights discourse tends to think of itself as the only one. In my words, it leads to arrogance. In Panikkar's words, it leads to blindness. To quote him: 'Human rights are one window through which one particular culture envisages a just human order for its individuals. But those who live in that culture do not see the window'. He continues:

For this they need the help of another culture which sees through another window. Now I assume that the human landscape as seen through the one window is both similar to and different from the vision of the other . . . (ibid.: 78–79)

This passage reminds me of a garden I am particularly fond of. The garden looks completely different, and yet the same, whether one looks at it from a window on the ground floor or from one on the second floor. The same goes for moral philosophies to the extent that they cannot conceive of other, equally valid, visions.

Our particular case is a typical example of the *pars pro toto*: from the optic of the inside it looks like the whole; from the outside it looks like a part, a fragment. Similarly, Human Rights are universal from the vantage point of modern Western culture, and not universal from the outside looking in . . .
  The answer which claims to discover the *totum in parte* is appealing, but not convincing. This is the temptation of the intellectual, who senses that any affirmation has the inbuilt tendency to be universally valid . . .
  Here lies the crux. We cannot but aim at the *totum*, and yet we often forget that all we see is the *pars* which we then take *pro toto*. (ibid., 94).

Panikkar asks us not to forget that our truth is not the whole truth. The best way to do this, he says, is to engage in a dialogue with the 'other', who will tell us his or her truth. In his words (ibid: 95), 'In brief, we need [to engage] in a *dialogical dialogue* . . . We must accept what our partner tells us: simply that we take the *totum pro parte*, when we are aware of the *pars pro toto*'.

We think we understand the position women who have excision performed on their daughters are in and what is best for them, but do we? Melissa Parker (1995) wonders whether it is the way we conceive of and practice sexuality in the West that leads us to an obsession with denouncing what we call female genital mutilation. Hazel Summerfield (1993) suggests that the infibulation of Somali women in London may represent the key to their relatively good mental health, because they are allowed more freedom of movement than their Bangladeshi counterparts. Rhoda Howard (1993) points out that Western women do not have solutions to the problems associated with sexuality, as the incidence of anorexia demonstrates, for example. We should be wary of pronouncing judgements on other people's ways. At least we should not assume that we necessarily know better than they do.

  This is not to say that we should be against human rights. Panikkar, for one, is not. On the contrary, he concludes his essay by saying that their defence constitutes a 'sacred duty' in the contemporary political arena (Panikkar 1982: 101). However, he urges more room for other world traditions, and hopes for the creation of an 'intermediary space' that would help bring forth, through a 'dialogical dialogue', the construction of a 'new myth'. While I agree with him that it is crucial to engage in a dialogue and not to assume that we know the 'other' before we have talked or listened to him or her, I am less convinced by his suggestion of a new myth in an intermediary space. Such a myth, I

think, would only displace the problem. I suggest that we need to accept
the discomfort of moving in-between, as a pendulum. In this sense,
Panikkar's *via media* is different from the unstable in-between position
that I advocate.

The difference in our perspectives probably stems from the fact that
we are not talking about the same thing. Panikkar has in mind the very
concept of human rights and its alternatives around the world. He is
talking all along about principles and moral norms. He is not concerned with the dilemma French judges and juries face when they have
to decide whether parents who have had their daughters excised
should be condemned or deserve sympathy, with the flux between
being drawn towards the universal and back to the particular again.
What he seems to be after is the meeting of two would-be universals.[20]
The same interest guides Corine Kumar (1998) when she talks of
culture as a real alternative to human rights formulations and forget-
tings. She tells us that culture can be good, that it need not be
conceived as something which mitigates or even annihilates human
rights. By contrast, when I try to understand why women are driven to
have their daughters excised or when Heather Montgomery (in this
volume) discusses what prompts Thai children to prostitute themselves
to Western men, we are questioning how principles can (or cannot) get
applied. In other words, we are looking at the interface between
principle and practice.

In other words, my aim is not to suggest that the concept of human
rights needs to be displaced, but to call for a concept that allows local
circumstances to be taken into account, to be part of the equation. Note
that I am avoiding the word culture. Let me explain my position further.

Against the 'footnote 10' phenomenon

Anthropologists are used to thinking in terms of binary oppositions: left
and right; low and high; nature and culture; raw and cooked; myth and
history. Here we are concerned with yet another binary opposition:
universalism and relativism. As I have indicated, my position is that one
pole cannot exist without the other. This is what Louis Dumont
suggested in his analysis of the caste system in India, when he coined the
phrase 'encompassment of the contrary' (1979). In this study, Dumont
discusses the opposition between hierarchy and equality, and compares
the Indian experience to the Western one. The former seems to be
governed by hierarchy, the latter by equality. However, Dumont argues,
one pole never manages completely to exclude the other; rather, it
encompasses it. Thus, in India, the dominant principle may be the

hierarchical one, but it includes the drive towards equality. By contrast, in the West, the dominant principle may be equality, but this cannot eliminate hierarchical tendencies and practices. In other words, the dominant pole cannot but encompass its opposite. The application to my topic is straightforward: universalism cannot exist without relativism, and vice versa. *True + particularities also change*

This directly follows Hatch's suggestion that ethical relativism presents us with a paradox: even though we cannot live with it, it is not clear how we can avoid it (1997: 371, 373). Hatch remarks that he first presented his paper at a session of the American Anthropological Association on the significantly formulated theme of 'Human Rights: Universalism versus Relativism'. He writes: 'Adapting a Derridian argument, the question of human rights and general standards of ethical judgement are never a mere "presence", something to be established in their own right, but exist only in relation to their opposite, which is relativism' (ibid.: 373). As I have said, one pole does not exist without the other. This is simple enough to understand. And yet this basic 'truth' easily gets forgotten.

The title of Hatch's essay 'The Good Side of Relativism', is highly revealing, because it implies that universalism is the dominant pole in the binary opposition, the term that can be taken for granted. It is as if it did not need to be argued for in the debate about the universality (note which word appears again) of human rights. Can you imagine coming across an article entitled 'The Good Side of Universalism'? Such an occurrence is unlikely because the *prima facie* value of universalism is generally not contested. There is more: universalism can so much be taken for granted that the other pole of the equation, relativism, can get almost totally overlooked. This leads me to what I shall call the 'footnote 10' phenomenon.

A footnote of that number recently appeared in a book from a leading law publisher which contained almost 800 pages of text and materials on international human rights (Wallace 1997). In a work of this length, one might have expected more than a lip-service to the universalism *versus* relativism debate. However, the one reference to the debate is hidden in a seven-line footnote (the tenth) to the effect that cultural relativism is 'an issue of such depth that it falls beyond the scope of this work' (ibid: p. x). With this acknowledgement, the book is written as if the universality of the human rights provisions it reproduces raises no issues whatsoever. This is consonant with the dominant attitude in the field. The question of the universality of human rights is of interest to anthropologists and to a few others who take it up at meetings especially convened to discuss it (like the AAA session in which Hatch first presented his paper), as if the rest of the world could forget about this fundamental issue.[21] It cannot.

Recognizing the ubiquity of the debate

I would go even further and say that the need for relativism is *so* fundamental that it is bound to crop up in places where we would not expect it. One such place is the European Court of Human Rights.

Anyone familiar with the case-law of the Court will have heard about the doctrine of the 'margin of appreciation'. Through this doctrine, the Court recognizes that national governments can be better placed than itself to appreciate local circumstances and local needs, and thus human rights claims. The OPI case[22] is one of the many cases where the Court has applied the doctrine. The case involved the seizure and destruction in Tyrol of a film which offended Christian feelings. The question the Court had to decide was whether, in so acting, the Austrian authorities had violated the right to freedom of expression. The Court decided there had been no such violation. It argued:

The Court cannot disregard the fact that the Roman Catholic religion is the religion of the overwhelming majority of Tyroleans. In seizing the film, the Austrian authorities acted to ensure religious peace in that region and to prevent that some people should feel the object of attacks on their religious beliefs in an unwarranted and offensive manner. It is in the first place for the national authorities, who are better placed than the international judge, to assess the need for such a measure *in the light of the situation obtaining locally at a given time*. In all the circumstances of the present case, the Court does not consider that the Austrian authorities can be regarded as having overstepped their margin of appreciation in this respect (*my emphasis*).

This represents a standard application of the doctrine of the margin of appreciation. The ironical effect it has to allow states to remain 'off the hook', so to speak, while the aim of the European Convention of Human Rights is to supervise state action, has not been lost on lawyers (Steiner & Alston 1996: 631–634). But we can look at the doctrine in another light. We can see it as a way for the Court to deal with the 'unspoken' pole in the universalist-relativist equation. The Court does not do so by naming relativism, but by inventing a new expression: 'the margin of appreciation'. The result is the same, in that the doctrine makes it possible for the non-dominant pole to be encompassed in the dominant one. It makes it possible to take into account local circumstances, ie what some would call – arguably, regrettably – culture (see Brems 1997: 162).

Conclusion

During the workshop from which this book arose, Peter Fitzpatrick remarked that the universal can never establish itself because it must be approached from the specific. The UN Declaration provides a good example, I think, of what he means. The Declaration pretends to universality, but it was in fact drafted by people who looked at the world from a particular window. Its drafters were addressing a particular situation, which they had experienced and did not want to see repeated.[23] While they were hoping to achieve the universal, they were doing this from a specific position. The same is true of all human rights conventions: they strive to reach the universal, but address the problem they wish to confront from a particular position. Fitzpatrick talked of a mutual compensation between the two poles, in which each constitutes the other. He was careful to point out that the achieved resolution is not knowledge; rather it is a constant effort to find one's way. I agree with him. This is why I say that the in-between position I advocate is an unstable one and have opted for the image of the pendulum.[24] Rather than a theory which invites us to choose one of the two poles, we need one which recognizes that neither is tenable without awareness of the other. We may also have to accept that, in practice, we shall remain torn between them.

ACKNOWLEDGEMENTS

I have developed the argument presented here over the years and especially thank the Centre for Cross-Cultural Research on Women (Oxford), the North–South Coalition (Oslo) and the Centre for Socio-legal Studies (Oxford) for the opportunity to share some of my ideas. I have borrowed the idea that relativism and universalism are unsustainable in isolation from each other from Peter Fitzpatrick, who articulated it at the Sussex workshop on which this book is based. Linda Weil-Curiel granted me two interviews and Anouk Guiné provided material on the Koita trial. The European University Institute, Florence, funded a research trip to Paris in June 1995. Richard Wilson and Jane Cowan offered perceptive and challenging comments on an earlier draft. Lysbeth Gehrels edited the text.

NOTES

1 Traditional African land property, often presented as being communitarian, is a case in point. Vanderlinden (1996, pp. 94–98) shows how such a view

grossly simplifies the reality, which is arguably more akin to a European model of property than is generally imagined.

2 See for example Dembour 1996: 22–24; Donnelly 1989: 5; Marks 1998: 481–482, 523–514.

3 This research is mainly literature-based, although it includes two interviews with Linda Weil-Curiel in Paris (June 1995 and March 1997) and one with Efua Dorkenoo in London (June 1995).

4 This is exactly the point made by Christine Walley (1997) in a subtle article which urges us not to understand female genital operations in either/or terms.

5 For anthropological references, see for example Boddy 1982; Erlich 1986; Talle 1993.

6 To be noted that international human rights legislation calls for the abolition of female genital mutilation either directly (see article 2(a), for example, of the 1994 Declaration on the Elimination of Discrimination Against Women) or by targetting traditional practices prejudicial to health (e.g. Article 24 (3) of the 1989 UN Convention on the Rights of the Child). Female circumcision makes up the lion's share of the various 'harmful cultural practices' that outrage feminists (Brems 1997: 148).

7 In support of this view, one can observe that the roots of the Universal Declaration of Human Rights lay in the French Revolution (Marks 1998).

8 For details on these and the other cases cited below, see Table 3.1.

9 Winter speaks of October 1982 as the date of this trial (1994: 944), but Lefeuvre-Déotte gives the date as October 1984 (1997: 23).

10 Under French law a *partie civile* is the individual or an organization representing the interests of the victim(s) in a criminal case. As a party to the case, the *partie civile* is entitled to its own lawyer(s), whose arguments typically parallel those of the Prosecution.

11 For a transcript of the arguments put forward at a particular trial, see Lefeuvre-Déotte (1997, chapter 1).

12 To give two examples: in *Warrior Masks*, Alice Walker recounts that she 'wanted to take [the little girls] in [her] arms and fly away with them' (1993: 49); half a century before, the anthropologist de Villeneuve (1939) expressed similar shock, although in a different style.

13 See also the testimony of Fadumo in Abdalla (1982: 105–107).

14 Interestingly the Prosecution's line has been relatively softer, as demonstrated by its lack of action until Bobe Traoré's death made the headlines, its initial satisfaction that excision cases were to be dealt with by correctional tribunals, and its frequent request for sentences against parents to be suspended.

15 The president of the court nonetheless assured that 34–year-old Teneng Jahate, who had been breastfeeding the youngest of her 8 children during the proceedings, would be freed that night, as he was going to request the application of a rarely used legal mechanism, which allows for the sentence not to start being served until the judgement becomes final.

16 See *Newsletter* no 14 of the Inter-African Committee on Traditional Practices Affecting the Health of Women and Children (July 1993: 6).

17 This fight does not consist in a criminal strategy only. It also includes an

education programme, consisting of posters, leaflets and most notably a short, entertaining, and excellently produced film entitled *Bintou à Paris*.

18 This is consonant with an approach which looks at human rights as having been invented to check the arbitrariness of the modern state.

19 He notes that the Svadharma vision should not be rejected just because it fails to live up to its own standards, as the system of castes and especially the treatment of the untouchables demonstrate. What he says about Svadharma can also be said of the human rights ideology. It is not because human rights are constantly violated that the ideal which they represent should be rejected.

20 For Christoph Eberhard, who works in the wake of Panikkar, what is important is to use a dialogical and pluralistic approach to go beyond (as opposed to stay in-between) the universalist and relativist poles.

21 The parallel with women's rights is striking. Although men cannot exist without women (and vice versa), women's issues tend to be forgotten and relegated to special forums, without ever managing to become mainstream.

22 *Otto Preminger Institute* vs. *Austria*, Judgment of 20 September 1994, Series A, No.295–A; (1995) 19 European Human Rights Reports 34.

23 On the impact of the Second World War on the development of the International Bill of Human Rights, see Morsinck 1993.

24 This image has limitations. In particular, it could suggest a mechanical reversal at a definite point from one pole to the next. Of course I do not suggest this.

REFERENCES

Abdalla, R.H.D. 1982. *Sisters in Affliction: Circumcision and Infibulation of Women in Africa*. London: Zed Press.

Boddy, J. 1982. Womb as Oasis: The Symbolic Context of Phraonic Circumcision in Rural Northern Sudan. *American Ethnologist*, 682–698.

Brems, E. 1997. Enemies or Allies? Feminism and Cultural Relativism as Dissident Voices in Human Rights Discourse. *Human Rights Quarterly* 19, 136–164.

Curzon, L.B. 1979. *Jurisprudence*. Aylesbury: MacDonald & Evans.

Dembour, M-B. 1996. Human Rights Talk and Anthropological Ambivalence: The Particular Contexts of Universal Claims. In *Inside and Outside the Law: Anthropological Studies in Authority and Ambiguity*. (Ed.) Olivia Harris. London: Routledge.

de Villeneuve, A. 1937. Etude sur une coutume somalie: Les femmes cousues. *Journal de la Société des Africanistes* 7, 15–33.

Donnelly, J. 1989. *Universal Human Rights in Theory and Practice*. Ithaca: Cornell University Press.

Dorkenoo, E. 1994. *Cutting the Rose. Female Genital Mutilation: The Practice and its Prevention*. London: Minority Rights Group.

Dumont, L. 1979. *Homo Hierarchicus. Le système des castes et ses implications*. Paris: Gallimard.

Eberhard, C. 1999. Pluralisme et Dialogisme: Les droits de l'homme dans une mondialisation qui ne soit pas uniquement une occidentalisation. *La revue du MAUSS semestrielle* 13, 261–279.

Erlich, M. 1986. *La femme blessée. Essai sur les mutilations sexuelles féminines.* L'Harmattan. Préface de Marc Augé.

Favell, A. 1998. *Philosophies of Integration: Immigration and the Idea of Citizenship in France and Britain.* Houndsmills: Macmillan.

Fitzpatrick, P. 1992. *The Mythology of Modern Law.* London: Routledge.

Hargreaves, A. G. 1995. *Immigration, 'Race' and Ethnicity in Contemporary France.* London: Routledge.

Harris, J.W. 1980. *Legal Philosophies.* London: Butterworths.

Hatch, E. 1997. The Good Side of Relativism. *Journal of Anthropological Research* 53, 371–381.

Howard, R. 1993. Social Degradation and Female Self-mutilation in North America. In *Human Rights in the 21st Century: A Global Challenge.* (Ed.) Kathleen Mahoney. Amsterdam: Nijhoff.

Kumar, C. 1998. South Wind: On the Universality of the Human Rights Discourse. In *Human Rights: Universal or Culture Specific.* North–South Coalition Information Bulletin No1, 111–150.

Lefeuvre-Déotte. 1997. *L'excision en procès: Un différend culturel?* France: L'Harmattan.

Lightfood-Klein, H. 1989. *Prisoners of Ritual: An Odyssey into Female Genital Mutilation in Africa.* New York: Haworth Press.

Lindholm, T. 1998. The Plurality of Normative Traditions and the Need for Cross-cultural Legitimacy of Universal Human Rights. In *Human Rights: Universal or Culture Specific.* North–South Coalition Information Bulletin No. 1, 10–46.

Lord Lloyd of Hampstead and M.D.A. Freeman. 1985. *Lloyd's Introduction to Jurisprudence.* London: Stevens and Sons.

Marks, S.P. 1998. From the 'Single Confused Page' to the 'Decalogue for Six Billion Persons': The Roots of the Universal Declaration of Human Rights in the French Revolution. *Human Rights Quarterly* 20, 459–514.

Morsink, J. 1993. World War II and the Universal Declaration. *Human Rights Quarterly* 15(2), 357–405.

Panikkar, R. 1982. Is the Notion of Human Rights a Western Concept? *Diogenes* 120, 75–102.

Parker, M. 1995. Rethinking Female Circumcision. *Africa* 65(4), 506–523.

Pollis, A. and P. Schwabb (Eds.). 1980. *Human Rights: Cultural and Ideological Perspectives.* New York: Praeger.

Steiner, H. & P. Alston. 1996. *International Human Rights in Contex: Law, Politics and Morals.* Oxford: Oxford University Press.

Summerfield, H. 1993. Patterns of Adaptation: Somali and Bangladeshi Women in Britain. In *Migrant Women: Crossing Boundaries and Changing Identities.* (Ed.) Gina Buijs. Oxford: Berg.

Talle, A. 1993. Transforming Women into 'Pure' Agnates: Aspects of Female Infibulation in Somalia. In *Carved Flesh/Cast Selves: Gendered Symbols and Social Practices.* (Eds.) Vigdis Broch-Due, Ingrid Rudie and Tone Bleie. Oxford: Berg.

Thomas, L.M. 1996. '*Ngaitana* (I will circumcise myself)': The Gender and

Generational Politics of the 1956 Ban on Clitoridechtomy in Meru, Kenya. *Gender and History* 8(3), 338–363.

Toubia, N. and A. Rahman. 2000. *Female Genital Mutilation: A Guide to Worldwide Laws and Policies.*

Touré, C. 1984. Des femmes africaines s'expérimentent. In *Les Mutilations du Sexe des Femmes d'Aujourd'hui en France.* Paris: Editions Tierce.

Vanderlinden, J. 1996. *Anthropologie juridique.* Paris: Dalloz.

Walker, A. and Prathibha P. 1993. *Warrior Masks. Female Genital Mutilation and the Sexual Blinding of Women.* New York: Harcourt Brace.

Wallace, R. 1997. *International Human Rights: Text and Materials.* London: Sweet & Maxwell.

Walley, C.J. 1997. Searching for 'Voices': Feminism, Anthropology, and the Global Debate over Female Genital Operations. *Cultural Anthropology* 12(3), 405–438.

Winter, B. 1994. Women, the Law, and Cultural Relativism in France: The Case of Excision. *Signs* 19(4), 941–974.

4   Imposing rights? A case study of child prostitution in Thailand

Heather Montgomery

Introduction

Anthropology has traditionally been associated with a relativistic understanding of moral issues, a position which is increasingly problematic in a period of globalization. The creation of an international community sharing the language of human rights and the values of liberalism considerably complicates the way anthropologists now have to think about the specific cultures with which they become engaged. Local understandings of culture, which anthropologists have hitherto emphasized, no longer seem to do justice to the demands of globalization, in which local law and custom are subsumed under international treaties and universal human rights legislation. Contentious issues such as child prostitution raise important concerns about whether a universal morality can exist and, if it can, what form it takes and whether it can, or should, be codified. The local knowledge of the anthropologist now has to engage with the universalizing propensity of international law and transnational obligations.

The issue of child prostitution problematises this new perspective not least by emphasizing how local variations and traditions challenge any simplistic reduction of local phenomena to universal facts. The idea of children selling sex provokes such feelings of abhorrence that one would expect child prostitution to be an area in which any potential conflict between 'rights' and 'culture' is easily resolved. One would accordingly argue that children have an overwhelming right to be protected from prostitution, and that there can be no place for a debate in which issues of culture, social background or local realities are taken into account. Yet I will argue that issues such as child prostitution are rarely as simple as they are portrayed. Nuances apparent in any discussion of this subject show very clearly the difficulties and dangers of realizing rights, even those that seem the most justified. In particular, I want to explore the issue of child prostitution in relation to the UN Convention on the Rights of the Child and how the universal rights that the Convention enshrines can be applied to a local reality.

The UN Convention on the Rights of the Child

Since its creation in 1945, the UN has been involved in the process of globalization. Its ideology is based on the ideal of universal standards that all countries can meet, and of certain inalienable rights that apply to everyone by virtue of their humanity. One of the most successful UN conventions has been the Convention on the Rights of the Child, which was adopted without a vote by the UN General Assembly in 1989 and has since been signed and ratified by almost every state.[1] Conventions such as this are presented as the benevolent side of capitalism and the 'New World Order'. While globalization may bring an unwelcome capitalist transformation to many countries, the UN conventions represent the gentler face of international development. They point to the gains that adopting Western-style democracy and concern for human rights can bring.

The Convention on the Rights of the Child is an integral part of the human rights discourse, as well as a culmination of six decades of work for children's rights and special protection for children. As far back as 1924, the special status of children was noted and marked out for protection in the Declaration on the Rights of the Child. This declaration was modified in 1959 and later metamorphosed into the Convention on the Rights of the Child (Van Bueren 1995). Alongside it ran various human rights treaties which expressly acknowledged the vulnerability of children and their right to special protection. The 1948 Universal Declaration of Human Rights, the 1966 International Covenant on Economic, Social and Cultural Rights, and the International Covenant on Civil and Political Rights, also introduced in 1966, all made distinct provision for the protection of children. None of these documents gave much indication as to how these provisions could be achieved, yet their inclusion into a larger framework of human rights emphasizes the indivisibility of human and children's rights (Alston 1994; Ennew 1998; Van Bueren 1995). While children may need special protection because of their age or emotional development the rights laid out in these conventions spring from the inalienable fact of their humanity. Indeed the writers of the Convention state this explicitly. The Preamble begins:

Considering that, in accordance with the principles proclaimed in the Charter of the United Nations, recognition of the inherent dignity and of the equal and inalienable rights of all members of the human family is the foundation of freedom, justice and peace in the world,

Bearing in mind that the peoples of the United Nations have, in the Charter, reaffirmed their faith in fundamental human rights and in the dignity and worth of the human person, and have determined to promote social progress and better standards of life in larger freedom,

Recognizing that the United Nations has, in the Universal Declaration of Human Rights and in the International Covenants on Human Rights, proclaimed and agreed that everyone is entitled to all the rights and freedoms set forth therein, without distinction of any kind, such as race, colour, sex, language, religion, political or other opinion, national or social origin, property, birth or other status,

Recalling that, in the Universal Declaration of Human Rights, the United Nations has proclaimed that childhood is entitled to special care and assistance.

The Convention on the Rights of the Child is premised upon the notion that concepts such as human rights or children's rights are not negotiable at the local level and that differences between cultures and between individuals within cultures can be ignored. The boundaries of childhood have become fixed and the parameters of a 'normal' or acceptable childhood have been set. The first statement in the UN Convention states that: 'A child means every human being below the age of 18 years'. Yet this is clearly problematic, ignoring the complex rituals and rites of passage that are part of the life cycle of many people. In Britain, people can marry, take legal responsibility and go to work – the defining features of adulthood in our society – while technically still children. In developing countries, the difficulties of a standard age are even more obvious. Boys and girls get married at puberty, they work as soon as they are able and they have their own children at an age we would count as within childhood. Anti-Slavery International has called child-marriage a form of slavery and has initiated a campaign to have it abolished (Anti-Slavery International 1995). But if we reject an arbitrary age of eighteen and accept local norms, the view that all early marriage is wrong becomes untenable. There may well be grounds for legitimate concern about the possibility of abuse when children marry early but it does not take an anthropologist to recognize that a child marrying at fifteen in full accordance with traditional norms and local custom in India is very different from a child marrying at fifteen in the UK.

Issues of cultural relativism *versus* universal notions of human rights have plagued UN conventions from the outset (Alston 1994; Cerna 1994). In 1947 the executive board of the American Anthropological Association withdrew from discussions that led to the Universal Declaration of Human Rights because it felt that there could be no universal standards of rights that could apply to all people regardless of cultural diversity (Alston 1994; Dembour 1996; Fluehr-Lobban 1995). Similarly, there have been regional differences about the wording of various human rights documents which have had an impact on the rights given to children. In 1948 the American Declaration of the Rights and Duties of Man was published by the Organization of American States (OAS). Although it resembled the UN Declaration, there were important differences, not least in the title, which emphasizes duties alongside responsibilities. Article 30 states that, 'It is the duty of every person to aid, support, educate and protect his children and it is the duty of children to honour their parents always and to aid, support and protect them when they need it.' Likewise, the African Charter on the Rights and Welfare of the Child, based on the 1979 Declaration on the Rights and Welfare of the African Child, states in Article 31 that 'Children have a responsibility to work for the cohesion of the family and to respect parents and elders at all times and to assist them in cases of need.' This tension around the balance between rights and duties is complicated, but it is where there is the most potential for discussing notions of universalism and cultural relativism. It is this tension that will form the basis of this chapter.

The UN convention tries to standardize an ideal of childhood and lay down guidelines for what is and is not acceptable for children (Alston 1994; Ennew 1998). It is an important document because it demands that children be given full legal and social status without denying their social and political disadvantages. Yet the ideal of childhood that it represents is based on a Western model which may not be appropriate for all societies. It implies that every child has a right to a childhood that is free from the responsibilities of work, money and sex: in other words, a Western-style childhood. But we know that children in developing countries have always worked, have always married and have always had children younger than their Western peers. They do not and clearly never will have any meaningful right to this sort of childhood. While setting up an ideal may be a benevolent (if naïve) wish, it is dangerous to codify an unchanging standard. Interestingly also, the Convention makes exceptions for different legal interpretations of childhood but makes no similar exceptions, or even acknowledgement, of cultural variations in the definition of childhood.

There are, therefore, problems for an anthropologist with the issue of universal children's rights. It has been suggested that children, like women, are a vulnerable group in society and therefore clearly need rights enshrined in law. However, women are a more obvious group. Although we can discuss 'woman' as a social construct, and draw a useful distinction between the biological given of sex and the cultural construction of gender, the boundaries between men and women are mostly fixed. The boundaries are much less clear when we talk about adults and children, not least because childhood is neither a permanent nor an homogenous state; when children become adults, their status and social identity changes. To speak of 'the child' as an ungendered isolate fails to acknowledge the differences inherent within children as a group. There are different expectations of children depending on their gender, their age or cohort set, and their position within the family (Ennew 1986; La Fontaine 1986). If generalizations about children are to be made, they must be qualified by these factors. It must be acknowledged that childhood is an inherently unstable concept and its ending – and even its beginning – differs widely according to culture and belief system. Notions of childhood are culturally and historically specific, and differ considerably according to time and place.[2] In any interpretations of the Convention it is important to avoid a teleology in which a Western view of childhood is imposed on other societies as 'normal' and which has a tendency to misinterpret, and even sometimes to demonize, other cultural attitudes towards children.

However it becomes extremely difficult to talk about children without defining childhood. A universal stance which claims that anyone under eighteen is a child is intellectually satisfying and expedient but leaves no room for the interpretations and needs of individual communities. To discuss children's rights in a meaningful way, therefore, we must also discuss local culture and confront the dichotomy between universalist and cultural relativist positions. We must ask: how does each society define childhood? What are the rights and duties conferred on childhood within that society? The issues involved in answering these questions are crucial and challenge the universalizing instinct of the Convention. To give an example, Article 16 proposes the right to privacy. In a Western context, with the emphasis placed on individualism, this is important. No one should open a child's letters or interfere with his or her beliefs and thoughts and adults must give children the physical and emotional 'space' to develop. But in other societies, where the community is placed above the individual, such a right is less relevant, and to leave a child alone and unguided is seen as a neglect of parental duty. In contrast, the African Charter on the Rights and Welfare of the Child stresses both the rights and the responsibilities of the child and gives equal weight to the concurrent responsibilities of the community towards the child. It recognizes that childhood is constructed differently in Africa and therefore that the realities of children's rights are played out differently in an African context. Indeed, it specifically refers to 'the historical background and the values of African civilization' as a starting point, rather than universal notions of human rights. One of the reasons why concrete attempts to implement children's rights are proving so difficult is because the notion that children are individual and equal members of society is alien to how they are seen in many communities.

The UN Convention, like other human rights documents, is caught in a contradiction between universal standards and their effects on individuals. While its provisions apply universally and equally to all children, it is individual children who suffer when their rights are infringed. The effect of human rights violations can only be felt by the individual and the consequences only suffered by the individual. Indeed, it is easier to measure the failures of the Convention when its articles are dishonoured than it is to measure its success. It is difficult to measure how much freedom from sexual exploitation children may have; we are only aware of the Convention when it has been disregarded and the abuse has occurred. Freedom of speech, freedom from hunger and freedom of thought become most evident when they vanish. Paradoxically, rights are most apparent when they are not respected in practice (Donnelly 1989). However, those who write the treaties, and even those who attempt to implement them, cannot legislate for individuals. They are compelled to pass laws and sign treaties on what they assume to be the greatest good of the largest number of children, even though these assumptions may not have been empirically tested or even be theoretically sound. Despite the importance of emphasizing the child as an individual, the realities of individual children are, by necessity, overlooked.

Child prostitution and the Articles of the Convention

Discussions of children's rights need not develop into a dichotomy between cultural relativism and universalism. Nor do these two extremes need to be viewed as irreconcilable. Yet the ways that sensitive issues such as child prostitution are dealt with reveal a dangerous lack of common ground between local experience and global expectation. The study of child prostitutes in this chapter brings many of the issues already cited into sharper focus. It is an extreme example that should, in theory, answer many questions about the desirability of universal rights. I will argue, however, that even this issue does not provide conclusive answers. Instead, it reveals many of the difficulties faced in implementing such rights and raises further questions about how rights can be both universal and comprehensive. The Convention on the Rights of the Child gives children multiple rights but, in practice, the assurance of one right often occurs at the expense of others. How these rights are prioritized is not culturally neutral and forms one of the greatest problems in their implementation. Even when there is worldwide acceptance (at least by governments) of children's rights, some rights will inevitably take precedence over others.

The sexual abuse of children has become a particular concern in the West and issues of child abuse, especially international child prostitution, have caught the public imagination and provoked new interest in the Convention on the Rights of the Child. Children's rights are quite clearly being violated when Western men travel to countries such as Thailand or the Philippines and have sex, whether paid or not, with children. The concern over this has mounted during the 1990s and in 1996 the World Congress Against the Commercial Sexual Exploitation of Children was held in Sweden, and was attended by political leaders from around the world. Child prostitution was variously referred to as 'a crime against humanity', 'slavery' and 'torture'.[3] It was clear that, at this Congress at least, ending the sexual exploitation of children was a priority, and the article of the Convention which enshrined the child's right to freedom from sexual exploitation was paramount.

Article 34 of the Convention declares that 'States Parties undertake to protect the child from all forms of sexual exploitation and sexual abuse.' For the majority of people, the morality of child prostitution is straightforward and Article 34 is one of the most heavily invoked and non-controversial Articles of the Convention. It is taken seriously throughout the world and the international codification of Western morality has undoubtedly gathered an indigenous momentum in local discourse. This discourse is fuelled partially by national governments, which have changed laws in accordance with the treaty, and practices that contradict it are outlawed (although these bans are not always policed). It has also been given impetus by local elites, especially those in the non-governmental organization (NGO) movement, which are fluent in the new global language of international conventions, and whose calls for changes in behaviour and for closer monitoring of those who do not live up to this new 'universal' law have had a large impact. In Thailand Dr Saisuree Chutikul, the Secretary-General of the National Youth Bureau, has stated that parents whose children become prostitutes should lose all their parental rights and even be actively discouraged from having children in the first place (Chutikul 1992: 5).

Although Article 34 is usually given top priority in discussions of children's rights linked to prostitution, paradoxically it may not prove to be the most useful in protecting children from sexual exploitation. Indeed, the emphasis on Article 34 can obscure other protections enshrined in the Convention that may often prove more useful to children. Articles which discuss the definition of childhood (Article 1), as well as those discussing children's identity and dignity (Article 2, concerning non-discrimination and Article 8, which deals with a child's right to identity), are as vital to an understanding of children's rights regarding sexual exploitation, because they deal with the very aspects which are violated when sexual exploitation takes place. Likewise, Article 12, which gives a child the right to give or withhold consent, or Articles 5, 8, 19, 26, 27, which deal with family support, must be seen as inherently relevant. However, too often they are seen as unrelated to each other and Article 34 is quoted in isolation, decontextualising sexual abuse and presenting it as the paramount difficulty that poor children face, without linking it to global issues of poverty, cultural background and discrimination. As Ennew *et al* have written (1996: 56):

The relevant articles of the Convention should not be limited to Article 34 or even to other articles relating to protection from abuse and exploitation. If eradication of sexual exploitation is the aim, then the maximum force of articles should be brought into action, in order to ensure that eradication campaigns do not consist merely of declarations of intent, legislation, prosecutions, rescue operations and rehabilitation of victims. Protection of children from sexual exploitation requires making use of all relevant articles.

Child prostitution: a case study from Thailand

It is easy to argue that the Convention gives a child his or her right to freedom from sexual exploitation by mandating all the steps that are necessary to prevent any harm, even to the extent of splitting up families. Indeed, Article 9 of the Convention specifically states that if it is in the best interests of a child, he or she can be removed from their parents. Parents who allow the sexual exploitation of their children are, by definition, bad parents and must be punished in order to protect the children. However, this may be harder to justify at the grassroots level, where the situation looks very different. As part of my fieldwork for an anthropology doctorate, I worked with a small slum community in Thailand for fifteen months. There were sixty-five children in this community who worked in prostitution, almost exclusively with foreign tourists. I spent my time there observing the children and asking them and their parents how they understood and justified prostitution. Their answers made me question how the multiple rights that the Convention gives children can be realized. They also forced me to examine the difficulties that I faced as an anthropologist in such circumstances.

The slum community that I worked in, Baan Nua, was based on the edge of a large tourist resort by the sea. It is famous for its sex tourism, which caters to the large numbers of foreign sailors who use the nearby port and also to Western and Japanese sex tourists drawn there by its lurid reputation. I came to know it through a local NGO which ran a small-scale educational and social project in the community. I lived away from this extremely poor community, feeling that a foreigner living within it would have drawn a great deal of unwanted attention. I chose instead to visit every day, as well as participating in some of the teaching programmes run by the NGO. The people in the community that I worked in were migrants to the area. They were attracted to the resort in the belief that where there were foreigners, there was money. Originally farmers from the north and north east, they had migrated to this resort around fifteen years earlier, looking for work as street traders or in the informal economy that grew up around the port. Linked by friendship and in some cases kinship, they arrived in the resort, found land which they originally squatted on but now rented legally, and put up makeshift houses made out of corrugated iron and scrap wood. Over the years, some of these houses had been rebuilt out of simple concrete breeze-blocks and had a more permanent feel to them, while others were patched together by whatever material came to hand. The land was barren and desolate and there was no room even for subsistence farming or a small patch to grow food. The number of households fluctuated throughout the year, ranging from sixteen to twenty as households changed, children moved out and built their own houses, and other houses finally collapsed and families move out. The inadequacies of the shelters were most apparent in the rainy season, which caused some people to move away, leaving fewer than eighty people in the community.

It is important to emphasize that these people were unrooted. There was limited contact with kin back in the home villages, but for the most part they referred to Baan Nua as home and saw no possibility of going back. Contact with the world outside Baan Nua was limited to a few children from neighbouring slums and the workers from the NGO. Because contacts outside the community were limited, kinship relations and community obligations took on a special significance within Baan Nua. The children had almost nothing, except their mothers, siblings and community. The majority of the children had been born in Baan Nua and knew no other way of life. The importance of kinship and social obligations cannot be overestimated, because it was through the duties that kin felt towards one another that the children who worked as prostitutes were able to rationalize and condone what they did. The community in which I worked shared the values of the wider society in its emphasis on filial duty. Children were seen a parental investment with an anticipated return and were expected to work for the family as soon as they were able.[4] The concepts of gratitude and obedience towards parents were taken seriously and the obligations towards parents were viewed as a child's primary responsibility. Even adulthood, marriage and having one's own children did not lessen these obligations (Hanks 1962; Phillips 1965; Sharp *et al* 1952).

Within Baan Nua, respect for parents equalled respect for mothers. There were very few men in this community. The young men left early, often for seasonal construction jobs, and showed little interest in marrying or settling down in Baan Nua. The younger boys stayed with their mothers and often worked as prostitutes themselves before drifting off in their late teens. It was the women of the community that held Baan Nua together. All the households, with one exception, were headed by women who controlled the labour and the income of everyone in the household. Even when one father was present, he did nothing to stop the prostitution of his children, who immediately handed their wages over to their mother to dispose of as she saw fit. *upsetting*

The duties that a child had to his or her mother were paramount. The mother/child relationship was viewed as the most important relationship of a person's life and the one that carried the heaviest burden of obligation and reciprocity (Hanks 1964; Muecke 1984; Muecke 1992). I was once told by one of my informants that 'even though Buddha showed his mother the way to enlightenment, he could not pay back the debt he owed her for giving birth to him'. The children in Baan Nua felt this obligation very strongly and saw it as their duty to support their mothers financially. Given the grinding poverty of the community, the *called:* wages of the children often made the difference between survival and going under, and were the means by which the community remained *sacrifice* intact. The children had tried a variety of jobs: selling sweets to the tourists, begging, scavenging for rubbish at nearby dumps, or occasionally working in unregulated garment factories making fake designer goods to sell to tourists. All these options were badly paid and exposed the children to further exploitation. Begging and selling sweets often resulted in theft or intimidation from older street children or the police. Working in a factory or on the rubbish dump was extremely hard in the heat and the unsanitary conditions, few children lasting long in either job.

In these circumstances, prostitution, especially with foreign clients, was a job which brought in relatively large amounts of money which could be used by the children as a way of fulfilling their perceived obligations. Prostitution brought in significantly more money than other jobs – usually five times as much as begging (Montgomery 1996) – and brought with it the chance to stay in luxurious hotels and eat well. Despite the stigma of prostitution, a powerful mitigating circumstance for many children was the fact that they were earning money to help their parents. Feelings of duty and responsibility were fundamental to all the young prostitutes; not to bring in money to support their parents would mean failure in their filial duties and obligations. One twelve-year-old, a very successful prostitute, was delighted the day that a client gave her enough money to rebuild her parents' house. She told me: 'I will be rewarded after this for looking after my parents'.

Both parents and children expected mutual indebtedness and obligation, but its extent remained ambiguous so that neither side was clear about exactly what they must do. The parents could be quite blasé about their children's prostitution and denied their involvement through justifications such as, 'I am his mother. If I ask my son to make money for me, he will go. I don't send him. He wants to go for me'. The children were sometimes less sure. One of the youngest children in my survey, a six-year-old girl, told me, 'I don't want to go with foreigners, but my grandmother asks me to so I feel I must.' Mothers would always deny asking their children to become prostitutes, but given the prevalence of prostitution in the slum, a child only had to look around and see what their sisters, brothers and friends were doing to know what was expected of him or her. Recruitment into prostitution was never through the mothers but through friends and neighbours. Children with regular clients would often be asked by these clients to find other children for them and, for a fee, they would recruit other children in Baan Nua. Mothers could therefore always claim that they knew nothing about their children working as prostitutes until it was too late. Both parents and children were working within the same cultural framework of reciprocity, but it was clear that there was uncertainty on both sides. Both adult and child were aware of the child's duties, but there was a degree of unease about how far a child had to go to fulfil them.

The jobs listed in Table 1 below are all the result of self-definition. I first asked the children if they worked and if they replied that they did, I asked them what they did and simply recorded their answers. Most children, disliking the term 'prostitute', told me they 'had guests', but as this is such a common euphemism for prostitution, I have assumed that everyone who used this phrase was a prostitute. However, not everyone is prepared to admit even this and there is therefore a large overlap between prostitutes and those in other categories, such as those 'supported by foreigners' or boxers who often work at bars where they meet clients. It is also possible that the jobs are not exclusive. Although the typical pattern of informal economic activity (Hart 1973) would suggest that the children had more than one source of income, in fact very few children seemed to work in several areas. Some children would occa-

Table 4.1. *Children's work by age*

	0–6 Mths	7–12 Mths	1–3 Yrs	4–6 Yrs	7–9 Yrs	10–12 Yrs	13–15 Yrs	Total
Not working	2	0	3	12	0	0	0	17
Have guests (prostitute)	0	0	0	4	7	8	7	26
Supported by foreigner	0	0	0	0	3	2	4	9
Street vendor/beggar	0	0	1	3	0	1	0	5
Garbage collector	0	0	0	3	1	0	0	4
Odd jobs	0	0	0	0	1	1	0	2
Boxer	0	0	0	0	0	1	1	2
Total	2	0	4	22	12	13	12	65

sionally beg and others would sometimes attempt to sell garlands or chewing gum in the streets but, on the whole, they listed their most regular and lucrative source of income as their work.

It is noticeable that all the children over seven years old work and bring in income, and that the vast majority of these jobs are related to the sex industry in some way. In both the 10–12 and the 13–15 age range, all the children rely on sex with foreigners for their earnings. In some cases this is disguised by the fact that, as the children have become older and less popular with Western paedophiles who want children of certain ages and sizes, they do not perform sexual acts anymore. Instead, they work as pimps and encourage other children to go with their old clients, a service for which the clients pay them. A similar pattern is evident in the next age range, although one child earns a living through odd jobs, including temporary construction work and running errands. There are only six children under three, only one of these works selling chewing gum on the streets of the larger tourist resort. It is the 4–6-year-old range that is especially interesting, as not only are there many children in this range but the majority of them do not work. Three of the working children beg among tourists, three sort rubbish on the nearby refuse tip and four of them (two boys and two girls) are already working as prostitutes. Although this seems to be a group of children who do not work, given the prevailing patterns in the older age groups, it seems unlikely that these children will *never* work. It also appears likely that they will work in the sex industry. No child over nine years old is working as a rubbish collector, and there is almost universal involvement in the sex industry after the age of nine which tends to suggest that earnings in prostitution draw children into the industry.

As I have already stated, there was no formal organization of prostitution in Baan Nua. Entrance into prostitution was through friends or older siblings who moved on to pimping whenever they could. The clients of these children were from a variety of European countries, with three individuals in particular having the most contact with the children. None of these men would be interviewed or talk to me, so my information about them came from the children. These three men had been visiting Baan Nua for many years and had formed relationships with many of the families. The children expressed no hatred for these men and over time, some form of relationship had been built up. They often sent money when they were not in the country or paid for large one-off projects like rebuilding houses or paying off debts. One client, an Italian in his thirties, was a regular visitor to the slum and both a client and a pimp of the children. He came to Thailand twice a year and stayed for a couple of months, during which time he videoed the children playing and took the tapes back to Italy to show friends and/or other men interested in having sex with them. For the children, the length of time that the men had been coming to them and the help they had given them meant that they could be classified as friends rather than clients. Almost all the children steadfastly refused to characterize the relationships with long-term clients as prostitution, abuse or exploitation. Another long-term client gave money to a couple of the girls if they asked for it and his most favoured partner always denied that he abused her. She said: 'He is so good to me. He gives me and my family money whenever we need it. How can he be bad?'

The mothers use the long-term nature of the relationship to characterize these men as 'good' men with whom they can trust their children. The fact that other men who come are friends of these men means they are accepted. The actual sexual acts take place away from the community, usually in apartments the men have rented. Generally the children live with their families in the village but sometimes stay out overnight with clients. In a few cases, the older children stay for a period of a month or two with visiting men, but frequently return to the village during the day. The effects of prostitution on the children are never discussed in the community. When I asked one mother about whether or not she was worried because her eight-year-old son was a prostitute, she looked at me blankly and replied: 'It's just for one hour. What harm can happen to him in one hour?' However, a child's body is too small for penetration by an adult, and some of the harm done by these men was evident in the bleeding and tearing that occurred during these encounters and which was ignored by many in the community.

Such encounters also brought my role as an anthropologist into question. On one occasion a boy was bleeding badly from his anus after a night with a client, so I took him to hospital, waited for him to be seen to and then took him back to the slum again. I had promised both him and his family that I would not intervene or try to stop him prostituting himself, but the extent of his injuries made me question this profoundly. Despite my beliefs about his right to have his wishes respected and to live with his family if he chose to, it was very hard, and not necessarily right, to have returned him there. Other rights, such as the right to be free from sexual exploitation and the right to protection from harm, were equally important. The fact that I was a supposedly neutral participant-observer did not mean that I could cast aside my own morality. To the contrary, I had very serious, and unresolvable, qualms about what I was doing.

Western men who use their structural, economic and political power to exploit the poverty of these children must not be seen as allowing such children to fulfil cultural obligations. Rather they are abusing and exploiting them. However, the children consistently gave different explanations for what they did and refused to view selling sex as inherently exploitative. To highlight this is not to offer a defence of child prostitution, nor is it to argue that children should not be protected because they have rationalized prostitution to themselves and to others; it is to acknowledge the difficulties of discussing children's rights when children and adults do not share the same viewpoint. The children certainly did not like prostitution and many rejected that label, saying instead that they 'had guests' or 'went out for fun with foreigners'. They refused to use the word 'prostitution', and constructed a view of the world in which their customers were guests, boyfriends or simply friends. One of the ways this was made easier for them was that there was no fixed rate for prostitution. The men paid them after sex but this was given as a 'gift' or a 'tip'. In other circumstances, a client might pay for the rebuilding or refurbishing of a child's family house.

Despite these rationalizations, both the children and their parents were acutely aware that what they did was considered wrong and shameful by those in the wider Thai society and that they could be punished for it. While Thailand has a long history of commercial sex, and even of child prostitution,[5] many Thais, especially in the media and in NGOs, bitterly resented the international spotlight being turned on their society. The focus for this anger, as a result, was not the indigenous Thai situation that had flourished for centuries but the newer, brasher model of prostitution when the tourist came in, bought whatever he wanted – including children – and left. The international press and NGOs had picked up on child sex tourism as an issue and, during the time I worked in Baan Nua, it was clear that the government was being forced into action by the campaigns. In 1993, stung by the international criticism of his country as a haven for child sex tourism, then Prime

Minister Chuan Leekpai ordered a crackdown on child prostitution. The people in Baan Nua were aware of this through the media and began to be very fearful for their own safety. Despite their own rationale and view of prostitution as something that supported the family and kept the community together, they acknowledged the opprobrium that it brought on them. Despite having little contact with the government and even less with the NGOs agitating to end prostitution, parents understood from the media that the prostitution of their children was no longer acceptable. For some this stigma become internalized: they stopped leaving their village and said they were ashamed to go out into the main town, where people might publicly condemn them. Others rationalized it on the grounds that they had no other options that paid them so well.

The children's justifications for working in the sex industry must also be set against their dependence on drugs and alcohol to get them through the day. There was a high level of drug and alcohol abuse in the slum, although the children always denied that they took drugs to cope with prostitution. Once the children had entered prostitution, they struggled to justify it and wanted to be seen as in control of their own lives and able to make informed choices. They were very reluctant to admit that they could not cope. To admit that they were addicted to certain drugs because they found life too difficult would have meant having to deconstruct a carefully built up self-image that many of them were unwilling and possibly unable to do. It is always dangerous to claim that informants have false consciousness and only the all-knowing researcher has a full insight into their actions, but the issue of drug abuse exposed the differences between what the children said and what they did, and also confirmed my own understandings of the effects prostitution had on them.

Imposing rights?

There is no doubt that child prostitution is physically harmful to children and that the international community should take what steps it can to eradicate it. At the same time, however, case studies such as the one presented here highlight the complexities of dealing with sexual exploitation and empowering children through rights legislation. Child prostitution is not necessarily the self-evident evil it appears to be for outsiders; in Baan Nua, ensuring a child's right to be free from sexual exploitation would mean violating their rights to live with their families and in their communities. Enforcing one right would mean infringing others that the children claim to value more.

The execution of this research raised many uncomfortable questions and dilemmas. The Convention on the Rights of the Child is explicit in offering children protection from sexual exploitation, and yet many of the children I surveyed claimed not to be exploited. In these circumstances is it acceptable, given the international legal precedent of the Convention, to ignore children's voices or disregard their worldview? Article 12 of the Convention states explicitly that:

States Parties shall assure to the child who is capable of forming his or her own views the right to express those views freely in all matters affecting the child, the views of the child being given due weight in accordance with the age and maturity of the child.

However, the Convention also lays particular emphasis on the child's best interests, which are compromised through prostitution. In these circumstances, multiple rights are impossible to enforce. It is extremely difficult to allow such children the right to be listened to and believed and yet not accept their explanations. Assuring one right only becomes possible at the expense of other rights – in this case to food, shelter and family unity, that is, precisely those rights which these families prioritize over the child's right to be free of sexual intervention. Equally, however, giving priority to the child's right to his or her own beliefs and freedom of expression (Articles 13 and 14), by claiming that there is no exploitation because the children do not recognize it, may jeopardize the premise of 'the child's best interests' and contradict other articles of the Convention, not least Article 34.

Undoubtedly, some of the children coped better with prostitution than others. Some rationalized it and claimed it was the life they had chosen; others denied that they were prostitutes; while others refused to speak about it, calling it 'ugly' and resenting my intrusion. Still others constantly sniffed glue and then denied that this was linked with prostitution. The reference point for all the children I interviewed, however, was the cultural belief in supporting their parents and their sense of filial duty. This is not to claim that culture demands that they prostitute themselves. While their cultural environment makes it more likely that they will become prostitutes, it does not mean that it is solely because of culture that they do it. Children undoubtedly gained satisfaction from being able to support their families and fulfil their kinship obligations, yet their agency was minimal and they remained socially and economically marginal. Their poverty and low social status consigned them to the edges of society, from where they had no structural power. With no welfare state or social security safety net, there were few options that enabled them to survive even at subsistence level. Both children and their parents told me that they chose prostitution and that

(poverty issue)

almost caste based

it paid better than other jobs, yet their explanations were not as unproblematic as they claimed. Parents placed overwhelming emphasis on their own cultural understandings and rationalizations and in doing so were unable to see the selling of their children in its wider political context. The Convention, and the NGOs who want Article 34 enforced at whatever cost, allow for no cultural specificity; in contrast, the people of Baan Nua allowed for no wider moral or political understanding. Whatever the children said about sex work, they did not have the complete knowledge to make a fully informed decision.

In these circumstances, it becomes impossible to sustain a dichotomy between cultural relativism and universal rights as alternative moral frameworks. Clearly there is a need for a dialogue between the two positions in order to ensure all the rights in the Convention are taken into consideration. It is obvious that cultural difference must not be used as a justification for harming children, especially when the abusers come, as they did in the case of these children, from Western countries which have condemned sexual abuse so strongly. As Judith Ennew has written, 'While cultural context must be respected, it is important to note that culture is not a "trump card" in international human rights' (1998: 8). However, it is equally clear that the process and consequences involved in implementing rights mean that not all rights are enforced equally and that some take precedence over others. In a Convention as complex as that of the Convention on the Rights of the Child, it is obvious that there are contradictions and problems and that not all rights can be realized equally for all children everywhere.

Local realities are important in understanding and resolving these dilemmas. It is only by acknowledging that children have a right to live with their families and to be protected from sexual exploitation, while simultaneously recognizing the cultural, historical, social and economic factors that have allowed child prostitution to flourish and taking steps to eradicate them, that children's rights can be practically implemented. When isolated from the other provisions and rights enshrined in the Convention, Article 34 fails to acknowledge all the complexities and realities behind the lived experiences of child prostitutes. Neither culture nor poverty on its own causes or sustains child prostitution. While it is possible to understand the children's view of prostitution through the cultural reference points of duty and obligation, this does not mean that child prostitution is an intrinsic part of Thai culture or that children have a right to prostitute themselves. However, their explanations and justifications are important and should not be dismissed by adults working in the child's best interests, without reference to the child. The Convention must be seen as a holistic document, allowing for a series of integrated rights and covering all aspects of a child's life. While children and adults may not share the same priorities, the Convention aims at a better life for all children. Discussions should not revolve around relativism versus universalism; rather, they should explore what is best for children given the unique cultural and economic circumstances of their lives.

Conclusion

The anthropologist is placed in an ideal role to mediate between cultural relativism and universalism: to study the priorities of individual communities and the effect that the rights discourse has at the local level, while being aware of globalization. This approach can also help deal with the contradictions inherent in enabling and empowering child prostitutes to claim the rights they deny they need because, as they explain, they are not being exploited. Instead of, on the one hand, imposing rights from above by removing children from their families in the name of universal human rights or, on the other, allowing children to remain unprotected rather than interfere with their 'culture', the anthropologist can offer a different way of understanding. It becomes possible to acknowledge the validity of the children's statements without dismissing them as misguided or wrong, while at the same time recognizing wider social and political issues of which the children may not be aware. It is possible for the anthropologist to view the children's references to filial duty or to clients as friends as cultural statements which acknowledge different cultural conceptions of children and childhood but, at the same time and more importantly, as rationalizations of an economic strategy which enable the families to retain dignity and achieve agency.

Given this understanding, rights, especially the right to be free from sexual exploitation, do not need to be imposed on children without their consent. Rather, they can be built upon the rights that children claim are important to them. It is not that the child prostitutes do not want the right to be free of sexual exploitation, as promised in the UN Convention, because it is part of an ideal that is culturally alien to them. It is, rather, that by taking that right out of context, and by disregarding the cultural prioritization of rights, its implementation is actually inimical to these particular children's well-being. By ensuring that their families could stay together and have a sustainable income, it would be possible to eradicate child prostitution without enforcing punitive measures against their parents. The commercial sexual exploitation of children does not exist in a vacuum. The material specificities which arise from

Thailand's position in globalized political and economic relations are as important as cultural specificities in perpetuating that sexual exploitation. As the International Tribunal for Children's Rights argued, it is 'important to take into account articles intended to provide support for parents (Articles 19, 26 and 27) so that the sexual exploitation of children does not become an inevitable income-generating mechanism within family survival strategies' (1998: 2). Article 34 would be redundant if the other rights enshrined in the Convention – rights that child prostitutes do so desperately want – could reliably be enforced.

ACKNOWLEDGEMENTS

This article was based on an earlier draft given at the conference on Culture and Rights held in Brighton in July 1997.

I would like to thank Jane Cowan, Marie-Bénédicte Dembour and Judith Ennew, whose comments and criticism helped me to reshape this paper and deepened my understanding of these issues.

NOTES

1 The US signed the treaty on 16 February 1995 but has so far failed to ratify it. Opponents of ratification in the US claim that the Convention violates principles of national sovereignity and American notions of the parent-child relationship (UNICEF 1998). The only other country not to have ratified the treaty is Somalia. According to UNICEF, 'Since Somalia does not currently have an internationally recognized government, ratification of the Convention on the Rights of the Child is not possible at this time'. (UNICEF 1998).
2 See for example Aries 1979; Ennew 1986; Holland 1992; La Fontaine 1986; La Fontaine 1990; Oakley 1994; Sommerville 1982.
3 Ecumenical Coalition on Thirld World Tourism 1990; Talierco 1993; Asia Watch 1993; Muntabhorn 1992.
4 See Havanon & Chairut 1985; Komin 1991; Muecke 1984; Mulder 1979; Tantiwiramanond & Pandey 1987; Vichit-Vadakan 1990.
5 See for instance *Black Shadow* 1940; Boonchalaksi and Guest 1994; Center for the Protection of Children's Rights 1991; Fordham 1993; Fox 1960; Hantrakul 1983; Thitsa 1980; Truong 1990.

REFERENCES

Alston, P. 1994. The Best Interests Principle: Towards a Reconciliation of Culture and Human Rights. In *The Best Interests of the Child: Reconciling Culture and Human Rights*. (Ed.) P. Alston. Oxford: Clarendon Press.
Anti-Slavery International. 1995. *Contemporary Forms of Slavery Requiring Action by Governments: Examples of a Large-Scale and Persisting Problem in the 1990s*.

Paper prepared in June 1995 by Anti-Slavery International for the United Nations Working Group on Contemporary Forms of Slavery.

Aries, P. 1979. *Centuries of Childhood*. London: Penguin.

Asia Watch. 1993. *A Modern Form of Slavery: Trafficking of Burmese Women and Girls into Brothels in Thailand*. New York: Human Rights Watch.

Black Shadow. 1949. *Dream Lover: The Book for Men Only*. Bangkok: Vitayakorn.

Boonchalaksi, W. and P. Guest. 1994. *Prostitution in Thailand*. Bangkok: Mahidol University Press. Centre for the Protection of Children's Rights. 1991. *The Trafficking of Children for Prostitution in Thailand*. Bangkok: unpublished manuscript.

Cerna, C. 1994. Universality of Human Rights and Cultural Diversity: Implementation of Human Rights in Different Socio-Cultural Contexts. *Human Rights Quarterly* 16, 740–752.

Chutikul, S. 1992. Child Prostitution in Thailand. Paper presented at the International Conference on Children in Prostitution, Sukothai University, Thailand.

Dembour, M-B. 1996. Human Rights Talk and Anthropological Ambivalence: The Particular Context of Universal Claims. In *Inside and Outside the Law: Anthropological Studies of Authority and Ambiguity*. (Ed.) O. Harris. London: Routledge.

Donnelly, J. 1989. *Universal Human Rights in Theory and Practice*. Ithaca: Cornell University Press.

ECTWT (Ecumenical Coalition on Third World Tourism). 1990. *Caught in Modern Slavery: Tourism and Child Prostitution in Asia*. Bangkok: ECTWT.

Ennew, J. 1986. *Sexual Exploitation of Children*. Cambridge: Polity Press.

Ennew, J. 1998. The African Context of Children's Rights. Paper presented at the ANPPCAN, CODESRIA, Childwatch International and Redd Barna Conference, The African Context of Children's Rights, Harare, Zimbabwe.

Ennew, J., K. Gopal, J. Heeran and H. Montgomery. 1996. *The Commercial Sexual Exploitation of Children: Background Papers and Annotated Bibliography*. Paper for the World Congress on the Commercial Sexual Exploitation of Children. Oslo: Childwatch International and UNICEF.

Fluehr-Lobban, C. 1995. Cultural Relativism and Universal Rights. *The Chronicle of Higher Education*. 9 June 1995.

Fordham, G. 1993. *Northern Thai Male Culture and the Assessment of HIV Risk*. Paper presented at the IUSSP Working Group on AIDS: Seminar on AIDS Impact and Prevention in the Developing World.

Fox, M. 1960. *Problems of Prostitution in Thailand*. Bangkok: Department of Public Welfare.

Hanks, J. 1964. *Maternity and its Rituals in Bang Chan*. Ithaca, NY: Data Paper 51 South East Asia Programme, Cornell University.

Hanks, L.M. 1962. Merit and Power in the Thai Social Order. *American Anthropologist* 64:6, 1247–1261.

Hantrakul, S. 1983. *Prostitution in Thailand*. Paper presented to the Women in Asia Workshop, Monash University, Melbourne.

Hart, K. 1973. Informal Income Opportunities and Urban Employment in Ghana. *The Journal of Modern African Studies* 11:1, 61–89.

Havanon, N. and W. Chairut (Eds.). 1985. *Nuptiality and the Family in Thailand.* Bangkok: Chulalongkorn University.

Holland, P. 1992. *What Is A Child?* London: Virago.

International Tribunal for Children's Rights. 1998. *First Public Hearings of the International Tribunal for Children's Rights: Extraterritorial Legislation on Response to the International Dimension of Child Sexual Exploitation.* International Tribunal for Children's Rights, Quebec.

Komin, S. 1991. *Psychology of the Thai People.* Bangkok: National Institute of Development Administration.

La Fontaine, J.S. 1986. An Anthropological Perspective On Children. In *Children Of Social Worlds.* (Eds.) M. Richards and P. Light. Cambridge: Polity Press.

La Fontaine, J.S. 1990. *Child Sexual Abuse.* Cambridge: Polity Press.

Montgomery, H. 1996. Public Vice and Private Virtue: Child Prostitution in Thailand. PhD Thesis. Cambridge: University of Cambridge.

Muecke, M.A. 1984. Make Money Not Babies: Changing Status Markers of Northern Thai Women. *Asian Survey* 24:4, 459–470.

Muecke, M.A. 1992. Mother Sold Food, Daughter Sells Her Body: The Cultural Continuity of Prostitution. *Social Science and Medicine* 35:7, 891–901.

Mulder, N. 1979. *Inside Thai Society: An Interpretation of Everyday Life.* Bangkok: Duang Kamol.

Muntabhorn, V. 1992. *Sale of Children.* Report submitted by the Special Rapporteur. New York: United Nations E/CN.4/1992/55.

Oakley, A. 1994. Women and Children First and Last: Parallels and Differences between Children's and Women's Studies. In *Children's Childhoods: Observed and Experienced.* (Ed.) B. Mayall. London: The Falmer Press.

Phillips, H.P. 1965. *Thai Peasant Personality.* Berkeley: University of California Press.

Sharp, L. and L. Hanks. 1952. *Siamese Rice Village: A Preliminary Study of Bang Chan 1948–49.* Ithaca, NY: Cornell University Press.

Sommerville, C.J. 1982. *The Rise and Fall of Childhood.* London and New Delhi: Sage.

Taliercio, C. 1993. *International Law and Legal Aspects of Child Sex Tourism in Asia: A Contemporary Form of Slavery?* Thesis. Sweden: University of Stockholm.

Tantiwiramanond, D. and S. Pandey. 1989. Dutiful but Overburdened: Women In Thai Society. *Asian Review* 3, 41–53.

Thitsa, K. 1980. *Providence and Prostitution: Women in Buddhist Thailand.* Women in Society Series No. 2. London: Change International.

Truong, T.D. 1990. *Sex, Money and Morality.* London: Zed Books.

UNICEF. 1998. The First Nearly Universally Ratified Human Rights Treaty in History. *Newsletter.* Geneva: United Nations.

Van Bueren, G. 1995. *The International Law on the Rights of the Child.* Dordrecht: Martinus Nijhoff.

Vichit-Vadakan, J. 1990. Traditional and Changing Values in Thai and American Societies: Bangkok: *AUA American Studies* 2, 27–52.

International and Regional Conventions

1924 Declaration of the Rights of the Child
1948 Universal Declaration of Human Rights
1948 American Declaration of the Rights and Duties of Man
1959 Declaration of the Rights of the Child
1966 International Covenant on Economic, Social and Cultural Rights
1966 International Covenant on Civil and Political Rights
1979 Declaration on the Rights and Welfare of the African Child
1981 'Banjul Charter' – African Charter on Human Rights and People's Rights
1989 Convention on the Rights of the Child

5   Gendering culture: towards a plural perspective on Kwena women's rights

Anne Griffiths

This chapter adopts a gendered perspective on rights and culture which highlights how women and men negotiate their procreative relationships and the claims that arise from this in daily life in Botswana. Based on research carried out in the village of Molepolole[1] between 1982 and 1989,[2] it is a local-level ethnographic study focused on the concrete and specific ways in which gender frames the relations of power up on which negotiations concerning family relationships among Bakwena[3] are founded, through social actors' perspectives and experiences. It thus is aligned with the shift from conceptions of 'culture' as representing a static, homogenous, coherent unity to a view of culture as practice, embedded in local contexts and in the multiple realities of everyday life (Bourdieu 1977; Sahlins 1976; Strathern 1980). This framework, which conceives of culture as an ongoing process, allows us to acknowledge heterogeneity in the social and legal practices shaping people's worlds and their relationship with rights (see Merry, in this volume). We may then bring together for consideration culture, rights and law in ways that undermine simple dichotomies between rights and culture.

Law, culture and rights: an ethnographic perspective

By taking account of the specificities of people's lives, my analysis reinforces the perspective on the relationship between culture, rights and law, that reorients the debate on human rights away from universalist/relativist polarizations. It rejects a notion of culture as bounded and focuses on the multiple configurations of meaning representing a 'network of perspectives' (Hannerz 1992: 265–266) that emerges from the situated contexts in which people live. What becomes key is how meanings are constructed, and how this raises questions about the power and authority to construct meaning, whether at a local, national or international level. Law forms part of this process, which in Botswana incorporates *mekgwa le melao ya Setswana* (Tswana law and custom), as well as European-style law, because when it gained its independence from Britain in 1966, Botswana elected to retain in its national legal system law made by its colonial overseers.

This legal system defines customary law as being 'in relation to any particular tribe or tribal community the customary law of that tribe or tribal community so far as it is not incompatible with the provision of any written law or contrary to morality, humanity or natural justice'.[4] In contrast, common law is 'any law, whether written or unwritten, in force in Botswana, other than customary law' (1969 Act s.2). Within the narrative of the Act that acknowledges their co-existence, two forms of law are defined in opposition to one another, representing systems that are mutually exclusive.

Inherited from the colonial period, this classification arose because the colonizers sought to uphold a clear divide between Europeans and Africans, which they marked, *inter alia*, with separate systems of law – common law for the former, customary law for the latter. Common law existed to govern the European 'self', while customary law governed the African 'other' (Hooker 1975). Such a perspective reflected a view of 'culture' that separated the European from the African in a way that promoted and upheld the concept of difference. Thus formal law engaged in the kind of essentialising of social categories and identities referred to by the editors in their introduction to this book. It also creates the conditions which lead to 'conceptual oppositions becoming frames of reference for comprehending culture', a standpoint that has been strenuously critiqued by Featherstone (1990: 2).

This process of differentiation stemmed from a colonial perception of Africans as possessing a group identity that was foreign to a European concept of law focused on the individual as the legal subject and bearer of rights. It is from this Eurocentric legal model, which was created out of the perceived relationship between state, law, and government that accompanied the growth of nation-states and the process of industrial development in Europe, that a rights discourse currently exhibiting global proportions has developed.

Colonialism has left as part of its legacy a model of law that continues to dominate legal discourse and praxis not only at a national, but also at an international level, in the form of various conventions on human rights. This model, often referred to as positivist, formalist or centralist, is one which promotes a uniform view of law and its relationship with the state (J. Griffiths 1986: 3), and establishes boundaries between legal and social domains and the rules associated with them. These domains exist in a hierarchical relationship so that the legal rules are not only set apart from, but acquire greater authority and precedence over, social rules (Galanter 1981: 20; Roberts 1979: 29) and are used to determine outcomes when conflict arises (Comaroff and Roberts 1981: 5; Roberts 1979: 20). Thus law, removed from the domain of social life, represents an autonomous field with immunity from the kind of considerations that permeate everyday existence. Through its autonomy and immunity from ordinary social processes – reinforced by the creation of specialist sources, institutions, and personnel – law claims to invoke neutrality and equality in its dealings with individuals who are subject to its remit, unlike the ordinary social world from which law studiously maintains its distance.[5]

Feminist perspectives

A positivist conception of law is greatly contested, especially by feminist scholars such as Mackinnon (1987), Smart (1989), Finemann (1991) and others, who argue that the inequalities existing between women and men as a result of the gendered structure of social, economic and political life continue to undermine women in the legal sphere. Attempts to rectify this situation have been made internationally through the 1979 General Assembly's UN Convention on the Elimination of All Forms of Discrimination Against Women (referred to as 'the Women's Convention'). The Convention contains guarantees of equality and freedom from discrimination by the state and by private actors in all areas of public and private life. In doing so 'it codifies the existing gender-specific and general human rights instruments containing guarantees of freedom of discrimination on the grounds of sex, though it adds some new provisions' (Byrnes 1997: 43). The concept of equality covers not only civil and political rights but also economic, social and cultural rights. At the core of the strategies offered by the Convention is Article 2(f), which imposes an obligation on states to modify or abolish existing laws, regulations, customs and practices that constitute discrimination against women. Thus Article 16 requires that married women and men shall have equal access to procreative remedies and equal rights in marriage and divorce. While the convention has no direct applicability, states are required under Article 18 to submit regular reports on the steps they have taken to effect their obligations under the Convention, and these are monitored by the Committee on the Elimination of Discrimination against Women (CEDAW), which consists of 23 independent experts elected to serve in their personal capacity by the parties to the Convention.

The Convention, with its focus on equality and rights, has been criticized by African scholars (among others) within family and women's law, who have drawn attention to its Eurocentric character. Armstrong *et al* (1993) and Rwezaura *et al* (1995), for example, point out that as an instrument for social and legal change it is premised on a mixture of law, modernization theory and liberal Western feminist jurisprudence. But this type of jurisprudence, while undermining conventional legal scholarship of the kind associated with legal centralism (because of its failure to integrate gender into its analysis of law) has come under attack for failing to take adequate account of the voices, views and needs of women of colour.[6] It has been accused of engaging in racial essentialism by treating white women's experience as the standard that applies to all women, in other words, of making one cultural standard universal, or rather, appropriating the power of one particular standpoint to speak for all. The debate is in danger of polarization in terms of universalist or relativist perspectives which adhere to notions of 'sameness' or 'difference', not only with respect to the treatment of women in relation to men but also with respect to one another. To overcome this impasse a number of feminists[7] are working towards a form of dialogue that can accommodate the diversity of women's experiences while acknowledging that there may also be experiences which they share in common. This process requires a form of knowledge that goes beyond the abstract propositions that form part of Western-style law, a form of knowledge grounded in the specific contexts of women's and men's lives. To acquire such knowledge, concrete data for analysis both within and across cultures are required. As the editors of this volume stress, empirical studies offer the possibility of developing a more grounded dialogue between theory and practice.

Law as a resource: procreation and marriage

Such a dialogue is important because it highlights the tensions that exist between 'the desire to formulate generalizing principles and the need to apply these principles within particular circumstances and contexts' (Introduction, p.6). In dealing with family law in Botswana, my data highlight the complexities of engaging in rights-based strategies that operate to the advantage of some, but not all, women. I will examine what is at stake here, in the context of women's procreative relationships with men and the role marriage plays in these relationships. For endorsing equal rights for women during marriage and upon divorce, CEDAW favours the registration of marriage and the abolition of polygamy, and it has put pressure on some African nations to meet these objectives by changing their domestic law.[8] The rationale for these reforms is that polygamy is demeaning to women who, unlike men, cannot have more than one spouse. In providing for equality of treatment in marriage, so that only one relationship for any individual can have the status of marriage at any one time, there is even greater need for the certainty that registration upholds. Such reforms, however, are often in conflict with customary law, which in Botswana both endorses polygamy and does not require registration for a marriage to be valid. Such proposed reforms do not necessarily improve the position of women because they fail to take account of the gendered world in which women and men live and how this impacts on their range of options in family life, including access to marriage and the law. Thus, there is a need for micro-level studies to assess the efficacy of internationally-initiated law reform in improving the position of different groups of women in different life situations. This means that, rather than perceiving of marriage as an abstract proposition, it is necessary to take account of the range of contexts in which it is negotiated and the consequences that ensue.

The life histories obtained during my research in Molepolole demonstrate that women's access to resources, including marriage, is heavily dependent on the type of network to which they belong. Such networks embody two basic forms of existence that emerged during the course of colonialism and which mark the process of social differentiation in operation in Botswana today. One type of network is formed by people whom Parson (1981) has termed the 'peasantariat', a group whose existence is predicated on subsistence agriculture, the raising of livestock, and migrant unskilled labour. These people make up the majority of families in the country. They may be contrasted with those whom Cooper (1982) refers to as the 'salariat', whose existence is dependent upon education and the acquisition of skilled and secure employment, which among the younger generation is predominantly government based. This group, which represents a national elite, no longer engages in subsistence agriculture or in migrant labour of the type entered into by the peasantariat.

These are, of course, not rigidly fixed categories – the salariat could not exist without social mobility – but should be thought of as the polar regions, rather than end points, of an uneven continuum of socio-economic-political status. They do, however, accurately reflect the lived reality of the vast majority of Tswana lives, as the authors in Kerven (1982) demonstrate. There are families that span both groups, highlighting the consequences that membership has for individuals, especially women, for negotiating status and rights to property. The life histories culled from over two generations demonstrate that women's access to resources (including marriage) and their life choices are heavily dependent upon the type of network to which they belong. The histories underline the ways in which power, crucial to an individual's existence, is constituted in everyday life; they also highlight important factors that inform people's actions before disputes arise or when parties turn to courts to settle their differences.

Local genealogies: familial life histories

The wide difference in life chances is exemplified by the descendants of Koosimile from Mosotho *kgotla*,[9] who had two sons, Radipati and Makokwe, by different wives. Makokwe's descendants, who constitute the majority of families in their *kgotla*, engage in subsistence farming and unskilled labour of the type associated with the peasantariat. Radipati's descendants, however, pursue another form of existence, one founded on education and skilled, secure employment that places them among the salariat. Within these two family groups women are differentially situated from men in terms of the claims they can pursue with respect to status and property. Their position in relation to one another also varies according to their affiliation within a particular group, as we shall see with three women, Olebeng, Diane, and Goitsemang, who, although of the same generation and related, lead very different lives.

For families relying on a peasantariat subsistence base, marriage still plays an important role in providing access to the broader networks of supra-household management and cooperation on which they rely. This is the case with Makokwe's family, which retains a relatively high rate of kin marriage among members of the older generation (ranging from fifty to ninety years old), they represent a substantial proportion of the current population of Botswana. When it comes to marriage within this group, women find their choices shaped by male networks and structures of authority, which provide the resources for their existence. For example, women who have their brothers' support often have the option of whether to marry or not – an option not available to other women who lack such support. This gives rise to a situation in which those with choices, such as Olebeng, may opt not to marry, while those without access to the conditions under which such choice becomes available, like Diane, want to marry but are unlikely to be able to because they lack the resources required to contract marriage.

Life for the women in Makokwe's family revolves round the village and the agricultural lands. Living in the village for much of the year they are able to attend school, unlike their brothers who are away herding cattle at distant cattleposts. This means that they are able to acquire a greater degree of formal education than their brothers. Among this group, women's work is integrated with that of their male counterparts. Makokwe's only daughter, Olebeng, for example, has been part of a family network, exchanging her domestic and agricultural labour for her brothers' assistance with ploughing and support. She has never moved beyond this sphere of operations to undertake any form of paid employment, which means that throughout her life she has had to rely on support from her father, her brothers and her male partners. Her five older brothers have been generous, assisting her with ploughing and upholding her welfare. They have, for example, consented to her taking over the natal household since they have all married and established their own households elsewhere in the village. Compared with other women, she is in a relatively strong position in that her circumstances have permitted a certain degree of choice, including over whether or not to marry. During her life she has had several children (all of whom died at birth) with a number of male partners, all of whom are absent from the village working on South African mines for all but a few days every year, but has never married. This is out of choice, according to Olebeng, who maintains that from her very first pregnancy neither she nor her family had any interest in pursuing the issue of marriage.

But Olebeng's situation is unusual. In the rural and village sectors of Botswana economic emphasis is placed on subsistence agriculture, livestock and cash input from migrant labour. In this environment, marriage is particularly important for women, who, if unmarried, find themselves at the bottom of the social hierarchy in terms of political power and access to economic resources. Social position in this society derives not only from family status and at which point of the lifecycle the individual is at but also from an individual's capacity to generate or control resources.

Gendered worlds: women's differential positions

In these circumstances women find themselves constrained by the gendered world in which men have a greater degree of control over access to resources (Kerven 1984; Solway 1980), and now especially cash (Brown 1983; UNICEF 1993: 12–20), which all households depend on for their existence. Almost all of this cash is obtained from remittances from the absentee mine workers who are the male relatives and partners of village women. Money is not only required to support family members but to maintain the subsistence base through the purchase of seed, labour (where kin are unavailable or demand payment) and livestock (Cooper 1980: 14; Izzard 1982: 712). Women have fewer opportunities than men to generate such income (Alexander 1991; UNFPA 1989: 13) as they do not have access to the most common forms of male employment – in mining or construction – and the returns they receive from participation in the informal economy are insufficient to maintain their basic needs.[10] Most successful are married women whose husbands have paid the cash – obtained by migrant labouring – necessary to promote and sustain their activities. Women selling fat cakes, for example, need money to buy flour and oil from before their enterprise becomes self-sustaining. While women may have access to livestock and land, utilization of these resources is often mediated through men. This is because it is men or young boys who herd livestock at cattleposts and it is hard to challenge a herder's claim that cattle have gone missing or died. Most people still rely on cattle to plough; those with a team have control over ploughing and the sequence it follows. These are mostly married men who plough their own fields before those of their brothers, parents and, lastly, unmarried sisters.

Within this kind of network, an unmarried woman finds herself at a disadvantage.[11] While part of her family and kin are responsible for her and obliged to plough for her, her position is a vulnerable one in that her interests are subordinated to those of other family members. This is the case with Diane and her unmarried daughters, who have found themselves greatly disadvantaged by the constraints inherent in a kinship network. Unlike Olebeng, Diane has had a more fraught relationship with her male kin, namely her brothers. Abandoning her after father's death, they have not only left her to fend for herself but have also appropriated for their own use the land she was left by her mother. Without access to her brothers' network she has found herself relying on a series of male partners for support, in relationships of *bonyatsi* (concubinage) that preclude marriage. Despite this she still firmly expresses the view that 'it is natural with Batswana to marry. A woman must marry'. Her own life history, however, has excluded marriage as a viable option, given the number of children she has had with different men.

Women who form part of an emerging bourgeoisie find themselves with a greater degree of control over the choices that are open to them. This is because, within their family group, they are less reliant on the male networks that peasant women depend on for existence. Goitsemang is just such a woman. Despite the fact that her father, Radipati, was Makokwe's half brother, her family members have experienced very different life trajectories from Makokwe's children. Unlike his contemporaries, Radipati (who died in 1950) was an educated man who placed great emphasis on his children's education, which his wife Mhudi struggled to provide after his death. As a result his three daughters were educated (at a time when many women only received nominal education) and acquired formal employment. The eldest unmarried daughter, Goitsemang (aged fifth-two in 1989), worked first as a nurse in South

Africa, then in a management capacity for a construction company in Botswana, enabling her to build a house in Gaborone – something many people in the village aspire to but are unable to achieve. Her younger unmarried sister, Olebogeng, has also acquired a plot of land in Gaborone by working for the same company. Radipati's sons were educated and two of them, unusually for that time, went on to acquire university degrees. Through their access to education and skilled, stable employment, the family fits the profile associated with the emerging bourgeoisie. Its members' activities differ from those associated with an agricultural base and they no longer plough.

Within this family group, Goitsemang, like her contemporaries Diane and Olebeng, has had children and remained unmarried. However, unlike the other two, she has had access to a world in which she was beyond her family's control in terms of apportioning resources. This is because she has managed to remove herself from the pressures that accompany dependence on domestic and agricultural labour and the networks that sustain them. Through her education and training, she had access to alternative means of support, which empowered her to make decisions on her own account and made her less vulnerable to demands made by kin. Indeed, Goitsemang has felt able to challenge her brother David's claims to control over the natal household under customary law and has received sufficient support from *kgotla* members to continue running the household for the time being.[12] Her situation is very different from that of Diane, who is unable to contest her brothers' actions, or from that of Olebeng, who survives on the basis of a co-operative relationship with her brothers. At her stage in life, Goitsemang has no desire to marry, observing that 'marriage just brings quarrels'.

These life histories highlight the ways in which individuals, who form part of a 'local' community in terms of genealogical and spatial relationships, find their life courses and everyday lives shaped by wider geographic processes. As a result, Botswana has long been dependent on first South Africa and then Europe as markets for its cattle. Similarly, Batswana people – women as well as men – have sought markets for their labour on South African farms, mines and urban centres since the mid-nineteenth century; in this century the search has intensified. All of these markets have been subjected to the vissitudes of fluctuating world demand and wars (Parsons 1977; Parson 1981). Schapera (1947: 8) observed that 'the [Tswana] people have been drawn into an elaborate system of exchange economy through which they are linked up with and even dependent upon the markets of the world'. More recently Kerven (1982: 545) has commented that 'Tswana livelihoods are made within the minimal core of the family and the maximal universe of the southern African economy'. The government of Botswana itself (1991a: xxi, 95, 145) notes the ways in which the country's development is inextricably tied to decisions, processes and events that take place at a regional and international level beyond its national borders.

The life histories sketched above – dominated by labour migration, absentee labour, dependence on cash remittances, single-parent households and unstable relationships – give testimony to these inextricable ties beyond the village.[13] Thus the global becomes intertwined with the local in a multiplicity of contexts that gives rise to a concept of culture as something permeable and multifaceted, which intersects with individuals' lives in different ways and with varying consequences, according to the type of networks to which individuals belong and their access to resources.

Marriage, law and the language of rights

Marriage is one of these resources in both a social and a legal context which, in Botswana, covers both common and customary law. This raises questions about how a rights-based discourse of the type promoted by the Women's Convention, intersects with a more locally-based customary law. The issue is especially pertinent when dealing with marriage given CEDAW's push towards the abolition of polygamy and emphasis on registration. Botswana, like many African states, upholds polygamous marriage in certain circumstances and recognizes customary marriages that are not registered. Does this mean that under the terms of the Women's Convention, women in Botswana are being discriminated against, or is the interpretation of the convention by CEDAW one that represents an ethnocentric approach to law in that states are being pressurized to adopt a Western definition of marriage? To answer these questions it is necessary to take account of the circumstances in which marriages are constituted and how these affect women.

Under the domestic legal system individuals have a right to marry according to customary law or in terms of a civil or religious ceremony followed by registration under the Marriage Act (1970). Under this Act, polygamy is banned (see s.15), but its provisions do not apply to any marriages contracted under 'any customary law of Botswana' (s.2). While the Act prohibits an individual from engaging in polygynous marriage, under customary law it is permissible for a man to have several wives. Unlike a civil or religious marriage, which is registered, a marriage according to customary law is not necessarily associated with any particular, identifiable occasion. For Batswana, like many other

Africans, a customary marriage is a process that may take place over many years, involving reciprocal relations between families.[14] In this process, my research shows that Bakwena place great emphasis on a ceremony called *patlo*, which for them is a definitive marker of a customary marriage; however, even without *patlo* relationships are treated as marriages.

What gives rise to a customary marriage depends on a number of cultural elements which cannot necessarily be defined in advance, including an exchange of gifts, and other actions may become subject to reinterpretation over time. This flexibility creates ambiguity, which parties manipulate in their negotiations over marital status. Such negotiation is central to the construction of Tswana kin relations (Comaroff 1980: 176; Comaroff and Roberts 1981: 62) and on which the marriage process itself depends (Comaroff 1980: 172).

In this process Tswana women's narratives reveal the extent to which women's power to negotiate partnerships with men depends on their position in the social order and the number of children they have. Childbearing starts at a relatively early stage, with the result that 'more than one quarter of the females in the population become pregnant while teenagers' (Botswana 1988: 1). Faced with the proposition that procreation is a fact of life, women must nonetheless accommodate such childbearing within socially sanctioned parameters that dictate the terms for recognition of a relationship and the types of obligation that are assigned to it. This creates problems for women, not only because of the ambiguity surrounding the creation of a customary marriage, but also because of the social pressure to bear children. Being a mother not only marks the transition from girlhood to womanhood but gives the father an enhanced status among his peers, as proof of his masculinity (regardless of the actual status of the relationship). A woman must balance the social expectation that she will have children with an assessment of the circumstances surrounding her partnership with a man. There is no doubt that having children with a man places the relationship on another footing and may enhance its credibility; however, should that relationship break down, the woman and children may find themselves in a vulnerable position because of the difficulties they face in establishing grounds for support or compensation, or in enforcing their claims.

In these circumstances, to push for legislation to unify family law through upholding registration as the only marker of marriage would disenfranchise a significant proportion of women, because where marriage exists it is overwhelmingly marked by *patlo*.[15] Just over a third of marriages involve both *patlo* and registration[16] and less than a tenth represent registered marriages alone.[17] In numerous marital disputes, women would find themselves being denied marital status if registration had been required, and thus lose the opportunity and the right to pursue property claims against their partners.

In many cases, what amounts to marriage is open to interpretation, and procreation and marriage do not necessarily coincide (A. Griffiths 1989a: 587). In Botswana, there are now significant numbers of unmarried women with children who remain attached to their natal household.[18] This came about for historical reasons which cannot be discussed in detail here, but which include introduction to a cash economy and the effects of sustained labour migration, a decline in polygamy, and greater freedom of association between the sexes at school and at work (A. Griffiths 1997: 17–24). With young adults, especially men, away from home for long periods of time, marriage was postponed until an age much later than that recorded for many other parts of Africa (Bledsoe 1990: 117).[19]

This was accompanied by a decline in polygyny[20] brought about by different factors. These included the influence of Christian missionaries (Comaroff and Comaroff 1991: 46–48; Ngugi wa Thiong'o 1986), but even more significant was the absence of eligible marital partners of the appropriate age and the shrinking of resources available to service martial obligations within an extended family network. Kuper (1987: 138) observes that elites ceased to practice polygyny because it no longer represented the best means of acquiring power and resources, which could be accumulated through other, capitalist means. According to Comaroff and Roberts (1977) Tswana families responded to these developments by accommodating earlier marriage practices within a reformulated framework which moved away from polygyny toward serial monogamy, where both women and men tended to engage in a series of relationships investigating the potential of various partners and testing the benefits of such associations before committing themselves to marriage with one partner.

While polygyny remains an option under customary law and one that would protect some women from being abandoned or divorced by their spouses on the basis of old age or childlessness, it is not one that Tswana men choose to pursue because of the obligations they incur. A number of men from Molepolole expressed the view that they preferred to have one wife and several girlfriends precisely because they did not wish to take on the responsibilities associated with plural marriage. This leaves many women in a vulnerable position and open to claims by their former partners that they were never a wife but merely a *nyatsi* (concubine) when women seek to enforce rights to support or property.

Given the social and economic contexts in which marriages are negotiated in Botswana, and the differential relations of power that operate in the negotiations surrounding the acquisition of status, it is not in the interests of certain women to reform the law so that only registered marriages are recognized by the state, or to abolish polygamy. Although the ambiguity surrounding the constitution of a customary marriage can have adverse consequences for women whose claims to status are disputed or rejected, it provides others with more scope for negotiating such claims with their attendant property rights. It may be argued that polygamy, far from discriminating against women, provides for a more inclusive approach that is not necessarily at odds with women's interests. In a context where individuals engage in a plural set of procreative relationships, it may be more advantageous for women to have their varying interests recognized and accommodated, rather than setting them at odds with one another under a system that requires one women's interests to trump those of another through adhering to a concept of monogamous marriage. Elsewhere feminists[21] have criticised a rights-based approach to law on the grounds that it underpins a system of adversarial relations in which the rights of those who have power and privilege prevail over the competing claims of others, in ways which fail to take account of an individual's relationships with, and responsibilities towards, other people.

Hellum (1998) notes that in her research on Zimbabwe polygamy played an important role in protecting women's interests, especially where an older women was childless and in danger of being abandoned by her husband. It also operated to protect young women whose economic situation was such that it made them vulnerable to exploitation by men – in some cases, to provide for children that a man was unable to have with another woman. To some extent the government of Zimbabwe has recognized the problems women face when a man has a relationship with one woman that amounts to a customary marriage and then enters into a registered civil marriage with another. In this situation, under the Administration of Estates Act (1997), where a customary union precedes a registered civil marriage, the former is treated as a valid marriage for the purposes of intestate succession. In other words, the civil monogamous marriage does not supersede the customary union but is treated as if it were the second customary law union. In this way it accommodates the interests of both women, rather than leaving the first wife without any inheritance rights. In these situations, a rights-based discourse framed in terms of a Western-based marriage law acts to the detriment, rather than the benefit, of women.

Mmashaoudi and Pepere Gabarane

The vulnerable position in which older women can find themselves in their relationships with men is exemplified by the case of Mmashaoudi and Pepere Gabarane. This couple lived together in Molepolole for many years and had five children. There was some speculation in the village as to the status of their relationship, was not registered as a civil marriage, and there was some doubt as to whether it qualified as a customary marriage (although *kgotla* officials treated it as such). After many years Pepere, the man, went to live with another woman, called Goajewa. To provide for Goajewa's support, he appropriated the property that he and Mmashaoudi had acquired together. When Mmashaoudi complained to local officials, Pepere unsuccessfully attempted to divorce her in the chief's *kgotla*[22] on numerous occasions between 1972 and 1983 (A. Griffiths 1989b). According to Deputy Chief Mr. Kgosiensho, 'When we examined the case, [in 1982] we found that there was no fault with Mmashaoudi. We found fault with Pepere because in terms of Tswana custom it is wrong when a man has a *nyatsi* to move out from his family and stay at the nyatsi's place and forget his wife and children altogether'. As a result, 'this *kgotla* ordered Pepere to return to his wife and stay with her and the children and [that he] should not continue selling cattle to provide for Goajewa'.

Pepere, however, stubbornly refused to carry out the order, and he and Mmashaoudi were continually at loggerheads because he could not obtain a divorce and she could not stop him from appropriating family property. Mmashaoudi explained, 'I'd never queried his wish to marry a second wife. My concern was with his neglect of me and the children'. While customary law prevented Pepere from forcing Mmashaoudi to return to her parents' home, she had difficulty in getting local officials to call Pepere to account over his misuse of property. Eventually, when Mmashaoudi 'realized that the senior *kgosi* [chief] was clearly avoiding hearing my case, I was forced to go and report to the DC [District Commissioner] at that time'. When she realized 'that the *kgosi* and the DC were both avoiding my case, I went to Gaborone to consult with the Ministry of Local Government and Lands [where the Commissioner of Customary Courts is situated]'. This led to the *kgosi*, Linchwe II, being engaged to deal with the dispute. According to Mmashaoudi, When the chief heard the case in 1976[23]

I stated the facts. I said that my complaint was in connection with my husband's desertion and lack of support for me and the children. I stated that I had never been found at fault in any way [and] that my people have also proved that I am a law-abiding *kgotla* woman. My grief is that I and the children are starving. Amongst the head of cattle which my husband had there were cattle which I brought with me from my parents when we married and that my husband was making use of all cattle property, including mine, selling them and taking all the proceeds to spend at Goajewa's place.

Her presentation in this case adhered to the forms of conventional Tswana discourse in that Mmashaoudi highlighted her exemplary behaviour as a wife, while at the same time underlining all Pepere's faults and his failure as a husband. This in itself might not have been sufficient to tip the balance in her favour if it had not been for the fact that Pepere had forfeited support from all those male networks that were vital to his position by refusing to consult the men from his natal *kgotla* about moving to Goajewa's *kgotla*, and by alienating *kgotla* officials through his arrogance.

As a result Mmashaoudi explained that '*Kgosi* Linchwe decided that all the cattle were to be brought to Molepolole so that I could be given some cattle. [I received] fifteen cattle and three calves'. She did not know how many cattle to claim as 'at the time they were called for I did not know how many there were. For a long time my husband had been restricting me from going to the cattlepost'. Mmashaoudi confirmed that the 'eighteen head of cattle were for my free use while Pepere enjoys life with Goajewa'. But she also stressed that the award ignored the livestock she had brought into the marriage. These included two heads of cattle and four goats. Her brothers had given her the two cattle from her mother's estate, and the goats she had bought. According to Mmashaoudi, '*Kgosi* Linchwe did not take account of livestock of that nature, even those which I made it clear I bought out of *sorghum* [profits].' Mmashaoudi was not complaining, but merely voicing how hard it is for women to establish specific claims to livestock. She was well aware that her award surpassed any that might have been made by Kwena officials, who were of the view that, 'according to pure Tswana custom', *Kgosi* Linchwe's handling of the dispute 'was wrong'. Members of Molepolole's Maunatlala ward commented that they were shocked by what he had done, and that 'the decision was not based on old traditional Tswana ways of doing things; it was done by modern ideas'. This is because they considered that Pepere, as head of the household, should have been left with control over the family property. They would only have awarded Mmashaoudi one or two beasts at most. They did, however, understand the tensions, observing that the problem as they saw it in Pepere's case was that 'from the time he fell in love with the second woman he had the practice of coming to the kraals, selling cattle, spending some of the money. . .That is why according to the feeling of people today they had to divide the cattle between them so that his wife could support the children and herself'.

Thus a creative solution was found under customary law which enabled Mmashaoudi to remain living in the family household in Pepere's *kgotla* (which she would not have been permitted to do if there had been a formal divorce), while allowing both parties to retain control over a share of the family property. Such flexibility underlines a scope for manoeuvre that is not always available under a more rights-based Western discourse. It is also interesting to note that although Mmashaoudi and Goajewa were presented in the disputes as being in conflict, when Pepere died in 1984 they came together to organize his funeral. Goajewa provided Pepere's coffin as well as an ox for the meal that forms part of the funeral ceremonies. She behaved, and was treated by Mmashaoudi, as a second wife. This demonstrates the extent to which women's relationships may be mediated through men.

Unity Dow

Although a rights-based discourse framed on the basis of Western law fails to meet the needs of some women, there are situations in which it can be mobilized to promote women's interests. One such example is provided by the court case instigated by Unity Dow then a prominent lawyer in the capital city (and now a High Court judge) concerning the citizenship rights of children in Botswana. The case arose out of changes made in 1984 by the government to the Citizenship Act to restrict the categories of persons who could become citizens through birth or descent. Section 4 of the Act provided that children born to Tswana women who were married to foreigners no longer had the right to be citizens of Botswana by virtue of their birth there. This was reinforced by Section 5 of the Act, which dealt with citizenship by descent and which prevented such women from passing on Botswana citizenship to their children. These provisions did not apply, however, to Tswana men who married non-citizens, whose children were entitled to full citizenship. Nor did they apply to the children of unmarried Tswana women whose fathers were non-citizens.

Unity Dow challenged these provisions on the basis that they contravened Section 3 of the Constitution, which confers rights and freedoms on individuals in Botswana, as well as Section 15, which provides for non-discrimination.[24] Dow petitioned the High Court for a declaration that the provisions of the Citizenship Act violated some of the fundamental rights and freedoms she was guaranteed under Constitution. The basis of her argument was that she was prejudiced by the provisions of this Act because her gender prevented her from passing citizenship to her children, and that this denied her the equal protection of the law and the right not to be discriminated against on the basis of her sex (guaranteed under Sections 3 and 15 of the Constitution).

This was the first time in the history of the country that a woman had challenged the government in court. At the time that she raised her action she was a leading member of the feminist organization *Emang Basadi* (Stand Up Women) and a participant in the Women and Law in Southern Africa Project. Unity had three children, one born in 1979 when she was unmarried and two born after her marriage in 1984 to Peter Dow, a US citizen. As a result her first child was entitled to citizenship while her children born in Botswana after 1984 were not, although they had lived there since birth. In its response to Dow's challenge, the state appealed to 'culture' to justify its position, arguing that customary law and society in Botswana upholds a patrilineal structure that is male-oriented and that this had been taken into account when the Constitution was enacted. This meant that Section 15 of the Constitution, which deals with discrimination, expressly declined to cover sex. The argument was made that if such discrimination were to be outlawed, then customary law itself would cease to exist. Thus, the government invoked a 'right to a culture' argument – that is, to the continued existence of Tswana customary law which is patriarchal in nature – in order to deflect an individual human rights claim.

In resorting to culture, the government was attempting to mobilize one view of society in Botswana, while Unity Dow, supported by national and international feminist groups, promoted another, which upheld the concept of non-discrimination and equal treatment for women.[25] The High Court finally found in favour of the petitioner on the grounds that it 'would be offensive to modern thinking and the spirit of the Constitution to find that the Constitution was deliberately framed to permit discrimination on the grounds of sex' (p 17 of typed transcript). In reaching this decision the judge was heavily influenced by the provisions of the Women's Convention, although Botswana was not a signatory to it at that time. When the state appealed, the Court of Appeal reaffirmed the judgment of the High Court, rejecting the argument that the need to respect and preserve tradition and custom justified the deliberately gender-discriminatory legislation. Once again the court placed great reliance on provisions of international human rights instruments upholding non-discrimination, equal protection of the law, and the elimination of discrimination against women. As a result of this case the government reluctantly amended the Citizenship Act in 1995 to provide that children acquire citizenship from either parent, by birth if they are born in Botswana, and by descent if born outside the country.

Gender and discourse: pluralist perspectives

These cases should not be interpreted as exemplifying a conflict between cultures in terms of universalist or relativist positions with respect to human rights. Rather, they underline 'culture as a field of creative interchange and contestation, often around certain shared symbols, propositions or practices, and continuous transformation' (Introduction, p.5). What the cases highlight is the way in which discursive forms are manipulated by various actors in specific contexts in pursuit of certain ends. Because of the various ways in which this discourse may be structured there is no one account of culture that can represent Botswana as a whole, but rather a range of perspectives fashioned out of local, national and international elements. These are configured in numerous ways to provide for overlapping discourses in some contexts, while giving rise to contestation in others (Preis 1996). In this process, disagreement and conflict form part of culture which is ongoing, socially constructed and continually negotiated. The different discourses on rights in relation to culture employed by the parties in various legal forums reflects the kind of insights developed by Nader (1966) and Rosen (1989) with respect to the relationship between law and culture, where law is conceived of as a 'worldview or structuring discourse which shapes how the world is apprehended' (Introduction, 13).

Kwena women engage in this process but they do so from an understanding of themselves as forming part of the same society as that of Kwena men. Their primary aim is not to subvert or radically alter the premises of society but, rather like Pacific Islander women (Merry in this volume), seek to transform its practices in a direction more responsive to their needs. The Unity Dow case is a partial exception in that it seeks to equalize certain statuses of women and men. In doing so, however, it was merely seeking to restore citizenship rights to their position prior to the 1984 Citizenship Act. However, one might note that Kwena women's views are a consequence of the ontological operation of Kwena 'culture' from which their initial acceptance of patriarchy parallels that of men.

Whatever the tensions, law forms an integral part of this mutually constitutive process and is dependent on the power of individuals to construct a discourse that will effectively represent their claims. For some women, like Unity Dow, a rights-based law can effectively be used to promote women's interests when it comes to the citizenship of their children. For others, like Mmashaoudi, it is more productive to adopt a more relational kin-based perspective in pursuing their claims, rather than centring their attention on the individual as legal subject. When it comes to constructing these discourses, power is not confined to, or solely derived from, the formal legal settings in which it operates, but derives more generally from the broader domain of social life. Taking into account these considerations, which are absent from a legal centralist model of law associated with colonialism, enables a more accurate understanding of people's access to, and use of, law, which highlights the obstacles that women face in the legal arena and the interconnections between social and legal worlds.

Within this framework women, like Mmashaoudi and Unity, challenge the terms of reference with which they are presented, but their ability to do so varies according to the type of network to which they belong. Women associated with the salariat, like Unity Dow, find themselves in a very different position from women like Mmashaoudi whose resources derive from domestic, agricultural, and unskilled labour associated with the peasantariat. To acquire an understanding of what gives rise to these differences, it is necessary to engage in research which focuses on detailed case studies so that an analysis of gender and its intersection with culture, rights and law is not formulated in abstract terms but is located in specific, concrete experiences derived from people's lives. In feminist scholarship, this marks a move away from treating the category 'woman' as a universal and homogeneous entity (Collier and Yanagisako 1987; Pateman 1989: 125) or from any suggestion that there is a prototypical woman whose interests can shape a feminist agenda (Pateman and Shanley 1991: 9). As Strathern (1980) among others observes, the category is not universal but is always culturally and historically specific. Bearing this in mind, if the Convention on the Elimination of All Forms of Discrimination Against Women (to which Botswana became a party by accession in 1996) is to provide a meaningful framework for upholding women's interests and promoting legal change, then its application must be sensitive to context, in order to meet the needs of different groups of women. This gives rise to a pluralism that is neither universalist, essentialist, nor relativist, but which is grounded in the reality of people's lives.

NOTES

1 Molepolole is the central town of the Kwena *morafe* (polity). Situated in Kweneng district and the gateway to the Kalahari Desert, it is close to the South African border and railway and about seventy km by paved road from

the capital city, Gaborone. Its population has grown from an estimated 20,000 in 1983 (Botswana 1983: 7) to more than 35,000 in the 1991 census (Botswana 1991b: 42).

2 For details of this research see A. Griffiths (1997).

3 In Setswana the prefix 'Ba' represents the plural modifier of a noun designating persons, so 'Bakwena' is the plural form of Kwena people or persons and 'Batswana' represents the plural form of Tswana people.

4 Customary Law (Application and Ascertainment) Act No.51 (1969) s.2.

5 For further details see A. Griffiths (1997: 29–35).

6 See hooks 1989; Ilumoka 1994: 320; Lam 1994; Nesiah 1993; Oloka-Onyango and Tamale 1995:720.

7 For example Bentzon et al 1998; Brems 1997:158; Charlesworth 1994:63; Moore 1993; Oloka-Onyango and Tamale 1995; Young 1994.

8 See the CEDAW Committee's comments to Ghana's initial and second periodic reports (CEDAW A/47/38:25 para.74) and to Kenya's initial and second periodic reports CEDAW A/48/38:27 para. 139. The impetus behind these comments has been to encourage states to move towards a single legal system applying a uniform system of law.

9 A kgotla is an assembly centre (both in terms of a physical location and the body of members) of a group of households presided over by a male headman or wardhead. Kwena society, like that of other Tswana *merafe* (polities), revolves around a tightly organized hierarchy of coresidential administrative units beginning with households which grouped together form a *kgotla*, and extending through family groups and a number of *kgotlas* to form wards, which represent major units of political organization. There were six main wards and seventy-three *kgotlas* when I began my research in Molepolole in 1982.

10 From my own data and Datta n.d.

11 For a discussion of women and the politics of marginality see Motzafi-Haller (1986).

12 For further discussion see A. Griffiths (1998: 549–597).

13 Abundant empirical evidence for the repercussions of this engagement with global economies is found in the Rural Income Distribution Survey (Botswana 1976), the National Migration Study (Kerven 1982), and Wilmsen's (1989) political economy of the region.

14 Evans-Pritchard 1951; Kuper 1970: 468–469; Roberts 1977: 242; Schapera 1938: 125–47.

15 *Patlo* accounts for eighty-six out of ninety-two marriages.

16 That is, in thirty-five out of ninety-two marriages.

17 That is, six out of ninety-two marriages.

18 See A. Griffiths 1988a: 295; Gulbrandsen 1986: 29–30; Kocken and Uhlenbeck 1980:53; Molenaar 1980: 12; Molokomme 1991: 100.

19 See Kocken and Uhlenbeck 1980: 55; Molenaar 1980: 17; Schapera 1947: 173; Timaeus and Graham 1989: 392.

20 See Comaroff and Roberts 1977; Kuper 1970: 473; Schapera 1950:45; Schapera and Roberts 1975: 266.

21 See Beveridge and Mullally 1995: 241–244; Lacey 1992: 106–107; Palmer 1996: 225–226; Rhode 1986.

22 The chief's *kgotla* (often loosely glossed as the chief's court) lies at the heart of the chief's ward, Kgosing, which is the most senior of all Kwena wards in the polity over which it presides.

23 There is no written record of his decision.

24 For further details see *Unity Dow vs. The Attorney General,* High Court Misca. No. 124/90, and *The Attorney General vs. Unity Dow,* Court of Appeal, Civil Appeal No. 4/91.

25 Note the Amicus Brief lodged with the high court on behalf of Dow by the Urban Morgan Institute for Human rights, University of Cincinnati College of Law.

REFERENCES

Alexander, E. 1991. *Women and Men in Botswana: Facts and Figures.* Ministry of Finance and Development Planning, Central Statistics Office, Gaborone: Government Printer.

Armstrong, A. *et al.* 1993. *Uncovering Reality: Excavating Women's Rights in African Family Law.* Harare: WLSA Working paper No. 7.

Beveridge, F. and S. Mullally. 1995. International Human Rights and Body Politics. In *Law and Body Politics: Regulating the Female Body.* (Eds.) J. Bridgeman & S. Millns, Aldershot: Dartmouth.

Bledsoe, C. July 1990. Transformations in Sub-Saharan African Marriage and Fertility. *Annals of the American Academy of Political and Social Sciences,* 115–125.

Bentzon, A.S., A. Hellum, J. Stewart, W. Nucube and T. Agersnap. 1998. *Pursuing Grounded Theory in Law: South-North Experiences in Developing Women's Law.* Norway and Zimbabwe: Tano and Mond.

Bourdieu, P. 1977. *Outline of a Theory of Practice.* Cambridge: Cambridge University Press.

Brems, E. 1997. Enemies or Allies? Feminism and Cultural Relativism as Dissident Voices in Human Rights Discourse. *Human Rights Quarterly* 19, 136–164.

Botswana, Government of 1976. *The Rural Income Distribution Survey in Botswana 1974/75.* Ministry of Finance and Development Planning, Central Statistics Office Gaborone: Government Printer.

Botswana, Government of 1983. *Summary Statistics on Small Areas (for settlements of 500 or more people). 1981 Population and Housing Census.* Central Statistical Office and MFPD (Ministry of Finance and Development Planning. Gaborone: Government Printer.

Government of Botswana 1988. *Teenage Pregnancies in Botswana: How Big is the Problem and What Are The Implications?* Gaborone: National Institute for Development Research and Documentation and the University of Botswana.

Botswana, Government of 1991a. *National Development Plan 1991–1997 (NDP7).* MFDP and Central Statistics Office. Gaborone: Government Printer.

Botswana, Government of 1991b. *Population of Towns, Villages and Associated*

Localities. Central Statistics Office and MFDP, Gaborone: Government Printer.

Brown, B. 1983. The Impact of Male Labor Migration on Women in Botswana. *African Affairs* 82:328, 367–388.

Byrnes, A. 1997. Human Rights Instruments Relating Specifically to Women, With Particular Emphasis On The Convention On The Elimination Of All Forms of Discrimination Against Women. In *Advancing The Human Rights of Women: Using International Human Rights Standards in Domestic Litigation*. (Eds.) A. Brynes, J. Connors and L. Bik. London: Centre for Comparative and Public Law, University of Hong Kong, for the Commonwealth Secretariat.

Charlesworth , H. 1994. What are 'Women's International Human Rights'? In *Human Rights of Women: National and International Perspectives*. (Ed.) R. Cook. Philadelphia: University of Pennsylvania Press.

Collier, J.F. and S.J. Yanagisako. 1987. Toward a Unified Analysis of Gender and Kinship. In *Gender and Kinship: Essays Toward a Unified Analysis*. (Eds.) J. F. Collier and S. J. Yanagisako. Stanford: Stanford University Press.

Comaroff, J.L. 1980. Bridewealth and the Control of Ambiguity in a Tswana Chiefdom. In *The Meaning of Marriage Payments*. (Ed.) J. L. Comaroff. New York: Academic Press.

Comaroff, J.L. and J. Comaroff. 1991. *Of Revelation and Revolution: Christianity, Colonialism, and Consciousness in South Africa*, Vol 1. Chicago: University of Chicago Press.

Comaroff, J.L. and S.A. Roberts. 1977. Marriage and Extra-marital Sexuality: The Dialectics of Legal Change among the Kgatla. *Journal of African Law* 21, 97–123.

Comaroff, J.L. and S.A. Roberts. 1981. *Rules and Processes: The Cultural Logic of Dispute in an African Context*. Chicago: University of Chicago Press.

Cook, R.J. 1994. Women's International Human Rights Law: The Way Forward. In *Human Rights of Women: National and International Perspectives*. (Ed.) R.J. Cook. Philadelphia: University of Philadelphia Press.

Cooper, D. M. 1980. *How Urban Workers in Botswana Manage their Cattle and Lands: Selebi-Pikwe Studies*. National Migration Study Working Paper No. 4. Gaborone: Government Printer.

Cooper, D.M. 1982. *An Overview of the Botswana Class Structure and its Articulation with the Rural Mode of Production: Insights from Selebi-Phikwe* (dated 1980). Cape Town: Centre for African Studies, University of Cape Town.

Datta, K. n.d. *Research on Women in Economy and its Impact on Policy Making in Botswana*. Gender Research Programme, Gaborone: University of Botswana and National Institute of Development Research and Documentation.

Evans-Pritchard, Sir E.E. 1951. *Kinship and Marriage Among the Nuer*. Oxford: Clarendon Press.

Featherstone, M. (Ed.). 1992. *Global Culture: Nationalism, Globalization and Modernity*. London: Sage.

Fineman, M.A. 1991. Introduction. In *At The Boundaries of Law: Feminism and Legal Theory*. (Eds.) M. A. Fineman & N. S. Thomadsen. London: Routledge.

Galanter, M. 1981. Justice in Many Rooms: Courts, Private Ordering and Indigenous Law. *Journal of Legal Pluralism and Unofficial Law* 19, 1–47.

Griffiths, A. 1988. Support among the Bakwena. In *Between Kinship and the State*. (Eds.) F. von Benda-Beckmann *et al.* Dordrecht: Foris Publications.

Griffiths, A. 1989a. Women, Status and Power: Negotiation in Family Disputes in Botswana. *Cornell International Law Journal* 22:3, 575–622.

Griffiths, A. 1989b. The Legal Heritage of Colonialism: Family Law in a Former British Protectorate. In *Law and Anthropology: Internationales Jahrbuch fur Rechtsanthropologie*, No. 4. (Ed.) W. Bauer. Vienna: VWGO-Verlag and Wissenschaftlichen Gesellschaften Osterreichs; Hohenschaftlam: Klaus Reiner Verlag.

Griffiths, A. 1997. *In the Shadow of Marriage: Gender and Justice in an African Community*. Chicago: University of Chicago Press.

Griffiths, A. 1998. Reconfiguring Law: An Ethnographic Perspective from Botswana. *Law & Social Inquiry* 23:3, 587–620.

Griffiths, J. 1986. What is Legal Pluralism? *Journal of Legal Pluralism and Unofficial Law* 24, 1–55.

Gulbrandsen, O. 1986. To Marry or Not to Marry. *Ethnos* 51, 7–28.

Hannerz, U. 1992. *Cultural Complexity: Studies in the Social Organisation of Meaning*. New York and Oxford: University of Columbia Press.

Hellum, A. 1999. *Women's Human Rights and Legal Pluralism in Africa: Mixed Norms and Identities in Infertility Management in Zimbabwe*. Norway and Zimbabwe: Tano Aschehoug.

hooks, b. 1989. *Talking Back: Thinking Feminist, Thinking Black*. Boston, MA: Sheba Feminist Publishers.

Hooker, M. 1975. *Legal Pluralism: An Introduction to Colonial and Neo-Colonial Laws*. Oxford: Oxford University Press.

Ilumoka, A. 1994. African Women's Economic, Social, and Cultural Rights. Toward a Relevant Theory and Practice. In *Human Rights of Women: National and International Perspectives*. (Ed.) R. Cook. Philadelphia: University of Pennsylvania Press.

Izzard, W. 1979. *Rural–Urban Migration of Women in Botswana*. Final fieldwork report for National Migration Study, Botswana. Gaborone: Government Printer.

Izzard, W. 1982. The Impact of Migration on the Roles of Women. In *Migration inBotswana: Patterns, Causes and Consequences*. Final report of the National Migration Study 3. Gaborone: Government Printer.

Kerven, C. 1982. The Effects of Migration on Agricultural Production. In *Migration in Botswana: Patterns, Causes and Consequences*. Final report of the National Migration Study 3. Gaborone: Government Printer.

Kerven, C. 1984. Academic Practitioners and all Kinds of Women in Development: A Reply to Peters. *Journal of Southern African Studies* 10:2, 259–268.

Kocken, E.M. and G.C. Uhlenbeck. 1980. *Tlokweng: A Village Near Town*. ICA Publication No. 39. Leiden: Institute of Cultural and Social Studies, Leiden University.

Kuper, A. 1970. The Kgalagari and the Jural Consequences of Marriage. *Man* 5, 466–482.

Kuper, A. 1987. The Transformation of Marriage in Southern Africa. In *South Africa and the Anthropologist*. (Ed.) A. Kuper. London: Routledge and Kegan Paul.

Lacey, N. 1992. From Individual to Group? In *Discrimination: The Limits of Law*. (Eds.) B. Hepple and E. Szyszczak. London: Mansell. pp. 99–124.

Lam, M.C. 1994. Feeling Foreign in Feminism. *Signs* 19, 865–893.

MacKinnon, K. 1987. *Feminism Unmodified: Discourses on Life and Law*. Cambridge, MA: Harvard University Press.

Molenaar, M. 1980. 'Social Change within a Traditional Pattern: A Case Study of a Tswana Ward'. MA thesis, University of Leiden.

Molokomme, A. 1991. *'Children of the Fence': The Maintenance of Extra-marital Children under Law and Practice in Botswana*. Research report No. 46. Leiden: African Studies Centre.

Moore, H.L. 1993. The Differences Within and the Differences Between. In *Gendered Anthropology*. (Ed.) T. del Valle. London: Routledge.

Motzafi-Haller, P. 1986. Whither the 'True Bushman': The Dynamics of Perpetual Marginality. In *Proceeding of the International Symposium on African Hunters and Gatherers*. (Eds.) F. Rotland & R. Vossen. *Sprache and Geschichte in Afrika*, vol 7, No. 1. Sankt Augustin: Monastery of Sankt Augstin.

Nader, L. 1966. *Law in Culture and Society*. Chicago: Aldine.

Nesiah, V. 1993. Toward a Feminist Internationality: A Critique of U.S. Feminist Legal Scholarship. *Harvard Women's Law Journal* 16, 189–210.

Ngugi wa Thiong'o. 1986. *Decolonising the Mind: The Politics of Language in African Literature*. London: James Currey.

Oloka-Onyango and S. Tamale. 1995. 'The Personal is Political', or Why Women's Rights are Indeed Human Rights: An African Perspective on International Feminism. *Human Rights Quarterly* 117, 692.–731.

Palmer, S. 1996. Critical Perspectives on Women's Rights: The European Convention on Human Rights and Fundamental Freedoms. In *Feminist Perspectives on the Foundational Subjects of Law*. (Ed.) A..Bottomley. London: Cavendish.

Parson, J. 1981. Cattle, Class, and State in Rural Botswana. *Journal of Southern African Studies* 7, 236–255.

Parsons, N. 1977. The economic history of Kharia's country in Botswana, 1844–1930. In *The Roots of Rural Poverty in Central and Southern Africa*, ed. R. Palmer and N. Parsons, Berkeley and Los Angeles: University of California Press.

Pateman, C. 1989. *The Disorder of Women*. Cambridge: Polity Press and Oxford: Basil Blackwell.

Pateman, C. and M.L. Shanley (Eds.). 1991. *Feminist Interpretations and Political Theory*. Cambridge: Polity Press and Oxford: Basil Blackwell.

Preis, A.S. 1996. Human Rights as Cultural Practice: An Anthropological Critique, *Human Rights Quarterly* 18:286–315.

Rhode, D. 1986. Feminist Perspectives on Legal Ideology. In *What is Feminism?* (Eds.) J. Mitchell & A. Oakley. Oxford: Blackwell.

Roberts, S.A. 1977. The Kgatla Marriage: Concepts of Validity. In *Law and the Family in Africa*. (Ed.) S. Roberts. The Hague: Mouton.

Roberts, S.A. 1979. *Order and Dispute*. New York: St Martin's Press.

Rosen, L. 1989. *The Anthropology of Justice: Law as Culture in Islamic Society*. Cambridge: Cambridge University Press.

Rwezaura, B. *et al*. 1995. Parting the Long Grass: Revealing and Reconceptualising the African Family. *Journal of Legal Pluralism and Unofficial Law* 35, 25–73.

Sahlins, M. 1976. *Culture and Practical Reason*. Chicago: University of Chicago Press.

Schapera. I. 1938. *A Handbook of Tswana Law and Custom*. London: Oxford University Press for the International African Institute.

Schapera, I. 1947. *Migrant Labor and Tribal Life: A Study of the Conditions of the Bechuanaland Protectorate*. London: Oxford University Press.

Schapera, I. 1950. Kinship and Marriage among the Tswana. In *African Systems of Kinship and Marriage*. (Eds.) A. R. Radcliffe-Brown and D. Forde. London: Oxford University Press for the International African Institute.

Schapera, I. and S.A. Roberts. 1975. Rampedi Revisited: Another Look at a Kgatla Ward. *Africa* 45:1, 258–279.

Smart, C. 1989. *Feminism and the Power of Law*. London: Routledge.

Solway, J. 1980. *People, Cattle and Drought in the Western Kweneng District*. Rural Sociology Report Series, no. 16. Gaborone: Botswana Government Publications.

Strathern, M. 1980. No Nature, No Culture: The Hagen Case. In *Nature, Culture and Gender*. (Eds.) C. MacCormack and M. Strathern. Cambridge: Cambridge University Press.

Timeaeus, I. and W. Graham. 1989. Labor Circulation, Marriage and Fertility in Southern Africa. In *Reproduction and Social Organization in Sub-Saharan Africa*. (Ed.) R. Lesthaeghe. Berkeley and Los Angeles: University of California Press.

Population Fund (UNFPA). 1989. *Gender Population and Development*. Report on the High-level Seminar for Chiefs and District Commissioners. (Eds.) L. Divasse & G. Mookodi. Gaborone: Macmillan Botswana.

UNICEF. 1989. *Children, Women and Development in Botswana: A Situational Analysis*. A consultant's report compiled for the joint GOB/UNICEF Programme and Planning and Co-ordinating Committee. Gaborone: UNICEF and Minstry of Finance and Development Planning.

UNICEF. 1993. *Children, Women and Development in Botswana: A Situational Analysis*. Report prepared by Mandeleo (Botswana) for the Government of Botswana and UNICEF.

Wilmsen, E.N. 1989. *Land Filled with Flies: A Political Economy of the Kalahari*. Chicago: University of Chicago Press.

Young, I. 1994. Gender as Seriality: Thinking about Women as a Social Collective. *Signs* 19, 713–738.

6   Between universalism and relativism: a critique of the UNESCO concept of culture

Thomas Hylland Eriksen

Introduction

In a scathing attack on the classic Herderian–Boasian concept of culture and its potential for generating both relativism and chauvinism, Alain Finkielkraut (1987) notes that although the United Nations' Educational, Scientific and Cultural Organization (UNESCO) was initially founded in an Enlightenment spirit loyal to the universalist legacy of Diderot and Condorcet, it almost immediately degenerated into a tool for parochialism and relativism. Uninhibited by the possible constraints implied by detailed knowledge regarding the topics under scrutiny, Finkielkraut was able to present a powerful, coherent and, in many people's view, persuasive criticism of the widespread culturalization of politics and aesthetics in the late twentieth century. Arguing that the meaning of culture has slid from *Bildung*[1] to heritage, from universalistic thought to relativistic anti-thought, his book on 'the defeat of thinking'[2] has been widely read and translated over the past decade.

In Finkielkraut's book, UNESCO is given a central role as a chief villain (along with social anthropologists, those dangerous purveyors of relativist nonsense). In this chapter, UNESCO's ideology of culture will serve as a point of departure, engaging current debates over culture and rights with the most recent and most comprehensive statement from UNESCO regarding culture in the contemporary world, namely the report on *Our Creative Diversity* (World Commission on Culture and Development 1995), a document which heroically and often skillfully attempts to manoeuvre in the muddy waters between the Scylla of nihilistic cultural relativism and the Charybdis of supremacist universalism. Fuzzier, less elegant and less consistent than liberal critiques of the Finkielkraut type, *Our Creative Diversity*, in spite of important shortcomings, is nonetheless more complex, presenting a multifaceted picture of the social world. While liberal critics frame the problem as being one of 'rights versus culture' (see the editors' introduction to this volume), the 'right *to* culture' is a stronger concern in UNESCO.

However, the authors do not explicitly address the possible contradiction between the two approaches. Nor do they see rights as culture: although they emphasize the value of cultural diversity, it appears largely as an aesthetic, rather than a moral, value.

An intriguing and ultimately disquieting context for the UNESCO model of culture is the work of Claude Lévi-Strauss on cultural relativity and culture contact, which, although peripheral to his structuralist *œuvre*, has been influential in UNESCO. The vision expressed in Lévi-Strauss' programmatic work on cultural diversity illustrates some of the difficulties inherent in *Our Creative Diversity*. The two pieces commissioned by UNESCO from Lévi-Strauss, *Race et Histoire* (Lévi-Strauss 1971 [1952]) and *Race et Culture* (Lévi-Strauss 1979 [1971]) highlight some of the dilemmas associated with a partition of the world into cultures. Central insights from these works can also be invoked against over-optimistic suppositions from scholars such as Finkielkraut that specific local circumstances and politics can be effectively divorced.

These problems recur: (Plato's Socrates, for one, discussed them with his contemporary relativists, Gorgias and Protagoras). These days frequently framed as communitarianism versus liberalism, or relativism versus universalism, there are some real baby-and-bathwater problems which can doubtless be dealt with eloquently and effectively, but not comprehensively, from an unreformed Enlightenment, cosmopolitan point of view. A discussion of these problems forms the substance of this contribution.

Our creative diversity

UNESCO has, since its foundation in 1945, planned and implemented a vast number of developmental and cooperative projects concerning education in a wide sense.[3] Cultural creativity, cultural rights and ethnic/racial discrimination have also been important concerns since the beginning – leading, *inter alia*, to its famous list of world cultural heritage sites, which recently expanded to include 'natural heritage sites' as well. Many writings supported or published by UNESCO have, over the past five decades, made important contributions to international debates about racism, ethnocentrism, cultural relativism, cultural hegemonies and quests for equal cultural rights. Although this body of work certainly has an applied perspective in common, it cannot be maintained that all, or even nearly all, the writings published under the aegis of UNESCO share a common perspective on culture, relativism and rights, despite Finkielkraut's insinuations.[4] A few publications nevertheless stand out as implicit or explicit policy documents. The most important example of the latter is clearly the report *Our Creative Diversity* (UNESCO 1995). Written by a characteristically global and interdisciplinary group,[5] the World Commission on Culture and Development (WCCD), the report was published simultaneously in several languages and later translated into yet others (thirteen at the latest count). This report seems a particularly fruitful starting point for a discussion of the global debates regarding cultural and political rights. It is a genuine intellectual contribution to the field. It can be read symptomatically as an expression of a certain 'UNESCO ideology'; its omissions are as interesting as the points it makes; it highlights – voluntarily and involuntarily – deep predicaments of culture; and last, but perhaps not least, being what it is, it will, by default, have real-world consequences of a magnitude most academics can only dream of for their scholarly work.

Like the UN report on the environment, *Our Common Future* (World Commission on the Environment 1987), *Our Creative Diversity* was a long time in the making. It was an expensive, prestigious and cumbersome project[6] and yet it has received comparatively little attention outside UNESCO's immediate sphere of influence. The reason may be that the Brundtland report was politically easier to relate to with great popular demand for its central concept – sustainable development – which elegantly embodied and concealed a kind of double-think characteristic of this risk-aware age of global capitalism. It presented a consistent description of the world and offered predictable and concrete policy advice of the kind heard from hundreds of environmentalist lobbyists for decades, including that provided by *Limits to Growth* the famous report of the Club of Rome (Meadows *et al.* 1974) completed a decade and a half earlier. The Brundtland report's analyses and advice were thus consistent with much of the Romantic and green autocriticism that has been inherent in modernity at least since William Blake's day. The more recent UNESCO report, by contrast, offers little by way of actual policy recommendations. It is difficult to summarize; it introduces issues that demand real intellectual engagement – and not merely the reiteration of pre-existing conceptions – to be properly understood; and finally, it must in all justice be said, it requires a considerable talent for double- and triple-think to see it as a coherent piece of work.

Reading *Our Creative Diversity* soon after it was published, I was, like many other social anthropologists, curious to discover how it related to the current academic debates over the use and misuse of concepts of culture and, in a more political vein, the still vigorous debates regarding the relationship between individual, group and state in the contemporary, post-Cold War world. These involved quibbles over multiculturalism in North America; philosophical exchanges between communitarians and liberals, moderns and postmoderns on both sides of the Atlantic and Franco-German faultlines; disagreements over the relationship between cultural rights and equal rights among immigrants in Western Europe; nationalist essentialism 'with no head' versus marketplace liberalism 'with no heart'; consumerism and identity; globalization and localization. Now, as will be evident from the critique below, the report is sensitive almost to the point of hypochondria regarding the concept of culture (which does not preclude some interesting self-contradictions). Yet identity politics hardly figures at all in the report as a topic. This omission is symptomatic of the report's shortcomings.

A very brief summary of the report's general conclusions – which are based on the statistics, anecdotal evidence, informed reasoning and humanistic ideology featured throughout – might read like this: although global cultural variation is a fact, it is necessary to develop a common global ethics, which should draw on values most religions have in common as a starting-point. Notably, respect and tolerance must be emphasized as central values. The world is culturally diverse, and it is necessary to pursue political models which maintain and encourage this diversity. Such variation functions creatively both because it stimulates the members of a culture to be creative, and because it offers impulses to others. Equality between men and women is essential, and children and adolescents must be given the opportunity to realize their creative potential on their own terms. Modern mass media must be used to strengthen local culture, not to weaken it. The cultural heritage must also be respected – and this should be taken to mean not only one's own but also the heritage of others. Ethnic and linguistic minorities, in particular, need protection, and have the right to retain their cultural uniqueness.

While these conclusions are so generally phrased that they may seem palatable to both moderate communitarians and moderate liberals, they, and the report as a whole, gloss over fundamental problems and fail to address politically volatile issues. This shortcoming, of course, makes the report less useful than it could have been. I shall deal with the most serious problems at some length, but in all fairness it should be added that some of them cannot be resolved once and for all in political practice, which is bound to tread the muddy middle ground of compromise.

Two problems of culture

The report is characterized by indecision regarding the use of the concept of culture. There are two separate problems here. The first, typical of work emanating from the UN Decade for Culture, concerns the relationship between culture as artistic work and culture as a way of life. At the outset of the report, Marshall Sahlins is quoted approvingly for spelling out the classic anthropological view that every human activity, including those relating to development and the economy, has a cultural component or dimension. As a result, the report periodically reads as a catalogue of human activities. There is a nevertheless strong and slightly unsettling bias in this regard towards looking at culture as *difference*: as those symbolic acts which demarcate boundaries between groups. If culture is a way of life, then buying groceries at 7-eleven is naturally neither less nor more cultural than taking part in Tudor revivalism or teaching English history; working in a large factory or software company is no less authentic than tilling the soil or producing local crafts for tourists and anti-tourists, and so on. Being exotic or different in the eyes of the 'we' of *our* creative diversity does not qualify for being 'cultural' in an analytic sense. Besides, the penchant for locally rooted solutions in the sections dealing with development is both mysterious and empirically misleading: it has largely been through the appropriation and local adaptation of imported technologies and imported forms of organization that poor countries have become richer during the past century. In other words, even the ostensible strengthening of local culture is irretrievably a hybrid activity as it draws on organizational and technological resources of modernity.

The second definition of culture – culture seen as artistic production – is also amply represented in the report, and little effort is made to distinguish between the two perspectives. This kind of inconsistency is, perhaps, *gefundenes Fressen*[7] to many a nitpicking anthropologist, but in my view it does little harm. It may be noted as a problem, however, that the examples of artistic production mentioned in the report, like the examples taken from everyday life, highlight the uniqueness of the local, the rootedness of cultural activity and the differences between 'ours' and 'theirs'.

The second problem related to the concept of culture in the report is more serious than the exoticist bias. In most of the report, culture is conceptualized as something that can easily be pluralized, which belongs to a particular group of people, associated with their heritage or 'roots'. On the other hand, the authors are also keen to emphasize that 'impulses', external influence, globalization and creolization are also cultural phenomena. This duality corresponds to two sets of concepts of culture prevalent in contemporary anthropology, the first characteristic of cultural relativism, structural functionalism and structuralism, the second typical of deconstructivist trends, as well as recent 'post-structuralist' work, taking the framework of cultural globalization as a starting-point for what are often comparative studies of modernities.

Culture is primarily seen as tradition by the WCCD, but a secondary meaning allows communication to be defined as cultural as well. The result is analytically unsatisfactory, but it does not necessarily entail an empirically wrong description. Culture can be understood simultaneously as tradition *and* communication; as roots, destiny, history, continuity and sharing on the one hand, and as impulses, choice, the future, change and variation on the other. The WCCD has laudably tried to incorporate both dimensions, but it remains a fact that the latter 'post-structuralist' perspective so typical of contemporary anthropological theorizing becomes a garnish, an afterthought, a refreshment to accompany the main course of cultures seen as bounded entities comprising 'groups' that share basic values and customs.

Since Lourdes Arizpe, writing on behalf of UNESCO, recently (1998) expressed incredulity in response to a similar criticism from Susan Wright (1998), I will highlight a few quotations from the report to substantiate this claim, which is an important premise for the rest of this piece. In Chapter 2, programmatically entitled 'No culture is an island', the authors write about 'respect for all cultures, or at least for those cultures that value tolerance and respect for others' (p. 54). As if cultures were social agents; pluralism is defined as 'tolerance and respect for and rejoicing over the plurality of cultures' (p. 55); on minorities, the authors say that '[t]hese groups share systems of values and sources of self-esteem that often are derived from sources quite different from those of the majority culture' (p. 57); and in the subsequent chapter, the authors write that 'most societies today are multicultural' (p. 61), meaning that they contain several cultures, implicitly assumed to be bounded. Throughout the report, cultures are implicitly and explicitly seen as rooted and old, shared within a group, to be treated 'with respect' as one handles aging china or old aunts with due attention to their fragility. (Like so many elite accounts of culture tinged with Romanticism, this report does not explicitly recognize the cultural dimension of mainstream or modern phenomena such as urban middle-class English culture, the culture of New York or Bombay, or the culture of contemporary Germans or the French etc.) Although it is said explicitly that any culture's relationship with the outside world is 'dynamic', UNESCO cultures remain islands or at least peninsulas.[8]

Global ethics and identity politics

This perspective has more to recommend it than many devastating, but often ahistorical, recent critiques from cultural studies and anthropology have been willing to admit. For decades, anthropologists have urged development agencies to take the cultural dimension into account, to become more sensitive towards local conditions and to understand that successful development processes necessarily take local conditions and local human resources seriously as factors of change. The report gives legitimacy to such a time-honoured anthropological view. However, the insistence on cultural difference and plurality as constitutive of the social world does not fit very well with the equally strong insistence on the need for a global ethics. Obviously, the WCCD wants to eat its cake and have it too; it promotes a relativistic view of development and a universalist view of ethics. Distancing itself occasionally from the 'vocal bullies' of identity politics and the mono-ethnic model of the nation-state, it does not, however, discuss the obvious contradictions between cultural relativism and ethical universalism, or the perils of identity politics at the sub-national level. While the Commission may defend itself successfully against academic charges of superficiality and dated-ness[9] by pointing out that the target group consists of ordinary educated people, not specialized and parochial scholars engaged in games of intellectual one-upmanship, the political innocence evident in the report is nothing short of stunning. In an age when nearly all armed conflicts take place within and not between states (see SIPRI 1997), and most of them could be designated as 'ethnic'; in an age when Croatian news-papers write about their successful national football team (during the 1998 World Cup) that it is genetically determined to win when notions of collective cultural rights and fear of foreign contamination direct anti-liberal or anti-secular political efforts in contexts otherwise as different as Le Pen's France, the BJP's India (or Hindustan) and the Algeria of the FIS, issues relating to cultural rights ought not to be treated lightly by a policy-oriented body such as UNESCO. To simply state, as the report does in many places and in different ways, that one is favourable to cultural rights simply will not do, whether the context is an academic one or a political one. The notion has to be circumscribed more care-fully. It is not self-evident what the term means, nor how it articulates with individual human rights. The programmatic 'right to culture' may conflict with considerations of 'rights versus culture'.

The rise of identity politics at the turn of the millennium is not caused by a widespread and contagious lack of tolerance to be mitigated by the implementation of a global ethics. Rather, it draws legitimacy from a

Romantic way of thinking about difference and similarity, which the UNESCO report, in spite of its humanitarian intentions, may involuntarily contribute to perpetuating. The political conclusions to be drawn from the description of the world inherent in the report are not necessarily the liberal, tolerant and universalistic ones suggested by the authors (and here, at least, one must approve of Finkielkraut's unreformed Enlightenment universalism-cum-provincialism). Separatists, difference multiculturalists championing exclusive criteria of judgement for 'my culture', nationalists seeking stricter border controls and restrictions on the flows of meaning across boundaries, inquisitors chasing the Salman Rushdies of the world into hiding, and myriad nationalisms writ small could find a sound basis for their isolationism and political particularism in the report, notwithstanding its periodical assertions to the contrary. These assertions stand in a mechanical, external relationship to the basic view of cultures as bounded and unique. Cultures need to talk to each other, as it were, and tolerate but they remain bounded cultures nonetheless.

Probably, as Klausen (1998) remarks in a comment on the report, it would have been both better and more credible if the internal tensions and disagreements within the committee had been made explicit. In that case, one might have explored the strengths and weaknesses of the two positions (rights *above* culture and the right *to* culture), and it would have been evident that one cannot always have one's cake and eat it too.

Hybrids, traditions, culturalism and modernity

Let me sum up the argument so far. *Our Creative Diversity* invokes several concepts of culture, but it is dominated by the classic view from cultural relativism – '1930s social anthropology', Wright (1998:13) calls it dismissively – of cultures as bounded entities with their own sets of values and practices. Their 'distinctiveness should be encouraged', Wright paraphrases the report (1998:13), 'as it is by looking across boundaries between distinct cultures that people gain ideas for alternative ways of living'. The image presented actually resembles Darwin's (1985 [1859]) distinction between artificial selection (as in pigeon-breeding) and natural selection: artificial selection is rapid and superficial; natural selection is slow and deep. Creole culture, hybrid forms, global universals such as McDonald's (and human rights discourses?) must thus be seen as superficial; while tradition, associated with 'roots' and the past, is profound. Since the report does not distinguish between culture and ethnicity, it may perhaps be inferred that the 'deep' culture of tradition is associated with ethnic identity, while the 'superficial' culture of modernity is not. As long as such a view is not supported by evidence, it must be questioned. The many passages on 'minority cultures', further, reveal a conservationist view of cultural diversity; in several places, diversity is seen as a value in itself. To whom? – the conservationists? The pluralism endorsed in the report does not seem to include post-plural hybrid forms, the millions of mixed 'neither-nor' or 'both-and' individuals inhabiting both global megacities and rural outposts in many countries. In other words, the right to an identity does not seem to entail the right *not* to have a specific (usually ethnic) identity.[10]

The report simultaneously emphasizes the right of peoples to cultural self-determination and the need for a global ethics – as if ethics and morality had nothing to do with culture. Of course, cultural self-determination may conflict with a global ethics, since morality is an important component of locally constructed worlds (see Howell 1996). Development is framed in context-sensitive, culturalist language; ethics is discussed in universalist terms. If minorities (and, presumably, majorities) share unique 'systems of values', these 'systems' may be expected to give moral instructions to their adherents; and if these 'systems of values' are to be defended from the onslaught of modern individualism, a call for global ethics seems a tall order.

At several points in the report, group rights are defended,[11] yet it is also committed to the Universal Declaration of Human Rights, which is unanimous in according rights to individuals, not groups. The obvious dilemma in this dual position – the inevitable conflict between collective minority rights and individual rights – is not discussed. Had the problem been taken seriously by the authors, surely they would also have taken on the important question of the ways in which individual human rights could be adapted to local circumstances. For example, Johan Galtung (1996) is fond of pointing out that if nomads were given a say in the formulation of the declaration of Human Rights, the universal right to own a goat would have been high on the list; and if Indian villagers had contributed a paragraph or two, an essential human right would have been the right to die at home surrounded by family members. These suggestions show how locally embedded values may be different from, but compatible with, individual human rights.

Finally, identity politics is treated briefly and not confronted with other parts of the report, where respect and tolerance for others, tradition and change are dealt with in laudatory terms. Along with the intellectual quagmire resulting from the insistence on unspecified cultural diversity *and* global ethics, this lack is the most disquieting aspect of the report. Can groups be free? When do group rights infringe on individual rights? How can a state strike a balance between equal rights for all its citizens and their right to be different? There is a very large literature grappling with these dilemmas,[12] which are not taken into account by the WCCP, which applauds 'minority cultures' while condemning majority nationalism, generally oblivious of the fact that minority problems are not solved, but removed to another level when minorities are accorded political rights on ethnic and territorial grounds (see the chapters by Cowan and Gellner in this volume). Fighting cultural fundamentalism (as in supremacist nationalism) with cultural fundamentalism (as in minority identity politics) is usually a zero-sum game.

In sum, surprisingly little attention is granted to the phenomenon of identity politics, whereby culture is politicized and used to legitimize not just exclusiveness, but exclusion as well. An epistemology grounding an individual's quality of life in his or her 'culture' does not pave the way for tolerance, respect and a peaceful 'global ecumene' (Hannerz 1989), and it is difficult to understand how the authors of *Our Creative Diversity* have envisioned the connection between the one and the other. In a recent volume on war and ethnicity, David Turton (1997) and his contributors show precisely how globalization and intensified contacts between groups in many parts of the world pave the way for the entrenchment of boundaries and violent identity politics, provided the political leaders are able to draw popular support from culturalist rhetoric. And as the anti-immigration lobbies of European countries might argue: 'Of course we respect others, but let them remain where they are, otherwise our culture of peace, inspired by UNESCO, will not stand a chance. A culture has the right to protect itself, and we are under siege from American vulgarity and Muslim barbarism!' This may not, in a word, be the most opportune time in world history for an organization committed to global humanism to provide arguments for cultural isolationism.

Culture and two Lévi-Strausses

It needs to be mentioned at this point that, although the previous paragraphs may have given the opposite impression, my attitude towards the UNESCO effort is largely sympathetic. Some of the shortcomings and self-contradictions of the report are, perhaps, inevitable given the composition of the committee and the need for compromise, and some of them cannot be easily resolved either in theory or in practice. Traditionalism and modernism, ethnic fragmentation and global unification are complementary dimensions of political processes in the contemporary world. Yet I have argued that the main conceptualization of culture in the book is naïve, and scarcely serves the explicit political purpose of underpinning a 'culture of peace'. In dealing with the relativity of cultures versus the universality of ethics, it seems that *Our Creative Diversity* unwittingly reproduces the old German distinction between *Kultur* and *Zivilisation*, which was especially popular in the interwar years. The former, sometimes associated with Tönnies' notion of *Gemeinschaft*,[13] is local, experience-based, unique and is passed on through socialization and the unconscious assimilation of local knowledge. The latter, the *Gesellschaft*[14] variety, is global, cognitive, universal and passed on through reflexive learning. It was frequently said about the Jews in the interwar Germanic world that 'they could acquire our civilization, but never our culture'. Does our creative diversity, then, refer to 'culture' or to 'civilization'? Doubtless the former, while the global ethics refers to the latter. Finkielkraut (1987) is therefore only partly right when he asserts that UNESCO quickly moved from a universalistic Enlightenment way of reasoning to a relativistic Romantic attitude: the recent report tries to encompass both, but it glosses over the contradictions rather than attempting to resolve them. As Finkielkraut rightly argues, any universal standards contradict any unqualified cultural relativism. This point was seen clearly a century ago by conservative French intellectuals like Maurice Barrès and Gustave Le Bon, when they argued against colonialism on ethnocentric, cultural relativist grounds: colonialism and the ensuing mixing of peoples would create confusion and moral erosion on both sides of the Mediterranean, and it should therefore be avoided. Now, this kind of view was already foreshadowed in Herder's writings against French universalism-cum-provincialism, but also in Franz Boas' cultural relativism, in later anthropologists' advocacy on behalf of indigenous peoples, in Le Pen's *Front National* program and that of apartheid, and in Claude Lévi-Strauss' work. Before moving to an examination of the two texts Lévi-Strauss wrote for UNESCO, it must be stressed, in order to preclude misunderstanding, that this does not imply that Boas' and others' defense of indigenous rights, apartheid and French supremacism are judged as similar political views; only that they draw on the same ontology of culture, namely the Herderian archipelago vision (cultures are discrete and bounded, if not entirely isolated) which lies at the historical origins of both cultural relativism and nationalism.

Claude Lévi-Strauss has arguably been the most influential anthropologist in the postwar era (which could be said to encompass the period 1945–80). While Lévi-Strauss' structuralism is a universalist doctrine about the way human minds function, his position regarding culture has always been that of a classic cultural relativist. He regards cultural variation as the necessary experimental foundation for his theory of universals at the level of cognitive mechanisms. To French critics of anthropological exoticism such as Derrida, Baudrillard and Finkielkraut, Lévi-Strauss – in spite of his 'ultimate' universalism, but because of his 'proximate' relativism – is the very embodiment of *l'ethnologie*, the art of viewing natives in their natural environment in order to identify, classify and reduce them to so many laboratory specimens.

The shadow of Lévi-Strauss looms large over UNESCO ventures into culture theory. He was an honorary member of the WCCD, and he is quoted intermittently in the report. Much more importantly, UNESCO, at an early stage in its existence, commissioned a short text on ethnocentrism from him. The small book, *Race et Histoire* (Lévi-Strauss 1961 [1952]), has become a classic of anti-racism in the French-speaking world; it has been reprinted many times, and every year, he is reportedly approached by secondary school students who are obliged to write an assignment on the book and who despairingly confess that '*nous ne comprenons rien*' (Lévi-Strauss & Eribon 1988: 208).[15] The book, arguing along lines that are familiar to every contemporary anthropologist, warns against genetic determinism; reveals the fallacies of ethnocentrism and facile cultural evolutionism; defends the rights of small societies to cultural survival; and revels in the intricacies of the symbolic systems of societies unknown to the vast majority of his readers. There is a subtle irony in the fact that *Race et Histoire*, which – like the beautifully romantic '*Tristes Tropiques*' (1955) has later been invoked as politically correct *tiersmondiste*[16] literature fit for consumption by third-generation *beurs*[17] in Parisian suburbs and Senegalese university students. Lévi-Strauss has never been *tiersmondiste*.[18] On the contrary, as he explained, 'the societies which I defended [in *Tristes Tropiques*] are even more threatened by *tiersmondisme* than by colonisation' (Lévi-Strauss & Eribon 1988: 213), adding that 'I thus defend those little peoples who wish to remain faithful to their traditional way of life, outside the conflicts that divide the modern world.' This attitude makes Lévi-Strauss a strange bedfellow for UNESCO, a body tightly allied with a *tiersmondiste* outlook and whose principal *raison-d'être* lies in the dissemination of standardized, state-monitored education and modern means of communication in the so-called Third World.

Nevertheless, the main message of *Race et Histoire* went down well in the post-war decolonizing world of the early 1950s: cultures cannot be ranked according to their level of development; they are – to use a currently fashionable phrase – equal but different. Incidentally, Lévi-

Strauss' universalism is a long shot from the global ethics of *Our Creative Diversity*, although it cannot be ruled out that his structuralism could, at a formal and not substantial level, form the basis of some kind of universal ethics. Nevertheless, these would hardly be recognized as such by politicians and UN officials.[19]

Nearly twenty years after the success of *Race et Histoire*, UNESCO asked Lévi-Strauss to contribute a new text on the topics of ethnocentrism, race and culture. He now wrote a shorter piece, *Race et Culture* (Lévi-Strauss 1979 [1971]), which was received with more mixed feelings than the first commissioned work. Like his earlier text, it begins with a critique of the idea of race, but instead of discarding it as irrelevant for his purposes, he shows how pervasive notions of racial difference are in human societies, and how they contribute to the integrity of the group. 'We have a tendency', he writes (1979: 441), 'to consider those "races" which are apparently the furthest from our own, as being simultaneously the most homogeneous ones; to a White, all the Yellows [*sic*] resemble one another, and the converse is probably also true'. He notes the potential consequences of population genetics for anthropology, such that large questions regarding cultural history, prehistorical migrations, differentiation and so on may at long last be answered. He also concludes, in his characteristic Copernican way, that far from it being the case that culture is the product of race, 'race – or that which one generally means by this term – is one of several functions of culture' (Lévi-Strauss 1979: 446). Racial differences are the long-term outcome of tribal fission and the ensuing isolation of the segments ('How could it be otherwise?'). Later, he writes that 'mutual tolerance presupposes the presence of two conditions that the contemporary societies are further than ever before from fulfilling: on the one hand, relative equality [in relation to other societies], on the other hand, sufficient physical distance' (458). Also arguing that intergroup hostility is quite normal in human societies, and that conflict is bound to result from culture contact, the master anthropologist adds, within brackets, that without doubt, 'we will awake from the dream that equality and brotherhood will one day rule among men without compromising their diversity' (461).[20] It is, naturally, this dream that the WCCD has not yet awoken from, despite subscribing to Lévi-Strauss' general description of a world partitioned into cultures.

Assumed perils of culture contact

When this second text was published, many of Lévi-Strauss' former admirers in the French public sphere held that there was a contradiction between the two texts, the one being a humanistic charter for equality, extending the ideas of the French Revolution to include the small and oppressed peoples, as it were; the other being a concealed defence for ethnic nationalism and chauvinism, in addition to speaking warmly of that dreaded discipline, human genetics. Actually, as Lévi-Strauss remarked much later (Lévi-Strauss & Eribon 1988: 206), the Communist newspaper *L'Humanité*, in attempting to show that Lévi-Strauss' views had changed, inadvertently quoted a passage from *Race et Culture* which he had actually lifted verbatim from *Race et Histoire*. Asked by Didier Eribon to elaborate on his views regarding immigration to France, as Lévi-Strauss is widely believed to be against mass immigration (see Todorov 1989), the master anthropologist replied that insofar as the European countries were unable to preserve or animate 'intellectual and moral values sufficiently powerful to attract people from outside so that they may hope to adopt them, well, then there is doubtless reason for anxiety' (Lévi-Strauss & Eribon 1988: 213). Confronted with these contemporary complexities, in other words, Lévi-Strauss prefers the simple assimilationist model from the Enlightenment to the cultural complexity represented by unassimilated immigrants. In sum, Lévi-Strauss' perspective on culture and intergroup relations is unhelpful as a theoretical matrix for UNESCO.

Many cultures or none?

Read closely, there is no doubt that the argument in *Race et Culture* is consistent with *Race et Histoire*. Towards the end of the earlier work, Lévi-Strauss stresses that in order to learn from each other, cultures need to be discrete; in the latter work, he reminds his readers and UNESCO that love of one's own culture, which is necessary for a strong group identity, implies a certain distance, which may easily flip into hostility *vis-à-vis* others. The seeming contradiction – which turns out to be a complementarity – between the two texts goes to the core of UNESCO's predicament. If an archipelago vision of culture is maintained, then it is easy to defend cultural rights and to support endeavours aiming at the strengthening of symbolic and social cohesion among collectivities seen as culture-bearing groups; but in that case, the notion of global ethics becomes difficult to maintain. In addition, there is no guarantee that this notion of culture will be used in a 'tolerant and respectful' way (the *Race et Histoire* perspective) and not in a hostile and defensive way (as in *Race et Culture*).

Another, related question concerns whether Lévi-Strauss' conceptualization of a world composed of small, discrete societies can offer a useful concept of culture with which to analyse the contemporary world. He seems to deny it himself, regarding our time as a period of emergency when small societies are being obliterated (not least by their 'Third World' governments – there is no unanimous North-South manicheism here), the world is becoming too small for humanity, and contacts across cultural boundaries blur distinctions and threaten not only identities but also the comparative project providing structuralism with its data. Lévi-Strauss is, and has always been, an admirably consistent critic of universalistic ambitions of modernity, and his worldview is deeply at odds with the modernizing spirit that justifies UNESCO's development endeavours. UNESCO's attempts to accommodate notions of group rights and a concept of culture modelled on a more or less chimerical pre-modern tribal world contradict its basic commitment to individual human rights, universal education and global modernity. Individual rights, as defined since Locke, are sanctioned by a state, while group rights are associated with a collectivity at the sub-state level. One can simultaneously be a member of a cultural community and a citizen, but the social contract guaranteeing the equal treatment of citizens obtains between the citizen and the state. For this reason, it is misleading to speak of group rights, or even minority rights, if the issues pertain to, say, freedom of religion or linguistic pluralism.[21]

In real life, double standards are rarely twice as good as single standards, but in studies of social life, two descriptions are usually better than one. Not least for this reason, the UNESCO committee should be praised for attempting to arrive at a multifaceted description of culture in the contemporary world. Arne Martin Klausen, an old teacher of mine and a long-time critic of, and consultant for, development projects, often comments – slightly tongue-in-cheek – on the recent scholarly confusions over definitions of culture by proposing that several distinct concepts of culture are better than none. In his brief critique of *Our Creative Diversity*, Klausen says:

It is of course regrettable that other people [non-anthropologists], who have started to acknowledge the importance of the cultural dimension, are now operating imprecisely within one single concept of culture that is so comprehensive that it becomes meaningless and inoperative, but we must nevertheless continue to underline the importance of between two and four different, but precise, concepts of culture as vital tools for understanding social complexities (Klausen 1998: 32).

My own conclusion is precisely the opposite of Klausen's, although it takes a similar description of the contemporary world as its point of departure. Since the concept of culture has become so multifarious as to obscure, rather than clarify, understandings of the social world, it may now perhaps be allowed to return to the culture pages of the broadsheets and the world of *Bildung*. Instead of invoking culture, if one talks about local arts, one could simply say 'local arts'; if one means language, ideology, patriarchy, children's rights, food habits, ritual practices or local political structures, one could use those or equivalent terms instead of covering them up in the deceptively cozy blanket of culture. In a continuous world, as Ingold puts it (1993: 230), 'the concept of culture . . . will have to go'.

To be more specific:

(i)   What are spoken of as cultural rights in *Our Creative Diversity*, whatever they may be, ought to be seen as *individual* rights. It is as an individual that I have the right to go to the church or mosque or synagogue or not, to speak my mother-tongue or another language of my choice, to relish the cultural heritage of my country or prefer Pan-Germanism, French Enlightenment philosophy or whatever. As an individual I have the right to attach myself to a tradition and the freedom to choose not to.

(ii) There is no need for a concept of culture in order to respect local conditions in development work: it is sufficient to be sensitive to the fact that local realities are always locally constructed, whether one works in inner-city Chicago or in the Kenyan countryside. One cannot meaningfully rank one locality as more authentic than another. What is at stake in development work is not cultural authenticity or purity, but people's ability to gain control over their own lives.

(iii) Finally, it is perfectly possible to support local arts, rural news-papers and the preservation of historic buildings without using mystifying language about 'a people's culture'. Accuracy would be gained, and unintended side-effects would be avoided, if such precise terms replaced the all-encompassing culture concept. The insistence on respect for local circumstances, incidentally, would alleviate any suspicion of crude Enlightenment imperialism *à la* Finkielkraut. And, naturally, Radovan Karadzic and Jean-Marie Le Pen would not be pleased with such a level of precision.

If the mystifying and ideologically charged culture concept can be discarded, the case for a global ethics also seems stronger. As *Our Creative Diversity* shows, there can be no easy way out. The classic Enlightenment model (surprisingly applauded by Lévi-Strauss in re-sponse to a question about immigrants) represented by post-revolu-tionary France and contemporary Turkey, to mention two spectacular examples, has achieved a high score regarding equality, but a lament-able record concerning the right to difference. Within this political model, homogeneity is seen as desirable for all, and the state-designated barbarians (Basques, Bretons or 'Mountain Turks' – Kurds – as the case may be) ought to be grateful, as it were, that someone bothers to integrate them into civilization. A classic Romantic model drawing on an archipelago vision of culture was evident in the apartheid system in South Africa, providing groups with 'cultural autonomy' and thereby preventing them from becoming integrated in greater society; bluntly put, it had a high score on the right to be different and a low score on the right to equality. Anyone who tried to talk about cultural rights to an ANC member before the transformation would learn a lesson or two about culturalist politics and the political pitfalls inherent in Romantic ethnology.

It is between these extremes that contemporary politics must man-oeuvre, and neither notions of culture nor rigid universalisms have helped so far. It is for this reason that the unreformed Enlightenment position represented by Finkielkraut is unacceptable: A lesson from this past century of extremes must be that any imposition of homogeneity, whether from a state or from the self-appointed spokespersons of a 'group', is ultimately at odds with a notion of rights; and that, in Bauman's words (1996: 18), 'If the *modern* "problem of identity" is how to construct an identity and keep it solid and stable, the *postmodern* "problem of identity" is primarily how to avoid fixation and keep the options open'. This position does not imply that cultural creolization, flux and perpetual change are the only viable options; conservative choices are as valid as radical ones. Who, after all, is going to stand up and say that Borneo tribespeople, in the name of liberalism and universal human rights, should get a haircut and a job, start a trade union, or at least go and vote in the next elections? (Ironically, UNESCO is liable to stand up and say just that, given its positive view of state-monitored development.)

With a French thinker I began this piece, and with a French thinker I will end it. Tzvetan Todorov, in his thoughtful and beautifully written *Nous et les Autres* (1989), ends his long and winding journey through French conceptions of cultural (and racial) difference from Montaigne to Lévi-Strauss with an ambivalent conclusion, saturated with his own and others' struggles between ethnocentrism and relativism, universalism and particularism, individualism and collectivism:

A well-tempered humanism [*un humanisme bien tempéré*] can protect us against the faults of yesterday and today. Let us break up the simple connections: to respect the equal rights of all human beings does not imply the renunciation of a value hierarchy; to cherish the autonomy and freedom of individuals does not oblige us to repudiate all solidarity; the recognition of a public morality does not inevitably lead to a regression to the times of religious intolerance and the Inquisition [. . .] (Todorov 1989: 436).

Since the word culture divides but an unqualified rejection of the relevance of local circumstances oppresses, this kind of cautious and ambivalent position is the only valid starting-point for a humanistic politics that tries to achieve the impossible: equality that respects difference, 'a sense of belonging to a community larger than each of the particular groups in question' (Laclau 1995: 105). To achieve this end, the concept of rights is more useful than the concept of culture.

Postscript: winds of change in an anthropological semiperiphery

At the initiative of Marit Melhuus, the anthropology department at the University of Oslo inaugurated in 1997 an annual series of topical debates inspired by the success of the GDAT debates in Manchester (Ingold 1996). The first debate concerned conceptualizations of culture, and the motion to be discussed was actually purloined from *Our Creative Diversity*. A particularly clear passage from the executive summary, it read as follows:

Cultural freedom, unlike individual freedom, is a collective freedom. It refers to the right of a group of people to follow a way of life of its choice [. . .] It protects not only the group, but also the rights of every individual within it (UNESCO 1995:15).

Two members of staff were enrolled to argue in favour of the motion, and two were asked to argue against it. Signe Howell and Harald Beyer Broch, the supporters of the motion, had both carried out extensive fieldwork among indigenous peoples – Howell in Malaysia and Indonesia, Broch in Canada and Indonesia – and had in the course of their fieldwork witnessed the more or less enforced encounters between vulnerable indigenous groups and modern state apparatuses. The two opponents, Halvard Vike and myself, had been working in modern, complex societies where the populations tended to turn towards the state rather than away from it in order to have their rights sanctioned – Vike had recently completed his PhD on local politics in a Norwegian county, while I had carried out research on ideology and the politicization of culture in the poly-ethnic island states of Mauritius and Trinidad and Tobago. Speaking from very different ethnographic horizons, the antagonists not only reached opposite conclusions, but also failed to engage in a proper dialogue: they tended to depict each other, in the heat of the debate, as hopeless Romantics and cynical modernists, respectively. The two in favour of the motion argued from the vantage-point of indigenous peoples in Indonesia against state dominance, language death and global capitalism (see Samson's chapter in this volume). The opponents spoke about the multi-ethnic (and in some cases, post-ethnic) nature of contemporary European and North American society, and how the politicization of culture had drawn public attention away from issues of rights and distribution of resources. In other words, the debate mirrored the more general controversies surrounding the communitarianism–liberalism divide in contemporary politics and political philosophy, and also illustrated the fact, un-surprising to an anthropologist, that where you stand depends on where you sit.

After the debate, the audience was invited to vote on the motion. At the final count, seventy-eight voted for it and seventy-five voted against it. Although all academic categories were represented, the audience mostly consisted of undergraduates. Ten or fifteen years ago, there would almost certainly have been a massive 'yes' vote, anthropology undergraduates having been for decades notorious for their Romantic bent and for regarding indigenous peoples' struggle for autonomy as a general model for politics. Perhaps the tide will turn again. In any case, it is likely that the questions summarized in the above quotation from *Our Creative Diversity*, and which have been discussed in this piece, will be increasingly central to the global political agenda in the decades to come. If this prediction holds, anthropologists – no longer the bearded and greatcoated explorers plying remote waters in search of radical difference – may, provided they are as flexible as the identities they theorize about, attain a pivotal societal role as political analysts.

ACKNOWLEDGEMENTS

An earlier version of this text was presented at the Culture and Rights Workshop, at the University of Sussex in July 1997.

I would like to thank the organizers and the participants for a lively and stimulating interdisciplinary exchange of similar and dissimilar ideas. Thanks also to Richard A. Wilson for persuading me to write this up, and for the comments on the draft by Wilson, Marie-Bénédicte Dembour and two anonymous referees.

NOTES

1 In English, 'formation'.
2 The English translation of *La défaite de la Pensée* is called, somewhat idiosyncratically, *The Undoing of Thought* (Finkielkraut 1988).

3 In order to exemplify the wide scope of the organisation's activities, let me mention that my father was employed by UNESCO in the 1970s to supervise and help organise a number of rural newspapers with a clear educational bent in various African countries.

4 UNESCO's current slogans read:

Strategies for development

    promoting lifelong education for all;

    assisting in the advancement, transfer and sharing of knowledge;

    enhancing the concept of cultural heritage and promoting living cultures;

    promoting the free flow of information and the development of communication.

Strategies for peace-building

    encouraging education for peace, human rights and democracy, tolerance and international understanding;

    promoting human rights and the fight against discrimination;

    supporting consolidation of democratic processes;

    encouraging cultural pluralism and dialogue between cultures;

    contributing to conflict prevention and post-conflict peace-building. (Source: http://www.unesco.org)

5 The World Commission on Culture and Development (WCCD) responsible for the report had thirteen full members with academic, political and artistic backgrounds, from Mexico, Nigeria, Pakistan, the USA, Greece, Norway/ Sápmi, Senegal, Switzerland, Brazil, Egypt, Japan, Russia, Zimbabwe and Argentina. In addition it had *ex officio* observers from India and Mozambique, as well as honourary members including Burmese human rights activist Aung San Suu Kui, West Indian poet Derek Walcott, Belgian physicist Ilya Prigogine, American writer Elie Wiesel, a couple of Arab princes in succession, and Claude Lévi-Strauss. The Commission's work was led by Peruvian Javier Pérez de Cuéllar, former Secretary-General of the UN.

6 'Once the Commission was in place', explains Lourdes Arizpe, Assistant Director-General for Culture, UNESCO (Arizpe 1998), 'the three years that followed comprised nine consultations in the different continents in which some 120 speakers took the floor'.

7 In English, 'a heaven-sent opportunity'.

8 On the archipelago view of culture, see Eriksen 1993.

9 See for example Arizpe's (1998) response to Wright (1998).

10 As an exemplification of this point, the high suicide rates among youth in Finnmark county, Norway, an area associated with the formerly transhumant Sami, is often attributed locally to identity problems: the young Sami can neither fulfil the expectations of Sami traditionalists nor of Norwegian modernists; they are condemned to leading a hybrid life with no fixed identity. From the viewpoint of culture theory, it must be asked whether the problem lies in their cultural repertoire or in the local ranking of people according to their ability to fit stereotypes of bounded cultural identities.

11 For example in paragraph 3, 'The protection of minorities', in the chapter on global ethics.

12 See for example Kymlicka 1989, Taylor *et al.* 1992, Wilson 1997.
13 In English, 'community'.
14 In English, 'society'.
15 Literally, 'we don't understand anything'.
16 In English, 'third-worldist'.
17 French slang word for second- or third-generation immigrants from North Africa, living in the suburbs.
18 On this background, Finkielkraut's (1987) coupling of 'fourth-worldist' Lévi-Strauss with Frantz Fanon in *La défaite de la pensée* is curious, to say the least. *Tiersmondisme*, 'third-worldism', is a modernist emancipatory ideology promoting self-determination and equity for poor countries, while 'fourth-worldism' defends the traditional culture of tribal societies. Needless to say, the two do not combine well in practice, as many visitors to Sandinista Nicaragua in the 1980s discovered when they looked into the conditions for the indigenous Miskito.
19 See Lévi-Strauss 1983, ch. 12 for intimations to this effect.
20 Commenting on Lévi-Strauss, Todorov (1989:108) says: 'If one really has to choose between the two evils – cultural relativism and unilineal evolutionism – the latter is preferable, on the cognitive level as well as on the ethical level', before reassuring his readers that there are alternatives to these extremes.
21 See Eriksen 1997 for a full discussion of this dilemma in Mauritius; see Kymlicka 1989, ch. 7, for a Canadian example.

REFERENCES

Arizpe, L. 1998. UN cultured. *Anthropology Today* 14:3, 24.
Bauman, Z. 1996. From Pilgrim to Tourist; or A Short History of Identity. In *Questions of Cultural Identity.* (Eds.) S. Hall and P. Du Gay. London: SAGE.
Darwin, C. 1985 [1858]. *The Origin of the Species by Means of Natural Selection, or The Preservation of Favoured Races in the Struggle for Life.* Harmondsworth: Penguin Classics.
Eriksen, T.H. 1993. Do Cultural Islands Exist? *Social Anthropology* 1b:1.
Finkielkraut, A. 1987. *La défaite de la pensée.* Paris: Gallimard.
Galtung, J. 1996. Personal communication.
Hannerz, U. 1989. Notes on the Global Ecumene. *Public Culture* 1:2, 66–75.
Howell, S. (Ed.). 1996. *The Anthropology of Moralities.* London: Routledge.
Ingold, T. 1993. The Art of Translation in a Continuous World. In *Beyond Boundaries: Understanding, Translation and Anthropological Discourse.* (Ed.) G. Pálsson. Oxford: Berg.
Ingold, T. (Ed.). 1996. *Key Debates in Anthropology.* London: Routledge.
Klausen, A.M. 1998. Our Creative Diversity: Critical Comments on Some Aspects of the World Report. In *Our Creative Diversity: A Critical Perspective.* Report From The International Conference on Culture and Development, Lillehammer 5–7 September 1997. Oslo: Norwegian National Commission for UNESCO.
Kymlicka, W. 1989. *Liberalism, Community and Culture.* Oxford: Clarendon.
Laclau, E. 1995. Universalism, Particularism and the Question of Identity. In *The Identity in Question.* (Ed.) J. Ratchmann. London: Routledge.

Lévi-Strauss, C. 1955. *Tristes tropiques*. Paris: Plon.

Lévi-Strauss, C. 1961 [1952]. *Race et histoire*. Paris: Denoël.

Lévi-Strauss, C. 1979 [1971]. Race et histoire. In *Claude Lévi-Strauss*. (Eds.) R. Bellour and C. Clément. Paris: Gallimard. (Originally published in *Revue internationale des sciences sociales* 23:4).

Lévi-Strauss, C. 1983. *Le regard éloigné*. Paris: Plon.

Lévi-Strauss and D. Eribon. 1990. *De près et de loin, suivi d'un entretien inédit 'Deux ans après'*. Paris: Odile Jacob.

SIPRI. 1997. *SIPRI Yearbook 1997: Armaments, Disarmaments and International Security*. Oxford: Oxford University Press.

Taylor, C. *et al.* 1992. *Multiculturalism and the 'Politics of Recognition'*. (Ed.) A. Gutmann. Princeton, NJ: Princeton University Press.

Todorov, T. 1989. *Nous et les autres. La réflexion française sur la diversité humaine*. Paris: Seuil.

Turton, D. 1997. Introduction: War and ethnicity. In *War and Ethnicity: Global Connections and Local Violence*. (Ed.) D. Turton. Woodbridge, Suffolk: University of Rochester Press.

World Commission on the Environment. 1987. *Our Common Future*. Oxford: Oxford University Press

Meadows, D. *et al.* 1974. *The Limits to Growth*. Report for the Club of Rome's Project on the Predicament of Mankind. London: Pan.

World Commission on Culture and Development. 1995. *Our Creative Diversity*. Paris: UNESCO.

Wilson, R.A. (Ed.). 1997. *Human Rights, Culture and Context: Anthropological Perspectives*. London: Pluto.

Wright, S. 1998. The Politicization of 'culture'. *Anthropology Today* 14:1, 7–15.

Part II

Claiming cultural rights

The four chapters included in the second part of the book explore how activists involved in grassroots cultural or ethnonationalist movements have been claiming rights based on what they perceive as 'their culture'. While these local-level case-studies are concerned with realities taking place in various continents – Europe, Southeast Asia, Central America and North America, respectively – they make similar points. One is that the articulation of such claims, which oppose the politically dominant view in the country where they are made, has been directly dependent on an international arena and a global forum which have encouraged their expression, at the same time as local circumstances have shaped the precise form of this articulation. Another point is that the significance and ultimate motive of these claims can only be understood by paying attention to the local context, as moulded by history. Finally, the essentialization of culture is inherent in the making of such claims. Each author, in his or her own way, reveals how such rights processes lead to particular predicaments.

In her study of Macedonian minority claims in Greece, Jane Cowan introduces the concept of 'minoritization'. With this term, she refers to the transformation of a fluid identity into one of supposedly ontological quality in order to fit legal and political criteria. In the region Cowan has studied, this transformation has been accomplished since the mid-1980s by activists whose words resonate in international fora ready to take on board the activists' message without asking whom they represent. Cowan shows, however, that the question of representation – and of numbers – is a crucial one. In the wake of a complex regional history, many of those ostensibly represented by the activists do not themselves claim a Macedonian identity in so far as this entails rejecting their Greekness. Nor do they necessarily refer to the non-Greek language they use in some circumstances as Macedonian. While there are indeed people who perceive themselves as members of an oppressed minority, their numbers should not be inflated. Cowan acknowledges the courage of their fight for recognition but she regrets the denial of prevalent cultural ambiguity that their claims entail.

A specialist on Nepal, David Gellner addresses the question of what respect for cultural difference means in a country in which religion and culture have always tended to be conflated and which – uniquely in the world – declares itself Hindu and thus endorses a religious principle of group hierarchy. From the mid-eighteenth to the mid-nineteenth century, under the National Legal Code supposedly inspired by the French Napoleonic code, the Nepalese population was classified into five hierarchically-ranked groups, which encompassed all *jats* (castes and tribes). The modernizing Panchayat regime, which followed in 1960, proclaimed the equality of all citizens, without, however, challenging traditional customs and religion. In 1990 a new constitution, in response to cultural nationalist requests, came to define the Nepalese state as multiethnic and multilingual, fuelling multicultural initiatives. Gellner shows how the conventional divisions between people in political discourse and practice defy a more complex reality of often mixed identities. He proposes that the state should find ways of engaging with, and encouraging, this reality, instead of reactively accepting the conventional categorizations used by ethnic activists and the wider society.

Taking as their focus the 1995 peace accord which specifically recognizes the rights of Guatemala's indigenous people, Rachel Sieder and Jessica Witchell examine how the international normative order on which this settlement draws has shaped and constrained the strategies of local actors. While acknowledging that the fight for cultural rights must be understood as a response to deep-rooted historical legacies of discrimination, they observe that the reductionist orientation of law encourages a strategic essentializing of indigenous culture by both social movements and policy makers. This is particularly evident in projections of an idealized, 'harmonious' Mayan customary law. Sieder and Witchell argue that such reifications do not represent a complex social reality in which indigenous communities are often bitterly divided as a consequence of the vicious counter-insurgency war. They warn that discourses, strategies and legal frameworks that reify and imagine a harmonious and 'traditional' indigenous culture risk further marginalizing indigenous people from national processes, and may even deny access to justice for the most disadvantaged sectors of the population, such as women.

In the last case-study in this section, Colin Samson explains how the formerly nomadic Innu have been forced into 'participating', on unequal terms, in the state practices and discourses that exclude their own practices and worldview. Samson argues that the Innu, who value

an egalitarian and communal way of life organized around hunting, have
been recently subject to intense colonizing pressures by the Canadian
state. He explains that in the mid-twentieth century, Canadian authorities assumed that a policy of sedentarization, achieved by granting
Innu welfare benefits, access to private property and other rights, would
safeguard the interests of the Innu. However, access to these 'rights'
came at the expense of their rights to land, which only began to be
considered seriously in the 1990s in the context of land claims procedures and Environmental Impact Assessments (EIA) assessing the
effect of industrial developments such as mining on the social and
physical environment. Innu came to be consulted in these procedures
but, Samson remarks, without any chance of being heard. This is
because their sense of knowing as an active process and of truth as
found in real experience does not fit the bureaucratic processes or
categories such as 'traditional ecological knowledge' that the EIA
incorporates. The irony is that Innu can hardly refuse to 'participate' in
these processes, even though they are aware that they will only be
granted participatory rights through a denial of their cultural difference.

The last case-study is arguably the most depressing, concerned as it is
with a situation where people have been forced to claim rights that in
fact represent losses to them. The other three case-studies trace the
emergence of movements that see themselves engaged in efforts to gain
important rights for their members. Such emergence points to the
possibility of effecting political and social change through negotiation
and engagement with rights discourses and institutions. At the same
time, the project of claiming cultural rights suffers from serious shortcomings, which derive from the necessary but ultimately sterile and
possibly even counterproductive reification of culture it entails. As the
case-studies show, such pitfalls arise whether the cultural rights claimed
are those of a national minority, disprivileged castes, indigenous people
making up the majority of the national population, or a small group of
indigenous hunters confronted with Western development projects.

Missing from the accounts presented in this section are situations in
which the ultimate political aim for making cultural claims is not
recognition but to get the other excluded, even annihilated. In his
contribution to the previous section of the volume, Thomas Eriksen
stressed the importance of being aware of this danger, especially in an
era in which most wars are ethnic ones.

7

Ambiguities of an emancipatory discourse: the making of a Macedonian minority in Greece

Jane K. Cowan

Introduction

In 1991, in the wake of Yugoslavia's violent disintegration, the Federal Republic of Macedonia bid to establish itself as an independent state. It sought international recognition under the name Macedonia. On its flag it placed a sixteen-pointed symbol – identified as a star south of the border, and a sun north of it – drawn from archeological finds in a recently excavated ancient tomb claimed as that of Phillip of Macedon in the Greek village of Vergina. These actions were read by many Greeks as a 'theft of history' and tantamount to territorial claims upon the portion of Macedonia incorporated into Greece in 1912–13. Greek reaction was swift and intense. Shop receipts, telephone cards, billboards and graffiti proclaimed 'Macedonia is one and it is Greek'. On St Valentine's Day 1992, Greeks in their thousands poured into Salonika to demonstrate support for this claim. The 'Macedonian Question', dormant since the close of the Second World War, was reawakened.

The tumult of these mass demonstrations and of Greek diplomatic manoeuvres within the European Union over the name obscured another dimension to the controversy. It concerned the revival of the never fully resolved controversy within Greece over the existence within her borders of a distinctive Slavic Macedonian people. As early as the mid-1980s, self-defined Macedonian activists had come into conflict with police and local authorities when they sang songs in Macedonian and used Macedonian terms for dances and for local place names during village festivals (Danforth 1995: 121). Significantly, activists' gestures, like their complaints about official attempts to suppress them, were framed in terms of a discourse of human rights and minority recognition.

The Macedonian case is just one example of the recent proliferation at the global level of rights discourses used by and on behalf of 'oppressed' groups. In making cultural difference both the grounds for, and the object of, claims, it also exemplifies what Nancy Fraser, in *Justice Interruptus*, has called 'the shift in the grammar of political claims-making' from struggles for social equality to those for group recognition (1997: 2). This grammatical shift has occurred in the context of a wider 'politics of recognition', 'the name [which] political theorists have given to "an emancipatory politics that affirms group difference" and to the demand by minority groups for "recognition of their identity and accommodation of their cultural differences"' (Rosenblum 1998: 321).

International and transnational institutions of law and human rights have responded to this clamour for group recognition by opening up the previously narrow legal-political space devoted to cultural difference. Once perceived as a challenge to a universal human rights regime, cultural diversity is now celebrated, and an archipelago view of a world composed of discrete, bounded islands of culture prevails (see Eriksen in this volume). The conceptual and ethical commitment to distinct cultures has enabled the invention of new categories of rights for collectivities, such as indigenous rights, that were previously unrecognized in international law. It has also underpinned an expansion – and simultaneously, a rephrasing – of the more established area of minority rights, where the pendulum has swung away from exclusive reliance on protecting individual rights and towards some recognition of group rights.[1] The greatly expanded scope for recognizing culturally distinctive sub-national units (peoples, cultures, and minorities), as well as increasingly vigorous monitoring and adjudication procedures by international and supranational bodies for ensuring their rights, is widely viewed as constituting an emancipatory trend.

In this paper, I explore certain ambiguities of the emancipatory discourse of protecting and promoting vulnerable cultures and embattled minorities by examining the making of the Macedonian minority in Greece. In describing this as a 'making', I do not mean that it has been invented out of thin air. Rather, I want to highlight the ways in which a specific population's social and linguistic distinctiveness, whose nature and salience have long been contested, have been *recast* in the past two decades through transnational legal categories and institutional practices. A discourse of 'minority', 'culture' and 'human rights', I argue, dictates how difference can be formulated and defended, and is thus partially constitutive of the groups the international community purports merely to recognize. Claims for the *recognition* of the Macedonian minority, its culture and its human rights, have therefore not been simply *concurrent with* its construction as a novel cultural-legal category and socio-political constituency; *they have been the very means of that construction.*

Since the mid-1980s, activists within a movement for Macedonian human rights have pursued what I call a 'minoritization of culture'. They have attempted to narrow and fix the meanings of certain cultural forms such that they may underwrite and authenticate a particular minority identity. They have also urged a reformulation of the subject from one whose identities are multiple, fluid and situational – grounded as they are in an array of cultural practices, only some of which are distinct from those of the majority (in particular, the use of a Slavic language) – to one predefined in terms of separateness and subordination *vis-à-vis* the Greek majority, oppression *vis-à-vis* the state, and entitlement to special rights guaranteed by the international community.

The project of constructing and consolidating minorityhood has been taking place in different domains. At a local level, activists and their supporters have sought, and continue to seek, to persuade people who today call themselves *dopii* ('locals') or *dopii Makedones* ('local Macedonians') to embrace the name 'Macedonian' for themselves, their language and their culture, and to think of themselves as a 'minority'. At the same time, they are seeking to consolidate the existence of 'the Macedonian minority' in the international law and the human rights community, and by that means to compel the state to recognize it.

Yet the population to which this designation is meant to apply is politically fractured, with multiple subjectivities reflecting different histories, different modes and degrees of accommodation to a hegemonic Greek national culture, and different levels of interaction with neighbours of different linguistic and cultural backgrounds. The activists' reformulation of identity has consequently met with considerable suspicion and even hostility from *within* the *dopii* population. Most members of this population identify themselves today as 'Greeks'. This has already raised within the population, and signals for us, important issues of representation and accountability.

My analysis reveals a plethora of ambiguities: about the intended referent for the term 'Macedonian minority', about its scope, and about the activists' 'real' objectives. Above all, I am concerned with the ethical ambiguities of a discourse which may constrain, as much as enable, many of those it is meant to empower, by forcing their expressions of difference into a dichotomous interpretive frame that misrepresents their complex identities and rests on the same logic as the nationalism it ostensibly contests.

Minority and minoritization

Within discourses of international law and human rights, the older legal concept of 'minority' functions very much like the concept of 'culture'. Although the international community has never found a universally-acceptable definition of 'minority', the category is normally construed through reference to cultural criteria. Consider the widely-cited definition of 'minority' by Francesco Capotorti:

a group numerically inferior to the rest of the population of a State, in a non-dominant position, whose members – being nationals of the State – possess ethnic, religious or linguistic characteristics differing from those of the rest of the population, and show, if only implicitly, a sense of solidarity, directed towards preserving their culture, traditions, religion or identity. (cited in Thornberry 1991a: 11)

A minority is considered as a matter of 'fact', whose existence can be ascertained on the basis of certain objective or subjective criteria, or some combination of both (Eide 1996; Thornberry 1991a, 1991b). Even without state recognition, a minority's existence may be acknowledged within the international sphere.

As a legal or technical category, 'minority' partakes of the essentialising and reification entailed in all legal regimes, which demand clearly defined, context-neutral categories of identity and membership. 'Minority' and 'majority' are presented as discrete, clearly bounded entities. A minority is normally taken to be a pre-existing social group into which individuals are born. However, given the individualist human rights framework within which minority rights are situated, international law recognizes that 'members of a minority have two ways of expressing their identity': either by associating themselves with the strong desire of a group to preserve its characteristics, or by exercising their choice not to belong and instead to assimilate into the majority (UN 1992: 10). By positing membership as ultimately voluntary; the 'minority' remains conceptualised as a cohesive group.

The attribution of cohesion to a minority within discourses of international law and human rights has significant consequences. It leads to a representation of struggles over minority rights as merely dyadic, involving conflicts or competing claims between the state and the minority, or the majority and the minority. Such representations are frequently infused with a Manichean moralism, and a romance of resistance, positing powerful oppressor states and vulnerable, victimised minorities. They leave unaddressed the minority's internal dynamics, as well as the larger global context framing, and animating, these struggles.

The related assumption that a minority is ontologically pre-given is also problematic. A minority is better understood as a product of particular ideological, social, political and economic processes, rather than a clear-cut component of a pre-existing multiplicity. In most cases, minorities are formulated at the moment of state formation. The post-1989 catalysms – the break-up of the Soviet Union and parts of Eastern Europe, especially Yugoslavia – and the subsequent political reordering into new states offer one opportunity to explore minorityhood (like statehood) as an emergent phenomenon. Although the minorities created in this process tend to be viewed as pre-existing culturally-defined social groups, merely renamed under new political conditions, in fact, they frequently involve significant transformations.[2]

The ways in which changes in the wider political framework can give rise to new social groupings, as well as recast the meanings and boundaries of established ones, invites attention to 'minoritization'. This is the process – which may also be a project – by which the identities of a diverse population and the meanings of its cultural practices are reformulated to fit within the framework of the moral, conceptual and legal category of minority. Minoritization is a distinctive strategy within a global political field, that eschews territorial objectives and seeks rights within existing national borders; it may develop as a *reformulation of* and an *alternative to* an explicitly nationalizing project. Yet it has many similarities and potential overlaps with nationalizing projects. A minoritization project may embrace and use the nation even as it refigures it, leaving the relation between minoritization and nationalism highly ambiguous.

Before minoritization: fragmentation

Although the international human rights community mostly takes 'the Macedonian minority' as a self-evident entity, I argue that it is still in a precarious state of becoming, and that its scope is not yet fully clear. For the population the Macedonian human rights movement sees as 'its own' and seeks to enlist in its collective project, is profoundly fragmented. From the late nineteenth century until the Balkan Wars, and long after national boundaries were established after 1919, Macedonia's Slavic-speaking peasants (usually called 'Bulgarians' in that era) found themselves alternately wooed and terrorized by competing national movements.[3] In rural Macedonia, even wholly Slavic-speaking villages often became divided, sometimes into two sides ('the Greek side' versus 'the Bulgarian side'), but in other cases, given the rifts within the latter camp between those favouring autonomy for Macedonia and those seeking union with Bulgaria, into three (or more) factions. Religiouscum-national antagonisms were frequently mapped onto old communal factions, or expressed enmities based on status or material inequalities between poorer and wealthier peasants (Gounaris 1996). Yet lines of alliance and conflict were not necessarily enduring. Individuals and communities, under pressure from nationalist educators, clergy and armed bands, shifted their national allegiances – in some cases, repeatedly – in response to perceived threats or interests.

After a portion of Macedonia became incorporated into Greece in 1912–13, this fragmentation was sustained, even exacerbated, by myriad factors: by the consequences of individuals' and communities' political choices, both before and after incorporation (and especially during the Resistance and the Civil War period of the 1940s); by the relations of particular communities and regions with the Athenian centre (largely mediated by local elites); by experiences, idiosyncratic to each community, of inward and outward migration (reflecting massive but unevenly distributed shifts in population affecting all the region's inhabitants); and by the vagaries of individual family fortunes. In each region, varying even from village to village, Slavic-speakers were incorporated into the Greek national project less or more effectively. They worked, lived, interacted and intermarried with other groups to very different degrees. They had no common name, in the sense of one acceptable across the whole population – neither 'Bulgarian' nor 'Macedonian' nor 'Greek'. They shared in a continuum of mutually intelligible dialects, rather than a common language. They had widely diverging political and material interests. They were united only, if at all, by external ascription, an ambiguous mark of otherness placed on them by an ambivalent Greek society.

The nation-building process gave rise to many subjectivities. These subjectivities have been produced always in dialectical relation to a historically fluctuating but, to some degree, enduring ambivalence of the Greek state and society toward its Slavic-speaking citizens. Were they to be considered 'us' or 'others'? 'Slavophone Greeks' or 'Bulgarians'? Loyal citizens who had voluntarily remained in their own, freely chosen nation, in contrast to their emigrating brethren, or potential, even actual, enemies within? Consequently, depending on the situation and the historical moment, the Slavic-speaking subject found herself alternately included in the Greek national community, on the argument that 'national consciousness' trumped language, and rejected as 'the Bulgarian' or 'the Slav' other.

Most of the subjectivities produced have entailed identification both with Slavic elements and with aspects of the hegemonic Greek norm, but in highly varied combinations. Today, many such persons say that they and their families have 'always' been Greek. This is not always a product of Greek nationalist rewritings of the past. Such persons may be descendents of 'Bulgarian-speaking' peasant women who, at the turn of the century, remained loyal to the Greek-speaking priest of her community's Patriarchist Orthodox Church; or their ancestors may have fought on the side of the 'Greeks' against the 'Bulgarians' in that era's Macedonian struggle. Many others, however, came to identify with the Greek national dream much later: some willingly or with resignation, most out of a complex combination of choice, compulsion and even trauma. Many revised their declarations of who they were several times throughout their lives. The question of how to theorize these complex, and often transmutating, subjectivities remains an open one. In any case, no one theory would illuminate the diversity of cases. But it is clear that, for the majority who today declare themselves Greek yet maintain some sense of difference, whether this be conceptualised in terms of hybridity, or layered or situational identities, they have found a way to be not either/or, but rather, both/and.

Interestingly, the term adopted for this population through the whole region of Macedonia, *dopii*, or *dopii Makedones*, marks, and makes possible, the accommodation of a double identity. *Dopios (m)* or *dopia (f)* (a 'local'), deriving from the word, *topos* (place or territory), is a common term throughout Greece. It refers to a long-term resident, connoting historical and ethical connection to a place and entitlements stemming from it. At a formal linguistic level, it is culturally or ethnically unmarked, leaving the bearer's Greekness assumed. Only in the north of Greece does the term have an additional resonance not found elsewhere. Here, with some exceptions (see for example Karakasidou 1997a:xv), it is understood to refer to Slavic-speakers long resident in the area. It came into use, replacing *Voulgaros*, on the arrival in Macedonia after 1923 of some 650,000 Orthodox 'refugees' uprooted from Turkey, victims of the compulsory population exchange which followed a failed Greek invasion into Asia Minor and Turkish retaliation – the 'Catastrophe' of 1922. The term *dopii* is thus ambiguous, declining to mark cultural difference linguistically but carrying this load through its contrast with other social categories: 'refugees', 'Vlachs', 'Gypsies' or 'Ponts' (Black Sea Greeks).

Under the heading of *dopii*, however, also fall those who did not in the past, and/or who do not today, feel Greek. In the period following Macedonia's incorporation into Greece, these included those who were 'on the Bulgarian side' of the Macedonian struggle, or who had been members of Bulgarian Exarchist churches and schools before 1912.[4] It also included those who, though not politically aligned, felt indifferent to or alienated from Greeks and the Greek national project. Such individuals may have resented the post-1923 redistribution of former Muslim properties, believing that the refugee incomers had been favoured over their own people, or they may have been targeted and punished – accurately or not – as pro-Bulgarian in their national sentiments. New defectors from the national project were created by the Metaxas regime (1936–41), whose repressive policies, such as the notorious practice of forcing individuals who spoke their Slavic mother tongue in public to drink castor oil, were directed even against *dopii* who had already come to identify as nationally Greek. Many of these people began to call themselves *Slavomakedones* when they became involved on the side of the left-wing Greek resistance organisation, EAM (National Liberation Front) and its army ELAS (Greek People's Liberation Army), or after 1943, in the sister organisation SNOF (Slav Macedonian National Liberation Front), against Axis occupation.

When the Axis forces retreated in 1944 and the country was plunged into civil war, some *Slavomakedones* fought as communists or partisans, alongside Greeks of similar political convictions, or in independent units of SNOF against relatives who had joined the monarchist government forces. Others redefined themselves uncompromisingly as *Makedones*, crossing into the fledgling People's Republic of Macedonia to join the Yugoslav Partisans (Koliopoulos 1997: 52). Many more Slavic-speakers associated with the Left, including up to 30,000 children, also crossed the border during the five years of civil strife, ending up in Yugoslavia and other communist countries in Eastern Europe and Central Asia. With the defeat of the Left in 1949, and the postwar aftermath of right-wing repression and economic neglect, the final stage of the exodus occured. Large numbers of *Slavomakedones, Makedones* or other non-Greek-identified Slavic-speakers departed, first – until 1950 – as political refugees, mainly to Soviet-affiliated countries, and later – in the 1950s and 1960s – as economic migrants, mainly to North America, Australia and Northern Europe. Once a considerable presence across Macedonia, but particularly in western Macedonia near the Yugoslav and Albanian borders, they gradually dwindled into a small section of the *dopii* population.

Minoritization: claims and counter-claims from within

In the early 1980s, a movement for Macedonian human rights began to articulate claims for the protection of Macedonian culture and the recognition of Macedonian identity. This movement is a loose concatenation of groups, some based in Greece and others in the diaspora, which has been active both locally and in the international arena (Danforth 1995: 108–141; Hotzidis 1997). Within Greece, the primary expression of the movement is the Florina-based political party Rainbow (*Ouranio Toxo* in Greek, *Vinozhito* in Macedonian). Established by some members of the Macedonian Movement for Balkan Prosperity (MAKIBE), Rainbow calls itself 'the Voice of the Macedonian Minority'.

The emergence of the movement at this particular moment reflects developments in dispersed locales and in very different social and institutional arenas which are nonetheless profoundly interconnected and mutually implicating within the global framework of rights processes. Very briefly, four developments of the past fifteen years have been crucial. First, in a small area of northwestern Greek Macedonia, principally around the prefecture of Florina, discontent over political and economic issues was expressed in an ethnic idiom, resulting in an intensification in the salience of ethnicity and an incipient mobilization around ethnic issues (Van Boeschoten 2000). Second, the Macedonian diaspora, particularly in Canada and Australia, became increasingly mobilized around issues of language and culture, partly under the influence of those countries' official multiculturalism. They set up Macedonian human rights committees, which offered moral and material support to relatives and compatriots in Greece; many have strong ties to the Florina region. Third, both international and European legal arenas began to expand the space for cultural claims and to strengthen mechanisms for protecting and promoting endangered cultures and minorities. Finally, the outbreak of war in Yugoslavia in 1991, followed by the establishment of the old Republic of Macedonia as a new state and diplomatic battles over 'the name', propelled the movement into the international limelight. In complicated ways, this (newly contextualized) visibility altered perceptions of its activities, both at home and internationally, and opened avenues for strategic action.

The movement is thus a product of transnational networks. It has always operated self-consciously within a global space. From its very first public action, the publication in August 1984 of a 'Manifesto of the Central Organising Committee for Macedonian Human Rights for Macedonians of Aegean Macedonia', it has directed itself not only to the national government, but to the international community.[5] The unresponsiveness of the Greek government, which until very recently refused to discuss the issues raised by the movement, has indeed prompted them to concentrate their efforts in the international arena. Discourses of minorities and of culture in this arena have partially shaped the way the movement articulates its claims. In the quest for recognition and an effective political voice, the movement has initiated a minoritization process.

Minoritization here draws on an older discourse of Macedonian nationalism, borrowing its symbols and its narratives of illicit occupation and anti-colonial struggle. But it also draws on human rights discourse, constructing minorityhood via unjustly 'denied' rights and recognition. The reformulation involves two related processes: first, a process of reduction in which the diversity, fluidity and ambiguity of cultural forms, practices and meanings are simultaneously fixed and transfigured; and second, a process of extension, in which the authoritative version is reprojected onto, or claimed for, the population as a whole. I consider here two issues currently being 'minoritized': the name of the group, and its language.

The issue of group definition

In as much as

[international] law has not been concerned with every conceivable classification of minority (lefthanders or redheads as possible categories) but with cohesive groups, the characteristics of which endure, and who regard themselves – or are regarded by others – as different to the mainstream of society (Thornberry 1991: 6)

the first fundamental task of the movement has been to transform an internally fractured population into a cohesive and distinctive group. Since naming brings an entity into social existence and defines its character (Bourdieu 1991: 120, 236) the choice of name has been critical. Activists have pressed for the acceptance of 'Macedonians' *(Makedones, Makedontsi)* as the authoritative collective name. They reject official Greek names such as *Slavophoni* (Slavic-speakers), *Ellines Slavophoni* (Greek Slavic-speakers) and *diglossi* (bilinguals) as 'denationalizing'. They condemn the label *Voulgari* (Bulgarians) – a term used by many outsiders and probably most insiders before the late 1930s – as insulting, not because it denies their Greekness (the source of outrage for many Slavic-speaking Greek citizens), but because it denies their Macedonianness. They similarly reject the term *Slavomakedones* (Slavomacedonians), used by the Left during the Civil War and still embraced as a term of self-ascription by some, as simply an excuse not to call them *Makedones*. The correct name of members of this community, 'the name they wish to be called', as their communications to the international community repeatedly assert, is 'Macedonians'.

Because, in Balkan societies, a name is also a claim to a conceptual and material inheritance (Sutton 1997), the matter of who has the right to call themselves Macedonians remains fundamentally contested. The internal debate about the name of the Slavic-speaking population cannot be separated from the international debate over the 'name' of the new republic (see Danforth 1993 and 1995; Roudometof 1996). However, because exactly *what kind* of affiliation *Makedonas* designates has been open to interpretation, local attention has focused on the qualifying phrases. Analyzing the 'minority discourse' of the Rainbow party's then-official periodical, *Zora* (Dawn), Hotzidis (1997) found that Rainbow defined itself as 'the organised political expression of *Makedones kata ton ethnos*' (Macedonians by ethnos), in Greece, or *ethnika Makedones*. *Zora* texts explain the Greek phrase *ethnika Makedones* as a continuation of the earlier term, *dopii*. *Dopii*, however, is redefined in a way that denies ambiguity in relation to the Greekness/non-Greekness of the identity and fixes it as non-Greek and possibly anti-Greek:

Dopii are the old residents of Macedonia, in counterdistinction to the refugees and the 'old Greek' government civil servants. Not, however, all the indigenous residents of Macedonia, but only those who didn't want to define themselves ethnically/nationally as Greeks or Vlachs (or ethnoreligiously as Jews) (*Zora* 8, July 1995).

The qualifier *ethnika* is meant to distinguish this use of 'Macedonian' from other competing uses – most importantly, 'Macedonian' as a regional term, applicable to *all* residents of the region (the Greek government's position). Yet the term *ethnika*, like *kata ton ethnos*, contains a central ambiguity, which has been at the centre of controversy *within* the Slavic-speaking population. *Ethnos* is normally translated as nation, making both *ethnika* and *kata ton ethnos* translate as 'national'. The terms 'ethnic' and 'national' were not distinguished until the early 1990s, when the neologism *ethnotika* was devised for 'ethnic' in its contemporary Anglo-American sense. For a Greek audience in the late 1980s and 1990s, Rainbow's use of the phrase *ethnika Makedones* signalled a decision to characterize this population as 'nationally' (rather than regionally, linguistically or culturally) Macedonian. Given that the discourse of nations posits national identifications as normally mutually exclusive, this characterization seemed logically to exclude the possibility that 'nationally Macedonians' (*ethnika Makedones*) could be 'nationally' Greek. In effect, Rainbow adopted a stance that appeared to ignore the self-definition as 'Greeks' of most of its potential constituency. This stance affected how local inhabitants used the term. In central Macedonia in the early 1990s, responding both to the movement's shifting of the term in non-Greek directions and to its association with the national project of the new Republic of Macedonia, many

Greek-identified *dopii* who had previously called themselves *makedones* or *dopii makedones* in an ambiguously cultural and regional sense stopped using the term for themselves (Karakasidou 1997: 22). In the Florina region, Vereni (personal communication, 1999) recently noted the converse: there, individuals of opposite national convictions are increasingly claiming to be Macedonians, defiantly unqualified.

In fact, Rainbow's apparently 'national' stance was not without ambiguity. By the mid-1990's it had adopted the neologism *ethnotikos*, describing its constituency as members of 'an ethnic group' (*mias ethnotikis omadas*) (Hotzidis 1997), while in its website postings in 1995, it translated *Makedones kata ton ethnos* as 'the Macedonian ethnical community'. This suggests an effort to renegotiate – indeed, to 'minoritize' – the meanings of *ethnos*, to detach it from territorial claims towards those of culture and identity. Rainbow officially repudiates all nationalisms and denies any aspirations for the revision of state borders. Yet its increasingly adamant demands for recognition of 'the Macedonian national minority' – though reframed in terms of rights to national culture, rather than territory – are for many people hard to distinguish from those of more traditionally nationalist and revisionist Macedonian diaspora organizations, many of which also operate as human rights groups.

Just as controversial for local reception as the qualifier *ethnika* has been the noun, 'minority' (*meionotita*). Within human rights discourse, 'minority' is treated as a neutral legal or technical descriptive term. This has drawn attention away from the term's specific history and semantic loading in any particular society, as well as from the disciplinary role of the international community in imposing a majority/minority logic. The degree to which local human rights non-governmental organizations (NGOs) in Greece are committed to the minority concept, even in the face of intense public scepticism, is evident in a report published by the Minority Rights Group – Greece/Helsinki Watch. This report acknowledges that 'many, if not most, Macedonian speakers appear to have a Greek national consciousness', a consequence of having been 'the victims of a usually systematic campaign of memoricide by the Greek state in the last half-century' (Greek Helsinki Monitor 1995: 57, 59). Yet it insists that this fact of a Greek national consciousness 'does not deprive them of the status of an at least linguistic minority . . .' (Greek Helsinki Monitor 1995: 59). Therefore,

it is important to do extensive research to establish what percentage of that minority should be considered as just a linguistic minority, what percentage as an ethnic minority, and what percentage as a national minority (Greek Helsinki Monitor 1995: 57).

This comment also hints at the wide-ranging discussions that have occurred within the movement, with its NGO allies, with other groups claiming minority status, and within Greek society, about whom the minority includes, the kind of minority – linguistic, cultural, ethnic, national – it is or should claim to be, and how it should define its origins and characterize its history. But all seem to have accepted the vocabulary of minority and majority as the necessary structure of the debate.

However, this is not yet an accepted social fact within Macedonia. Although some *dopii* now embrace the designation 'minority' for themselves, many have angrily rejected it. This is due not only to the *stigma* that minorityhood has traditionally carried in a society conceived as a single Greek ethnos. It is due equally to its associated claim of *separation* -social, political, cultural or national – from the majority. Products of a Greek nation-building project that dealt with cultural and linguistic difference through processes of incorporation and assimilation, most *dopii* today work with, go to school with, and intermarry with other Greek co-nationals (themselves with distinctive linguistic or cultural backgrounds).

Significantly, claims of Macedonian minorityhood find support primarily in those parts of western Macedonia where such social integration has been less extensive and where a sense of disadvantage already exists (Van Boeschoten 2000). Here, the locally-directed discourse of movement publications, both *Zora* and its competitor *Nova Zora*, found a receptive audience when they stressed historical and continuing economic conflicts of interest between *dopii* and 'the refugees' of the 1920s, and when they pointed to the recent resettlement of ex-Soviet 'Pontic Greeks' in the region as proof that the Greek state wishes, once again, to make *dopii* 'feel like foreigners in their own land' (Hotzidis 1997: 164).

The issue of language

The primary cultural object of Macedonian human rights claims, and of the minoritization process, is the 'mother tongue', which is made to symbolize a social boundary, while its beleaguered state is continually offered as evidence of the Greek state's efforts to annihilate that boundary – indeed, to annihilate the group itself by obliterating one of the foundations of its distinctiveness. Consequently the issue of the name of the mother-tongue, and its legitimation as a *bona fide* language, is central.

In taking up the issue of language, the movement broaches a subject charged with powerful but complex emotions. For a Slavic-speaker's experience of her Slavic language has always been marked by Greek authorities' ambivalence towards the language itself, and those who spoke it. Greek ambivalence was a response to the view in Europe, dominant throughout the nineteenth and much of the twentieth century and still pervasive, that language is the primary evidence of national belonging. Even though, in the special case of Macedonia, advocates of the Greek national project vigorously disputed the reading off of nation from language, insisting that criteria such as national consciousness, religion, customs and 'shared civilisation' were much more important in defining who belonged to the nation, they also felt under pressure from this dominant view, which many secretly shared. They responded, on the one hand, by trying to prove, through myriad 'scientific' linguistic studies, that the language was *actually* Greek. On the other hand, they denigrated it as impure and incomplete, and implemented policies intended to dissuade people from using it, while compelling them to use Greek instead (Ioannidou 1997).

Today, the language is spoken mainly by middle-aged and older people, in scattered sites throughout Macedonia. Apart from the western Macedonian region bordering the new republic, where it is widely heard in public and in cross-border economic interactions, the language is used mostly in private contexts. It operates as a language of intimacy among peers or family members, as a secret code in the presence of children or outsiders (including Greek authorities), as an 'idiom of belonging' (Cowan 1997), and as a medium for humorous reflection on its own political sensitivity (Van Boeschoten 1997). For most speakers, the two languages coexist in a dynamic and fluid relationship, and they liberally sprinkle the words of one language into the other, for effect. Code-switching – to invoke closeness or distance, to highlight an identity contextually, or to mark changes in the meanings of a social situation – is also common (Ioannidou 1997). Both the linguistic forms, and the connotations of using the Slavic language are contextually variable.

The greatest fear of many such Slavic-speakers is that their language will be taken, wrongly, as evidence of anti-Hellenic sentiments (Ioannidou 1997). Although some people call it *Makedonika*, *Makedonitika*, or *Makedonska*, many choose to distance themselves from political claims for the language by using ingenious circumlocutions. They may call it *Slavika*, 'Voulgarika-but-not-the-'real'-Voulgarika' (see Cowan 1997), *ta dika mas* ('our language', in Greek), *po nash* ('our language' in the tongue itself), *ta dopika* or *ta dopia* ('the local language'), or simply, *i glossa* ('the language'). They are consequently ambivalent about the movement's more assertive approach to naming. Activists are almost as impatient with these circumlocutions as they are with the phrases of Greek official discourse: 'the Slavic idiom' (*to slaviko idioma*), 'the Slavo-Macedonian tongue' (*i slavomakedoniki lalia*), 'the Slavonic language' (*i slavoniki glossa*) and 'the Slavonic dialect' (*i slavoniki dialektos*). These, activists say, either refuse it the status of a full language or skirt around its proper name. Activists insist that this range of dialects constitutes a language, and should be called, simply, Macedonian.[6]

Rainbow initially defined this Macedonian language exclusively in term of its local roots. In the first issue of *Zora*, in October 1993, they published a table of the Cyrillic alphabet used by 'our forefathers' early in the century, claiming that it 'contained all the elements that we need [today]'. Five months later, however, this older alphabet was dropped; songs, placenames and personal names, and ultimately the entire Macedonian portion of *Zora's* bilingual issues, were rendered in the Cyrillic alphabet used for standard literary Macedonian, the official language of the new Republic of Macedonia (Hotzidis 1997: 158). In this and other ways, Rainbow reaffirmed the putative link between language and nation – the source of so much contention.

Practically speaking, this linkage is probably unavoidable. Unless the language is to be maintained only as an oral form, and unless an altogether new literary language is to be devised, any formal language teaching needs to use an existing standard language with standard orthography. Literary Macedonian is clearly the best candidate. To this end, activists are naturalizing its link with these oral forms, and using supranational mechanisms to pressurize the Greek government to recognize and support Macedonian language education.[7] But it is indicative that no groundswell of support for formal teaching of Macedonian in the schools has so far emerged from within the *dopii* community. Alongside fears that such claims would generate public hostility against them (something government assurances would assuage), there is simply too little consensus about whether, how and in what form they should preserve their language, and too much suspicion of the activists' motives.

There have been no official restrictions on speaking the language for many years, and PASOK efforts in the 1980s to relax the atmosphere of anxiety surrounding it, and to increase the representation of *dopii* in its political organization have, in fact, led to its much wider public use. Even so, many speakers (and other sympathizers) would like to see a significant gesture by the Greek government to remove publicly the lingering stigma of it being seditious or anti-Greek. Their desire for the *de-politicization* of the language, however, puts them at cross-purposes with some supporters of the Macedonian human rights movement who, for example, boisterously sing old Macedonian revolutionary songs at village festivals, inviting police reaction and then complaining of violations of their human rights. Less militant *dopii*, who wish to distance themselves from such 'provocative' gestures of defiance, may, paradoxically, feel more reluctant to 'dance their own dances and sing their own songs'.

Parts for wholes and the problems/politics of representation

The controversy surrounding the existence of the Macedonian minority in Greece cannot be reduced to the state's refusal to countenance cultural difference. It is also related to a struggle within the contested population over how it is to be defined. I have sought to show that, although a significant number of individuals do now identify themselves as members of a Macedonian minority, many others object to this designation. This raises questions about the scope of the movement and the minority it claims to defend.

So, we need to ask again: *Who are the Macedonian minority, in the eyes of those who make claims on its behalf within a context of human and minority rights processes? Who is meant to be included in the term, and who is excluded?*

The widest and most totalizing definition is found in statements of certain Macedonian nationalist organisations in the diaspora. For these organisations, Macedonians include all Macedonian-speakers, or descendants of Macedonian-speakers, even when they no longer speak their ancestors' mother tongue. The 'Macedonian minority', defined by descent, comprises all such persons who live on Greek territory. Diaspora organizations deem Macedonians a 'national' entity, and consider it impossible to be *both* Macedonian and Greek. Significantly, these organizations often phrase their claims in a language of 'Macedonian human rights', and many of those involved in them acknowledge 'the self-ascriptive nature of national identity merely [as] a token gesture of respect, one . . . all too readily abandoned in favour of a more nationalistic approach' (Danforth 1995: 228).

Within the movement in Greece, there is a more complicated array of positions. The essentialist views described above are held by many. Yet others – notably the Rainbow leadership – have argued for a more constructivist understanding of nations and an emphasis on ethnic or national affiliation as a matter of choice. One can certainly discern a narrower usage of the term, 'the Macedonian minority' being those who declare themselves Macedonian, or who feel they have been disadvantaged by the Greek state and/or Greek society because of their background. Other public statements by Rainbow, however, seem to equate ethnic Macedonians and the national minority.[8]

When representatives of Rainbow make statements at meetings of Helsinki Watch or the Organization for Security and Cooperation in Europe (OSCE) about the persecution of the Macedonian national minority, are these meant to refer to explicitly self-identified national Macedonians – perhaps 10,000 people, according to Danforth (1995)[9] – or to all those of a Slavic-speaking background in Macedonia – which different claimants variously number from 10,000 to a million?[10] To whom do statements made by the Macedonian Human Rights Movement of Canada, or Greek Helsinki Monitor, refer? How are the statements of these organizations *heard* by the international community? I have argued that the view of a minority as a 'natural' ethnic unit prevails as common sense within international human rights discourse, even as it recognizes an individual's right to self-ascription. To this extent, such statements will be heard to refer to the larger entity. Anthropological work has inadvertently buttressed this impression: the rise of minority activism around Florina has created a veritable stampede of anthropologists to this small prefecture of 45,000, almost all of them examining 'ethnicity' and identity issues.[11] The cumulative effect of what I call 'Florinocentrism' (Cowan 1997b) in studies of the minority phenomenon, and in the human rights NGO literature, has overwhelmed individual anthropologists' own explicit disclaimers that the movement attracts a relatively small proportion of the *dopii* population across northern Greece (see also Gounaris 1997; Human Rights Watch/ Helsinki 1994).

The ambiguity around scope allows, in effect, the activists' case to appear stronger than may be warranted, while making Greek denials or minimization of the minority phenomenon appear simply absurd. This vagueness, along with the either/or, zero/sum nature of the debate, makes difficult any assessment of how widespread, and how intense, is the wish to be seen as a minority; how much support exists for the minority agenda; how widespread is the experience of 'denial of human rights' and of 'persecution'; how much of this is an ongoing problem, as opposed to problems of the past. In short, it makes it difficult to obtain any sense of proportion.

Above all, it raises questions of representation. Human Rights organizations regularly make statements about the wishes, identities and past and present experiences of 'the Macedonians of Greece', as they do for other minorities. But it is important to ask by what authority these organisations speak, and whose past and present experience is being made to stand as 'representative' for the group as a whole? Is a part of the group being taken for the whole? Whom, and how many, do the human rights organisations speaking on behalf of a minority actually represent?

Even though it was a primary impetus in the critique of universalism that led to a politics of identity, the question of representation is actually masked within a politics of recognition. No longer can national communities be argued to be homogeneous; yet the assumption of homogeneity has simply been pushed to another level, that of the ethnic or cultural group. Such groups are too often assumed to have shared or common interests, and to speak with a united voice. This allows a 'part for whole' logic to appear unproblematic. Of course, the fact that group members have differing views and interests does not preclude them from negotiating these and developing a common political platform, which may be seen with greater legitimacy to express collective wishes. And we need to acknowledge that an antagonistic attitude on the part of state authorities towards the expression of claims deemed politically sensitive or dangerous can constrain people's sense of their real choices and their willingness to speak out about what they want. However, when, as in this case, a vocal (and, one must admit, courageous) section within 'the Macedonian ethnical community' either explicitly purports to represent and speak on behalf of the group as a whole, or refrains from correcting that impression, questions about democratic representation and accountability can justifiably be raised.

This politics of representation also needs to be placed in a wider geopolitical context. Claims-making on behalf of Macedonian human rights is symbolically framed by a hegemonic political relationship between a peripheral and 'not-quite-European' nation and a dominant European centre. It is articulated through an Orientalist – or, as Todorova (1997) has argued, a 'Balkanist' – discourse, in which the enlightened, individualistic, democratic West is obliged to teach backward, tribalistic, ethnonational Balkan states the virtues of tolerance, multiculturalism, civil society, and respect for human rights (see also Burgess 1996, 1997). Minority rights activists operating in international human rights gatherings and fora comply with this cosmopolitan conceit, portraying themselves as progressive, model Europeans, striving for a post-national 'Europe of the Regions', while condemning their government for mere lipservice to European ideals. They may genuinely identify with these values, and their grievances may be legitimate; but from the perspective of *dopii* who do not share their agenda, the alliance between this movement and the international human rights community looks like just another version of an old Balkan story in which the cunning client cultivates the powerful and morally righteous foreign patron and persuades him to meddle in local affairs that he does not understand.

The imperialism of multiculturalism and the denial of cultural ambiguity

In their public statements in human rights fora, on their websites, and in their local publications, a spectrum of local and diaspora Macedonian human rights organisations, along with many national and international NGOs that support them, define the contours of the Macedonian minority. It is conceived as a 'community of suffering' whose members are persecuted merely for their cultural difference, because they do not fit within Greece's ideology of ethnic homogeneity. Seeking to challenge a state ideology of ethnic purity, the movement offers an alternative which is hardly less totalizing. In order to make their argument persuasive, they must impose unity and suppress differences *within* the population they claim to represent: hence, they have asserted singularity through a common name (Macedonians), and a common language (Macedonian), and they have tried to transform 'minority' from a stigmatized to a valorized and politically useful term of identity. They have claimed a common history, creating narratives that ignore or flatten out differences in the identities and affiliations within this population and present a monolithic account of assimilation processes. They have presented Greek policy as continuous across time. Their accounts are typically rendered in a language of 'oppressive states' and 'innocent victims', 'brutal assimilation', 'forced nationalization' and 'memoricide'.

The claims made by the Macedonian human rights movement are articulated largely as 'rights to culture' – the right to use the group's 'true' name, the right to speak the mother tongue, the right to sing its songs and dance its dances. The movement's call for the affirmation of these cultural forms has undeniably struck a chord within the wider community, especially a widespread desire for recognition of the legitimacy of the language, after decades of denigration. It has won some supporters, particularly in the western Macedonian region. It has, moreover, prompted a reconsideration of the meanings of being Macedonian. This process of unsettling identities and histories is still underway.

Yet to the extent that the movement's affirmation of specifically 'Macedonian' cultural forms is attached to an identity claim – of a *Macedonian national minority* linked historically and sentimentally to Bulgarian or Macedonian national movements for autonomy from Greece – its appeal within Greece will be limited, even if it is supported enthusiastically among its immigrants in diaspora. This identity claim has been, and probably will continue to be, rejected by most of those who themselves, or whose ancestors, have opposed, and defined themselves in opposition to, Bulgarian or Macedonian national projects in the past. This call, moreover, is unlikely to attract the majority of those *dopii* who, as the result of a complex, power-impregnated historical process, appear disinclined to choose once and for all, to be *either* Greek *or* Macedonian, a member of the majority *or* a member of the minority. Rather, such a person lives a life in which being *dopia* or Macedonian is salient at some moments, but not at others; she usually thinks of herself as 'Greek' yet sometimes speaks of 'the Greeks' as if the category did not include herself; and who is equally a woman, teacher, heterosexual, socialist, mother, and member of a particular family.

In the long embattled atmosphere which has surrounded Slavic forms within Greece, Stuart Hall's conception of cultural identities as 'nomadic', something one drifts into and out of according to circumstance, may appear inappropriately casual (1996). Yet as Brown (1999) has argued, it is precisely in a region such as Macedonia, where interminable contestation around the 'real' identities of its residents has created a long history of political instability, that people may develop an ironic view of the certainties of others (national defenders of whatever stripe, and their army of intellectual warriors and advocates), and of their naïve faith in the capacities of mutually exclusive categories to name the experience of those they claim to speak for. People may wish to distance themselves from such certainties, preferring to embrace ambiguity, to adopt more fluid strategies of identity, and to build relationships with myriad others in which identity and difference, collaboration and conflict, are contextual and negotiated, rather than predefined.

This is the central ambiguity of a minority rights discourse: that it must *deny* ambiguity and *fix* difference, in the realms of identity, and of cultural practice, in defence of distinct cultures. Recognition of one's culture is increasingly constructed and consequently increasingly experienced as a deep, primordial human need, as well as an inalienable right, one whose denial brings both suffering and indignation. Under such circumstances, I find the only tenable position for the engaged scholar to be a paradoxical one: to support the demands for recognition of the Macedonian minority, but as a category *chosen* rather than *imposed* (whether explicitly or de facto); yet at the same time, to problematize, rather than celebrate, its project, and to query its emancipatory aura, examining the exclusions and cultural disenfranchisements it creates from within. I feel obliged to stress the profound ambiguities and potential dangers of mechanisms which entrench and harden such identities, and which, even when meant to contest claims of national homogeneity, lock us ever more tightly into precisely the same national logic of purity, authenticity and fixity.

ACKNOWLEDGEMENTS

This paper has benefitted from comments by Georgios Agelopoulos, Keith Brown, Loring Danforth, Marie-Bénédicte Dembour, Thomas Hylland Eriksen, Vasilis Gounaris, Yannis Manos, Piero Vereni and Richard Wilson. Charles Gore, in addition to helping me clarify the overall argument, suggested the phrase 'the minoritization of culture'. I am grateful for the critical feedback of seminar participants when I presented a version of this paper at the universities of Sussex and Manchester. Finally, a British Academy grant enabled me to present the paper to the Council on European Studies Conference in Chicago in April 2000.

NOTES

1 The expansion includes the adoption in 1992 of the UN Declaration on the Rights of Persons Belonging to National or Ethnic, Religious and Linguistic Minorities, as well as minority rights and protections implemented at the regional level. In particular, Europe created a number of new measures in 1989 through the Council of Europe and the OSCE – Helsinki process (see Burgess 1996; Miall 1994; Poulter 1997; Wheatley 1996). For an overview of minority rights in international law, see Thornberry 1991b; for a review of debates on the rights of minority cultures, see Kymlicka 1995.

2 See, for example, David Laitin's (1998) account of the emergence of a 'Russian-speaking' (as opposed to 'Russian') identity in the new ex-Soviet republics, an identity embraced by some indigenous, non-Russian inhabitants.

3 This discussion is informed by a large corpus of anthropological and social-historical work on the region, including Agelopoulos 1997; Brown 1995; Carabott 1997; Cowan 1990, 1997a; Danforth 1995; Gounaris 1996; Gounaris *et al* 1997; Karakasidou 1993; 1997; Van Boeschoten 2000; Vereni 2000; Vermeulen 1984. I use the term 'Slavic-speakers', along with *dopii*, for this population in order to leave open the question of such individuals' ethnic and national identities, as well as to allow for their own range of claims about the national (or otherwise) character of the language they speak. When persons described identify their language as Macedonian, I retain that usage. For a strong position on the language as Macedonian, see Friedman 1975.

4 Many – perhaps 40 to 50,000 – of those with strong identifications as 'Bulgarians' or 'Macedonian Bulgarians' in a national sense fled to Bulgaria as refugees over the long period of intermittent conflict, from the late 1890s until the end of the 1920s. Around 92,000 others, (according to official Greek estimates), chose to migrate to Bulgaria and receive Bulgarian citizenship, in a voluntary and reciprocal migration scheme overseen by the Greek–Bulgarian Mixed Commission under the auspices of the League of Nations in the 1920s (Koliopoulos 1997: 49–51). Some Bulgarian-identified

persons, however, chose to remain. See Ladas 1932 and Pentzopoulos 1962.

5 Copies of the manifesto were sent to all foreign embassies in Athens, all European governments, the UN and several other international organisations (Danforth 1995: 125).

6 See, for example, Rainbow's website report on the Conference on the Slavonic dialect in the territory of Macedonia held at the Panteion University, Athens, on 31 October – 2 November 1998 (in which I participated). Summarising the discussion, Rainbow states: 'The discussion revolved around the issue of the existence of this Slavonic language in the past and present . . . At this forum, RAINBOW expressed its position citing the national character of the language. Some participants skirted around the issue of the national character and spoke of a so-called unified or singular Slavonic tongue, especially in relation to a 'Slavo-Macedonian' tongue and identity. . . ..Other participants, however, had no difficulty referring to the language properly as Macedonian without the addition of prefixes or suffixes. RAINBOW's presentation focused precisely on this matter. In its presentation RAINBOW reiterated the position that as a Macedonian national minority it seeks to bring proper recognition to the Macedonian language and have the literary standard Macedonian included within the framework of the Greek educational system'. (Rainbow, 'Language Conference-Athens', *www.florina.org)*.

7 After discussions with Rainbow, the Belgian member of the European Parliament, Nelly Maes, submitted in January 1999 an application before the European Commission asking that Macedonian be recognized as an official minority language in Greece, and that it be established in schools (from elementary level upwards) and in the mass media.

8 In 'Problems with Freedom of Expression' on Rainbow's website, it is stated that '. . . Greek authorities do not recognize the ethnic Macedonians as a distinct ethnicity and therefore a National minority in Greece' (*www.florina.org)*.

9 Although no direct correlation exists between Macedonian national identity and a vote for Rainbow, some electoral statistics from the last three European Parliament elections in the Florina prefecture, the heartland of the Macedonian human rights movement, are worth noting. Rainbow received 6 per cent of total votes cast in June 1994 (7,236 votes), 3.5 per cent in September 1996 and 3.5 per cent in June 1999.

10 The numbers of 'Slavic-speakers' (or 'Bulgarians', 'Macedonians') have been a matter of intense dispute, as well as wildly varying and frequently exaggerated claims since the nineteenth century. This is partly because those counting have used different criteria (language, religious affiliation, assumed national consciousness, explicit self-ascription) to calculate the numbers in their national camp. Probably, the number of persons of Slavic-speaking background in Greece falls somewhere in the region of 50,000 to 70,000, though with extensive intermarriage with other groups, such figures are not especially meaningful. On 'the war of statistics', see Mihailidis 1998 and Koliopoulos 1997.

11 Agelopoulos (1998) notes that following over sixty years of neglect, in the

seven years since 1991 at least ten anthropologists have undertaken long-term fieldwork in the Florina prefecture (not counting those on shorter research expeditions).

REFERENCES

Agelopoulos, G. 1997. From Bulgarievo to Nea Krasia, From 'Two Settlements' to 'One Village': An Ethnographic Account of Cultural Revaluations. In *Ourselves and Others: The Development of a Greek Macedonian Cultural Identity since 1912*. (Eds.) P. Mackridge & E. Yannakakis. Oxford: Berg.

Agelopoulos, G. 1998. Three Years of Living in the Margins: Between Autoethnography and Fieldwork at Florina. Paper presented at the conference Negotiating Boundaries: The Past in the Present in South-eastern Europe. University of Wales, Lampeter on 6–8 September, 1998.

Bourdieu, P. 1991. *Language and Symbolic Power*. Cambridge: Polity Press.

Brown, K.S. 1995. Of Meanings and Memories. The national imagination in Macedonia. PhD dissertation. Department of Anthropology, University of Chicago. Ann Arbor: UMI Microfilms.

Brown, K.S. 1999. Marginal Narratives and Shifty Natives: Ironic Ethnography as Anti-nationalist Discourse. *Anthropology Today* 15:1, 13–16.

Burgess, A. 1996. National Minority Rights and the 'Civilizing' of Eastern Europe. *Contention* 5:2, 17–36.

Burgess, A. 1997. *Divided Europe: The New Domination of the East*. London: Pluto Press.

Capotorti, F. 1991. *Study on the Rights of Persons Belonging to Ethnic, Religious and Linguistic Minorities*. New York: United Nations Publications.

Carabott, P. 1997. The Politics of Integration and Assimilation vis-à-vis the Slavo-Macedonian Minority of Inter-war Greece: From Parliamentary Inertia to Metaxist Repression. In *Ourselves and Others: The Development of a Greek Macedonian Cultural Identity since 1912*. (Eds.) P. Mackridge and E. Yannakakis. Oxford: Berg.

Cowan, J.K. 1990. *Dance and the Body Politic in Northern Greece*. Princeton, NJ: Princeton University Press.

Cowan, J.K. 1997a. Idioms of Belonging: Polyglot Articulations of Local Experience in a Greek Macedonian Town. In *Ourselves and Others: The Development of a Greek Macedonian Cultural Identity since 1912*. (Eds.) P. Mackridge & E. Yannakakis. Oxford: Berg.

Cowan, J.K. 1997b. Review of Loring Danforth, 'The Macedonian Conflict: Ethnic Nationalism in a Transnational World' (Princeton U. Press). *Journal of Byzantine and Modern Greek Studies* 21, 261–265.

Danforth, L.M. 1993. Claims to Macedonian Identity: The Macedonian Question and the Break-up of Yugoslavia. *Anthropology Today* 9:4, 3–10.

Danforth, L.M. 1995. *The Macedonian Conflict: Ethnic Nationalism in a Transnational World*. Princeton, NJ: Princeton University Press.

Eide, A. 1996. Classification of Minorities and Differentiation in Minority Rights. United Nations internal document E/CN.4/Sub.2/AC.5/1996/WP.2

Fraser, N. 1997. *Justice Interruptus: Critical Reflections on the 'Postsocialist' Condition*. New York and London: Routledge.

Friedman, V. 1975. Macedonian Language and Nationalism during the Nineteenth and Early Twentieth Centuries. *Balkanistica* 2, 83–98.

Gounaris, V., I. Mihailidis and G. Agelopoulos (Eds.). 1997. *Taftotites stin Makedonia [Identities in Macedonia].* Athens: Papazisis.

Gounaris, B. 1996. Social Cleavages and National 'Awakening' in Ottoman Macedonia. *East European Quarterly* 29:4, 409–426.

Gounaris, B. 1997. Anakyklondas tis paradoseis: Ethnotikes taftotites kai meionotika dikaiomata stin Makedonia [Recycling traditions: Ethnic identities and minority rights in Macedonia]. In *Taftotites stin Makedonia.* (Eds.) B. Gounaris et al. Athens: Papazisis.

Greek Helsinki Monitor. 1995. *Greek Monitor of Human and Minority Rights: Thematic Issue on Ethnolinguistic Minorities in Greece.* Athens: ETEPE.

Hotzidis, A. 1997. Arthrosi kai domi tou meionotikou logou: To paradeigma ton Moglenon kai tis Zora [Articulation and foundation of minority discourse: The case of *Moglena* and *Zora*]. In *Taftotites stin Makedonia.* (Eds.) B. Gounaris et al. Athens: Papazisis.

Human Rights Watch/Helsinki. 1994. *Denying Ethnic Identity: The Macedonians of Greece.* New York, Washington DC, Los Angeles, London: Human Rights Watch.

Ioannidou, A. 1997. Ta slavika idiomata stin Elladha: Glossoloyikes prosengisseis kai politikes apokliseis [Slavic idioms in Greece: Linguistic approaches and political exclusions]. In *Taftotites stin Makedonia.* (Eds.) B. Gounaris et al. Athens: Papazisis.

Karakasidou, A. 1993. Politicizing Culture: Negating Ethnic Identity in Greek Macedonia. *Journal of Modern Greek Studies* 11:1, 1–28.

Karakasidou, A. 1997a. *Fields of Wheat, Hills of Blood: Passages to Nationhood in Greek Macedonia 1870–1990.* Chicago: University of Chicago Press.

Karakasidou, A. 1997b. Women of the Family, Women of the Nation: National Enculturation among Slav-speakers in Northwest Greece. In *Ourselves and Others: The Development of a Greek Macedonian Cultural Identity since 1912.* (Eds.) P. Mackridge and E. Yannakakis. Oxford: Berg.

Koliopoulos, J. 1997. The War over the Identity and Numbers of Greece's Slav Macedonians. In *Ourselves and Others: The Development of a Greek Macedonian Cultural Identity since 1912.* (Eds.) P. Mackridge & E. Yannakakis. Oxford: Berg.

Kymlicka, W. 1995. *The Rights of Minority Cultures.* Oxford: Oxford University Press.

Ladas, S. 1932. *The Exchange of Minorities: Bulgaria, Greece and Turkey.* New York: Macmillan.

Laitin, D.D. 1998. *Identity in Formation: The Russian-Speaking Populations in the Near Abroad.* Ithaca, NY: Cornell University Press.

Michailidis, I.D. 1998. The War of Statistics: Traditional Recipes for the Preparation of the Macedonian Salad. *East European Quarterly* 32:1, 9–21.

Miall, H. (Ed.). 1994. *Minority Rights in Europe: The Scope for a Transnational Regime.* London: Pinter Publishers.

Pentzopoulos, D. 1962. *The Balkan Exchange of Minorities and its Impact upon Greece.* Paris and the Hague: Mouton.

Poulter, S. 1997. The Rights of Ethnic, Religious and Linguistic Minorities. *European Human Rights Law Review* 3, 254–264.

Rosenblum, N.L. 1998. *Membership and Morals: The Personal Uses of Pluralism in America*. Princeton, NJ: Princeton University Press.

Roudometof, V. 1996. Nationalism and Identity Politics in the Balkans: Greece and the Macedonian Question. *Journal of Modern Greek Studies* 14:2, 253–301.

Sutton, D.E. 1997. Local Names, Foreign Claims: Family Inheritance and National Heritage on a Greek Island. *American Ethnologist* 24:2, 415–437.

Taylor, C. 1992. The Politics of Recognition. In *Multiculturalism and the Politics of Recognition*. (Ed.) A. Gutmann. Princeton, NJ: Princeton University Press.

Thornberry, P. 1991a. *Minorities and Human Rights Law*. London: Minority Rights Group.

Thornberry, P. 1991b. *International Law and the Rights of Minorities*. Oxford: Oxford University Press.

Todorova, M. 1997. *Imagining the Balkans*. Oxford: Oxford University Press.

United Nations. 1998. Human Rights: Minority Rights, Fact Sheet No. 18 (rev. 1).

Van Boeschoten, R. 1997. The Political Dimension of Switching Languages. Unpublished paper presented at the International Symposium on Contact and Conflict, Brussels, 28–31 May 1997.

Van Boeschoten, R. 2000. When Difference Matters: Sociopolitical Dimensions of Ethnicity in the District of Florina. In *Macedonia: The Politics of Identity and Difference*. (Ed.) J.K. Cowan. London: Pluto Press.

Vereni, P. 2000. *Os Ellin Makedonas*: Autobiography, Memory, and National Identity in Western Greek Macedonia. In *Macedonia: The Politics of Identity and Difference*. (Ed.) J.K. Cowan. London: Pluto Press.

Vermeulen, H. 1984. Greek Cultural Dominance among the Orthodox Population of Macedonia during the Last Period of Ottoman Rule. In *Cultural Dominance in the Mediterranean Area*. (Eds.) A. Blok and H. Driessen. Nijmegen: Katholieke Universiteit.

Wheatley, S. 1996. Current Topic: The Framework Convention for the Protection of National Minorities. *European Human Rights Law Review* 6, 583–591.

INTERNET SOURCES

Greek Helsinki Monitor, www.greekhelsinki.gr
Macedonia for the Macedonians, www.geocities.com/~makedonija/aegean.html
Macedonian Human Rights Movement of Canada, www.mhrmc.on.ca
Ouranio Toxo/Vinozhito (Rainbow), www.florina.org

8

From group rights to individual rights and
back: Nepalese struggles over
culture and equality

David N. Gellner

Introduction: Nepal's South Asian context

'Cultural rights are now widely recognized as deserving the same
protection as human rights.'[1] So says an authoritative recent UNESCO
publication, which is examined in detail by Eriksen in chapter 6. The
rise of this kind of rights discourse, with its emphasis on the rights of
minority cultures, is, as the introduction to this book charts, a global
phenomenon; arguably it is itself an aspect of globalization. This
discourse of cultural rights is problematic on several counts. Within
liberal political and juridical theory it presents a fundamental challenge
to more traditional ways of conceiving rights. Are there any cultural
rights?[2] Do only individuals have rights or should groups defined by a
shared culture be granted rights that would enable them to impose their
standards on the individuals who belong to them? Furthermore, the
term 'cultural rights' can mean both (1) rights to culture, i.e. to
maintain cultural differences, with state and legal support if necessary,
and (2) differential rights to political and economic resources on the
basis of cultural difference. Perhaps most problematic of all, this
discourse assumes that every group possesses a shared and distinctive
culture which marks it off from other groups. In fact, in actual social
situations, as opposed to the thought experiments of philosophers, what
is to count as cultural difference, and who can claim it, are highly
political and often fiercely contested questions – a contention that will
be amply illustrated, I hope, by the case study presented in this paper.

The recent history of Nepal illustrates both the problems and the
temptations of 'rights talk' rather well. Throughout this time Nepal has
defined itself as a Hindu state, though how that has been understood,
and the degree to which it has been contested, have varied considerably.
I will sketch the last 150 years of Nepali history and the three contrasting
models of the political organization of culture that have prevailed in this
period. In doing so, I attempt to show how the language of cultural

rights has entered Nepali politics – what it is arguing *against* and what it is arguing *for*.

In traditional Nepal cultural difference was not relegated as a principle of social organization to marginal populations: it, along with the idea of hierarchy, was the key criterion by which the pre-modern Nepali state sought to organize society and rule over it. People had duties, as well as rights, as members of groups defined by their hereditary recruitment and by their relationship to the dominant division of labour. It was taken for granted that such groups had their own distinctive 'customs' or culture. In English these groups are usually known as castes or, in the case of more peripheral groups, as tribes. The most influential theorist of this division of labour is undoubtedly Louis Dumont in *Homo Hierarchicus* (1980). Critiques of *Homo Hierarchicus* have been many and varied, but Dumont's central contention that the dominant value of the caste system is and was hierarchy cannot, I think, be gainsaid.[3] The present paper is centrally concerned, then, with the transition from a fundamentally hierarchical situation to one in which equality, both of individuals and of groups, is the dominant value.

Another theme is the growing salience of religion rather than culture, or religion *as* culture, as a principle of identity. In the traditional situation religious identity was largely implicit for most of the population. Now that cultural differences are being eroded, religious allegiances have become both more self-conscious, more problematic, and much more politicized. In Europe most states are either secular republics or, if there is a connection between the state and a particular religion, as in England, the connection has been diluted so much in practice that it is no longer highly contentious. By contrast, in South Asia nationalism is relatively recent and, despite the best efforts of secularists such as Nehru, has taken a predominantly religious form (van der Veer 1994). As the frequency of constitutional amendments and new constitutions shows, the constitutional position of religion is a significant and sensitive issue in all the countries of South Asia.

India is officially a secular republic, with equal treatment of all its citizens guaranteed by the Constitution.[4] Pakistan, by contrast, came into existence because of Islam. Its successive constitutions have all guaranteed that Pakistani laws must not contradict Islam. Islamization has frequently been high on the political agenda and the controversy has often been over how, not whether, to implement it. Perhaps in reaction to the Pakistani experience, the constitution of Bangladesh enshrines secularism as a fundamental principle, though this has come under attack from Muslim activists. In Sri Lanka, the adherents of all four widely practised religions (Buddhism, Hinduism, Islam and Christianity) are supposed to enjoy equal status, but Buddhism has been given special status under the Constitution – a crucial step in the development of the ethnic war in the island.

Nepal is different from all of these examples because it was never formally a part of the British Empire. Although subject to various restrictions (for example, not being allowed direct dipomatic relations with other powers), it was not dictated to on internal affairs, as were the Indian princely states. From the 1930s Nepal was permitted to have an ambassador in London. Thus, as will be explored below, there was an important continuity between the period before 1950 and the Constitutions of 1960 and 1990: namely, the definition of Nepal as a Hindu state. That Nepal is, and has been, the world's only officially Hindu state is a matter of pride for many Nepalis, but has been increasingly controversial, especially since 1990.

The discourse of civil rights first began to arrive in Nepal early in the twentieth century. The autocratic Rana regime of the time was extremely sensitive to the slightest criticism, which it suppressed ruthlessly. At the same time, the Rana Prime Minister, Chandra Shamsher, abolished slavery in 1924, for which he was much praised by the British. From the 1930s to the 1960s, increasing numbers of Nepalis studied in India and imbibed the discourses of nationalism, Marxism, and civil rights which flourished there. Since that time many have continued to go to India, but increasingly others have headed for the West or the ex-Soviet bloc; nowadays the undisputedly most popular destination is the USA. The younger generation and the politically active today self-consciously align themselves with global developments, whether in music, fashion or human rights.

Within the lifetime of today's older generation, two radically different conceptions of individual and social rights have held sway within Nepal: a hierarchical, caste-based model, which reached its apogee in the Rana period, and a modernizing, individualist model, downplaying ethnic diversity, which was most characteristic of the Panchayat period (1960–1990). During the last ten or fifteen years a third, multiculturalist model has begun to be pushed by ethnic activists and has begun to receive some, though as yet limited, official recognition. In my conclusion I offer some reflections on its merits, but also on its contradictions and possible dangers.

Culture and Identity under the Rana regime (1846–1951)

The present state of Nepal was created in the late eighteenth century from geographically and ethnically highly diverse territory stretching

Table 8.1. *Five basic categories of Nepalese castes and ethnic groups according to the Law Code of 1854 (after Höfer 1979: 46)*

I.	Wearers of the sacred thread (*tagadhari*)
II.	Non-enslavable alcohol-drinkers (*na-masinya matwali*)
III.	Enslavable alcohol-drinkers (*masinya matwali*)
IV.	Impure but touchable castes (*pani na-calnya choi chito halnu-na-parnya*)
V.	Impure and untouchable castes (*pani na-calnya choi chito halnu-parnya*)

from Tibet in the north, through the rugged middle hills to the strip of Gangetic plain (the Tarai) in the south. The Rana regime began when in 1846 Jang Bahadur seized power by summoning all the leading nobles to a meeting and having loyal soldiers kill them all in the infamous Kot massacre. For the following 105 years he, his brothers, and their descendants held the hereditary prime ministership and, with it, all real power. The kings were reduced to the status of closely guarded figureheads.

By 1850 Jang Bahadur Rana had secured his position in Kathmandu and embarked on a trip to England and France (Whelpton 1983) – the first South Asian prince or king to breach the Hindu taboo on travelling across the ocean. The British government took care to impress on him its economic and military power. In France he was also impressed by the Code Napoleon, and this is supposed to have been the model for his National Legal Code (*Muluki Ain*) (Shaha 1982: 70). Although promulgated in 1854, it was not actually printed until 1870, shortly after the introduction of the first printing presses into Nepal (Hutt 1988: 132). Inspired by a Western model it may have been, but in its content the Legal Code was thoroughly traditional (Whelpton 1991: 218). All the groups in the country were classified into five hierarchically ranked divisions (see Table 8.1). In his thorough and seminal study of the resulting countrywide single caste hierarchy, András Höfer emphasizes that there is no indigenous distinction between caste and ethnic group or tribe (Höfer 1979: 46): all are equally *jat* ('kind' or 'species'). The ethnic groups or 'tribes' of the Nepalese middle hills were slotted into the hierarchy at levels II and III, placing them above the Untouchable service castes of the dominant Parbatiya group (level V) but below the Brahmans and Chetris (level I). They had little choice but to accept the ritual and social superiority of Brahmans and others. At the same time, they had the possibility of collective promotion from level III to level II.

The rights and duties of those subject to the Code were largely determined by their *jat* membership. No member of categories I and II could be enslaved. No Brahman was subject to capital punishment.

Although the Legal Code stated that occupation should not be governed by caste (ibid.: 119), in fact the law courts did support caste-exclusive occupations until the end of the Rana period: a non-Chitrakar who took up religious painting could be fined, for example. There were also numerous punishments for sexual liaisons across caste boundaries, the worst being reserved for those between low-caste men and high-caste women.

Professions were treated, in fact, like traditional customs. Anything established as a custom or ritual traditional among a given group was permitted, and deviation could be punished. When five Newars were ordained as Buddhist monks by a Tibetan lama in 1926, what incurred the wrath of the Rana authorities, leading them to expel the five from the country, was that one of them (Mahapragya, 1901–78) came from the Shrestha caste, mostly Hindus by tradition. On the other hand, Shresthas who traditionally received the ritual of tantric initiation from Buddhist priests rather than from (Hindu) Brahmans were explicitly given permission by the Legal Code to continue doing so (Höfer 1979: 160).

Thus, the Legal Code of Jang Bahadur Rana attempted to regulate the interactions and behaviour of all the subjects of the House of Gorkha on the following assumptions:

1) that everyone belonged to one and only one *jat*;
2) that people should only marry other members of the same *jat*;
3) that no one should adopt a profession that was traditionally the exclusive practice of another *jat*;
4) that all *jat*s fall into one of the five major categories, and that rights, duties and punishments should be determined in accordance with that status.

The details of the Code dealt with the anomalies and the practicalities of operating on these assumptions, for example, what was to happen in the case of inter-caste unions.

At the same time as its legal system operated on the assumption that each caste had its specific duties, or *svadharma*, the Rana regime also encouraged certain pan-Hindu values and practices. Foremost among these were the worship of cows and of Brahmans. Axel Michaels (1997) has shown how the Nepalese state, beginning in 1805, tried to introduce a ban on slaughtering cows to those, such as the Tamangs, Bhotiyas, and other populations with a tradition of eating beef. Essentially, the state compromised by imposing relatively small fines for the *unintentional* killing of a cow, as opposed to capital punishment or (after 1854) life imprisonment for doing so *intentionally*. (After 1990 the sentence still stands at twelve years in prison.) Consequently these populations were able to continue eating beef as long as the cow fell 'accidentally' to its death and was not intentionally killed.

As far as 'worshipping Brahmans' was concerned, the state did not impose cultural practices on its subjects, but rather led by example. In fact many non- or semi-Hindu populations were likely to have already been introduced to caste practices by the arrival of Untouchable castes in their locality: principally Damai (tailors), Kami (blacksmiths), and Sarki (leatherworkers). These were specialists whose services were welcomed. Interaction with them had necessarily to be carried on in Hindu terms, at least in public. This meant refusing water from their hands and keeping them outside their houses. Had the 'tribes' or ethnic groups of the hills not done so, they would themselves have fallen to the level of Untouchables. Nick Allen has elegantly described, for the case of the Thulung Rai, the gradual and almost imperceptible way in which this Hinduization occurred, with the people concerned lacking the concepts even to articulate how they had moved over a number of generations from viewing Brahmans as a separate people to accepting them as a superior caste (Allen 1997).

In addition to the right to carry on one's traditional customs provided they did not offend the elite too radically, there was also the right to change one's customs, with royal approval. Thus there are numerous examples of upward mobility where particular groups, including sometimes Brahmans themselves, petition to be allowed to give up certain customs, such as cross-cousin marriage or eating beef carrion, classed as low by Brahmanical norms (Pfaff-Czarnecka 1997: 428–32). By this means, there was a slow process of Sanskritization – the gradual and piecemeal adoption of Hindu practices – throughout the country.

Another way in which the state attempted to unify the country was by encouraging a single festival, Dasain, at the end of the harvest. Each local headman was expected to stand in for the king in the leading role. Ritual roles were distributed on a caste basis, with more demeaning roles being ascribed to 'tribals' or low castes (Pfaff-Czarnecka 1993). At the same time, the emphasis on animal sacrifice in Dasain – buffaloes in great number in royal centres, a goat for each individual household – engendered a Tibetan Buddhist counter-movement: many Tibetan Buddhist monasteries carry out rituals on behalf of the slaughtered animals and to make up for the sin of the killing.

By supporting Brahmans and Hindu renouncers; by enforcing, at least symbolically, universal cow worship; by giving caste distinctions the force of law; and by making Dasain a ritual of hierarchical inclusion for all their subjects, the elite of the nineteenth-century Nepalese state did more than merely endorse and perpetuate the cultural differences of the various peoples who were their subjects. It aspired to incorporate them into a single hierarchy. Thus the elite legitimated itself, and marked itself off from British and Muslim-dominated north India, with a self-consciously Hindu model of social order, thereby giving a substantial impetus to a process of Sanskritization that had already begun in some places before the eighteenth century (Whelpton 1997: 43). Many members of the 'tribes' or ethnic groups in the middle hills adopted both the language (Nepali) and the culture of the dominant group in the Rana period. By comparing the 1990 ethnicity figures with those for mother-tongue, Whelpton (1997: 59) estimates that language-loss among the major groups of the Nepalese hills has reached 68 per cent among the Magars, nearly 50 per cent among the Gurungs, 34 per cent among the Newars, 16 per cent among the Rais, 14.5 per cent among the Limbus, and 11 per cent among the Tamangs.

The Panchayat period: modernization by traditional means

The fall of the Rana regime is seen by Nepalis today as the end of a period of severe autocracy that was wholly deleterious to the country; the period after 1951 was experienced, and is still remembered, as a great liberation. However the first multi-party election in 1959 was quickly followed by their abolition and the introduction of a non-party, authoritarian regime: the Panchayat system. Although condemned as 'fascist' by its opponents, it would be wrong to see the Panchayat regime as having been as violent or as arbitrary as Rana rule.

The Panchayat regime went through a number of changes in the three decades between 1960 and 1990. Most importantly, student protests in 1979 led to a referendum in 1980 on whether to continue with the non-party system. Although the Panchayat system emerged the victor, with 55 per cent of the votes, the King conceded the principle of direct elections to the National Assembly. Before that, in accordance with the Panchayat ideology of building from the bottom up, which was supposedly in line with traditional Nepali national character, there had only been indirect elections, with village representatives nominating district-level representatives, who in turn selected national representatives.

Despite these developments, it is fair to say that there was a single guiding ideology of the Panchayat regime which persisted, with, no doubt, changes of emphasis throughout its thirty years. The regime itself attempted, through the official media and school system, to propound the need for such an ideology, which can be summed up as economically developmentalist, culturally integrationist and politically monarchical. It had a number of key elements, of which the following appear to have been the most important:[5]

1) leadership of the king, as the bringer and guarantor of 'democracy';
2) a system of bottom-up representation on the basis of what were argued to be genuinely Nepali village-level councils (*panchayats*), rather than through the supposedly foreign notion of political parties;
3) economic development (*bikas*), towards which aim all institutions were supposed to be subordinated;
4) equality of all citizens;
5) unity of the nation, as expressed in the slogan 'One language, one dress, one country' (*ek bhasa, ek bhes, ek des*), and the importance of 'building nationalism' (that is, feelings of national identification);
6) the banning of any non-governmental organizations, such as independent trade unions, that would represent sectional interests and increase internal conflict; they were replaced with official, supposedly non-political and non-conflictual 'class organizations' (*bargiya sangathan*) for youth, peasants, workers, women, students and ex-soldiers (Joshi and Rose 1966: 406–10);
7) Hinduism as the offical state religion, with Buddhism, Jainism and Sikhism seen as branches of Hinduism;
8) respect for traditional customs.[6]

There were bound to be tensions between these different items. Most obviously, the new value of equality was hard to reconcile with the 'traditional custom' of hierarchical exclusivity, as dramatically symbolized by the continued exclusion of Untouchables from the national shrine, Pashupati (Joshi and Rose 1966: 474; Höfer 1979: 204).

At the same time, the new regime did enact several modernizing legal measures, such as a law enabling unmarried women over the age of thirty-five to inherit a share of the ancestral property (Gilbert 1992) and several measures collectively referred to as Land Reform (1963–4). Under the latter, restrictions were placed on the amount that any individual could own (the rich registered land in the names of all the members of the family) and land rents were fixed in law, thus greatly reducing the tenant's traditional obligations. Both of these were signs of new values. The increasing monetization of the economy, especially in the Tarai and the cities, coupled with increased levels of education and a gradual decline in deference, inevitably brought new values in their wake.

Thus, the Panchayat period combined formal legal equality (but without any measures of positive discrimination), endorsement of traditional customs and religion, and an aspiration to national integration by means of the adoption of Parbatiya culture by minorities. With the collapse of the regime in 1990, it became evident that this had been no solution to the problems of cultural diversity, but had simply deferred them.

As with the treatment of low castes and excluded ethnic groups, the issue of conversion, as Richard Burghart has discussed, raises the serious question of how far pre-modern Hindu notions still applied, and whether there was individual freedom of religious expression. While individual practice of non-Hindu religion was legal, 'disturbing society' by causing people to convert was illegal, which led the British Liberal MP for Liverpool, David Alton, to protest at the treatment of Christians in Nepal in 1986. On this Burghart commented:

What Alton did not recognize, and possibly could not as a Liberal MP, was that the Kingdom of Nepal was not a civil society. Religious beliefs in Nepal are not merely a private matter between 'a man and his Maker'. . . . Rather society itself is an auspicious ritual unit. Religious conversions . . . disturb society as a whole. Something resembling religious tolerance exists in Nepal, but the constraints that operate on it are not the laws of contract appropriate for civil society. (Burghart 1996: 197)

In short, in the Panchayat period, the laws restricting employment to hereditary occupations, and punishing intermarriage between previously separate groups, had been rescinded, but religion had still not become entirely a matter of individual choice.

No one today wishes for a return to the Rana period, but there are many ordinary people who began to feel, not long after 1990, that things were better under the Panchayat regime: there was less corruption, less inflation, less disorder. However, the leading politicians of the Panchayat period do not, as yet, openly campaign for a return to the non-party system; officially their party, the National Democratic Party, has accepted the multi-party system and seeks success within it.

Post-1990: claiming new collective rights

In 1989–1990 a 'People's Movement' overthrew the by then morally bankrupt Panchayat regime.[7] A new Constitution in 1990 placed sovereignty firmly with the people, while confirming the position of the king. The old definition of Nepal as 'an independent, indivisible and sovereign monarchical Hindu Kingdom' was changed to 'a multi-ethnic, multilingual, democratic, independent, indivisible, sovereign, Hindu and Constitutional Monarchical Kingdom'.[8]

It is clear from this definition that ethnic and cultural differences have been given a legal and political recognition that was wholly lacking during the Panchayat period. The Constitution, while specifying Nepali as the 'language of the nation' (*rastrabhasa*), designated all languages spoken as mother-tongues in the country as 'national languages' (*rastriya bhasa*), and as such guaranteed the right to primary education in these languages. As far as I know, however, there is only one private school, funded by a Japanese social service foundation and with a large number of children from deprived backgrounds, where primary education is given in Newari. All other schools continue to teach in Nepali or, increasingly, in the rapidly expanding private sector, in English.

Meanwhile, from 1994 Radio Nepal started to broadcast the news for five minutes a day in languages with more than a million speakers.[9] The 1990 Constitution gives further support to a policy of multiculturalism in Section 26, subsection 2:

The State shall, while maintaining the cultural diversity of the country, pursue a policy of strengthening the national unity by promoting healthy and cordial relations amongst the various religions, castes, tribes, communities and linguistic groups, and by helping in the promotion of their language, literatures, scripts, arts and cultures.

Thus, alongside the entirely new recognition given to different cultural groups and to the necessity of promoting their cultures, the Constitution commits the state to a policy of national unity. It is a question of 'unity in diversity'. Furthermore, to the disappointment of many Buddhist and ethnic activists, the Constitution continues to define the kingdom as Hindu, despite an enormous demonstration demanding a secular ('religiously nonaligned') constitution. In short, the drafters of the constitution did not feel that they could place the term 'multi-religious' alongside 'multi-ethnic' and 'multi-lingual'. This failure led to an enormous increase in accusations of 'Brahmanism' (pro-Brahman policies and Brahman domination), charges further fuelled by the eventual introduction of news read in Sanskrit on the radio and the introduction of compulsory Sanskrit in schools. Secularists argued that non-Hindus were condemned to second-class citizenship and that therefore the Constitution was not fully democratic. Development expert and Newar activist Keshab Man Sakya declared that the Constitution instituted government 'by the people, of the people, for the Brahmins' (Sakya 1990: 10).

A range of groups, with different claims, have come forward to take advantage of the new multicultural situation after 1990. At the least contentious end of the spectrum, the Royal Nepal Academy has begun a new multilingual journal, *Sayapatri*, which publishes scholarly and literary articles both in Nepali and in other national languages with a parallel Nepali translation. A National Ethnographic Museum has been proposed, and agreed in principle by the government, in which all sixty-nine recognized ethnic groups and castes will be represented: the plot of land will be in the shape of the country, with a house for each group in its own traditional style. Despite the latter being a key demand of the activist groups, both initiatives have worked with the government and have attempted to be both multiculturalist and inclusive.

More oppositional, but still non-political in that it refuses to align itself with any political party, is an organization, formed in 1990, that calls itself in English the Nepal Federation of Nationalities (NEFEN), and in Nepali the Nepal Janajati Mahasangh (literally 'Union of Janajati Groups of Nepal'). As its English name suggests, it is supposed to be a federal umbrella group bringing together one representative member organization for each 'nationality' or *janajati* in Nepal, with more than thirty such ethnic organizations having joined by July 2000. The term *janajati* is a neologism that has come to be used for what used to be called 'hill tribes' and non-caste peoples of the Tarai. It excludes the Parbatiya castes, both the dominant Brahmans and Chetris, and their associated Untouchable castes (categories I, IV and V in Table 8.1), as well as the many castes of the more elaborate social hierarchy of the Tarai. These groups are supposed to be the non-indigenous incomers to Nepal, and NEFEN aims to speak for all the other, supposedly indigenous, groups. NEFEN is strongly anti-Hindu and anti-Brahman in its ideology; it aims to combat Brahman domination of the political, legal and administrative machinery, and to undo what it diagnoses as the cultural influence of Brahmans and Hindus on its member groups. It excludes Untouchables from membership but is willing to ally with Dalit (Untouchable) organizations in pursuing its aims.[10]

The essential issues, from NEFEN's point of view, can be seen in a survey by Nanda Kandangwa (1996: 25–30) of the three main parties' positions on twenty crucial questions. The questions were:
- proclamation of a secular constitution;
- end to linguistic discrimination;
- conversion of the upper house into a House of Nationalities;
- the right to self-determination;
- the right to the income from natural resources and the land;
- teaching in the mother-tongue;
- the right to use mother-tongues in the civil service entrance examinations and in courts and government offices;
- the right to have programmes, announcements and news in mother-tongues in the mass media;

- the provision of special arrangements to encourage *janajati* students in higher and technical education etc.;
- an end to compulsory Sanskrit [in secondary school];
- an end to the news in Sanskrit; conversion of the Sanskrit University into a campus for all languages, and conversion of the Sanskrit College and students' hostel into a college and hostel for students of all languages;
- the necessity of making government power and the running of the government public [that is, not confined to one group];
- protection and development of the places and items of cultural, archaeological, historical and religious importance to indigenous/*janajati* people;
- establishing institute(s) for the study of indigenous/*janajati* religion, culture and language;
- establishing an organization for the economic development of indigenous/*janajati* people;
- protection, development and management of indigenous intellectual property rights;
- giving guarantees of the human rights of indigenous/*janajati* people;
- giving national recognition of the culture and social values of indigenous/*janajati* people;
- to make corrections by rewriting and analysing the history, census data and numbers of indigenous/*janajati* people;
- that the government should use its influence to implement the UN's Decade of Indigenous Peoples.

It is no coincidence that these questions are in line with global discourses on cultural rights: they are derived and translated directly from them. Many of the activists working with or in NEFEN have studied and worked abroad and even those who have not are well attuned to international human rights issues. Access to the internet is easy in Kathmandu. One of the principal aims of organizations such as NEFEN is invariably to maintain contact with like-minded international bodies, to attend conferences abroad, and to invite international observers to attend their conferences in Nepal. In December 1996, for Human Rights Day, NEFEN published a Nepali translation of the Charter of the Indigenous-Tribal Peoples of the Tropical Forests; earlier the same year, the Nepal Tamang Ghedung, the NEFEN member-body for the Tamangs, which is run out of the same office as NEFEN itself, published a pamphlet containing Nepali translations of the Universal Declaration of Human Rights, the UN Minority Rights Declaration, the

UN Draft Declaration on the Rights of Indigenous Peoples, and the International Labour Organization's Convention on Indigenous and Tribal Peoples.

The awkward way in which the term *adivasi* ('indigenous', literally 'original dweller') has been incorporated into the ethnic activists' discourse is witness to the dependence of that discourse on international initiatives. The term *janajati* is also a neologism, unused and largely unknown even in activist circles before 1990. It has been adopted, by NEFEN and others, to pick out just those groups that are not part of the dominant 'Hindu' social order. The stress on indigenousness came later, with the UN's declaration of a Year of Indigenous Peoples in 1993. NEFEN argues that the two terms, 'indigenous' and *janajati*, refer in the Nepali context to the same people, but this overlooks the awkward fact that many *janajati* groups, or sections of them, have well-known myths locating their origin outside Nepal.

Alongside the politically non-aligned NEFEN, there are many much more radical bodies. Ethnic political parties such as the Mongol National Organization and the Nepal Rastriya Janajati Party, were refused recognition by the Election Commission in 1991 (Bhattachan 1995: 132; Whelpton 1997: 59). Other movements, such as the Khambuwan, Limbuwan, and Magar Liberation Fronts, claiming to speak for Rais, Limbus, and Magars respectively, have never sought electoral approval. Suresh Ale Magar, an outspoken proponent of ethnic rights, has established an Akhil Nepal Janajati Sangh or All Nepal Nationalities Organization (ANNO): unlike NEFEN, it is not a federal, officially non-political body, but is on the contrary a unitary organization aligned with the Maoist United People's Front (Bhattarai), also known as the Communist Party of Nepal (Maoist), led by Baburam Bhattarai and 'Comrade Prachanda' (Pushpa Kumar Dahal). The Maoists currently (1998–2000) control large parts of the western hills of Nepal. Bhattarai himself lives underground, but is widely assumed to be in Kathmandu, since his articles appear frequently in the national press and his rebuttals appear almost immediately. In his search for allies to overthrow the parliamentary regime, Bhattarai has aligned himself with ethnic activists such as the Khambuwan Liberation Front, and claims that he favours autonomous ethnic regions. Bhattarai was rather prescient when he declared, in a seminar in Delhi in 1990, years before the present Maoist agitation began:

Whereas the obscurantist forces headed by the king would try to put the clock back, the new ruling combine is a bundle of contradictions and a vascillating lot with more or less the same social base as the previous regime. The high democratic expectations of the long suppressed masses and the genuine aspirations of the ethnic, linguistic and regional minorities would exert tremendous pressure in the days to come upon the new regime. It is extremely doubtful whether anything quite short of a radical restructuring of the polity and the economy of the country can cope with the problems of such magnitude. (Bhattarai 1990: 17)

Support for this comes from the opposite end of the political spectrum. Pashupati Shamshere Rana, who was a powerful minister in governments of the 1980s and is now one of the leaders of the 'right-wing' National Democratic Party, writes in support of positive discrimination in favour of disadvantaged communities:

There is little doubt, that, whatever the perils, whatever the costs, the inescapable challenge of the day is to establish a more universal and assimilative pattern of institutional development, and a more egalitarian sharing of both economic and political benefits of development . . . The privileged castes and classes must rise above their narrow interests to espouse the cause of the disadvantaged and underprivileged to provide them with not merely equal but enhanced opportunities for improving their lot . . . Our multi-party democracy must create a multi-ethnic power structure. (Rana 1998: 82)

From castes to ethnic groups: common assumptions

What all Nepali political parties, pressure groups and revolutionaries seem to agree on is an essentialist view of the cultural divisions they argue over. All seem to agree that everyone in the country
(1) belongs to one and only one ethnic or caste group;
(2) is born into that group;
(3) cannot change their group.

There are two further universal assumptions, one procedural and one normative:
(4) though some groups are big and others small, they can, for practical purposes, be treated as groups of the same logical order;
(5) all groups should be treated equally.

For external sociologically inclined observers these assumptions are highly contestable and cannot be accepted as an analytically adequate description of how the social system operates or has operated, though they *do form* part of the folk model by which people guide their own conduct. Assumption (3) was refuted by the Ranas themselves, who raised their status from ordinary Chetri to that of the royal caste, Thakuri, by adopting the title 'Rana', forcibly marrying their sons and daughters to the children of the king's family, and adopting a prestigious Rajput genealogy linking them to India (Whelpton 1991: 187, 190–1). Likewise there have always been examples of inter-caste marriage or concubinage, with the offspring absorbed either into the father's or into the mother's caste, depending on the circumstances of the case. Assumption (4) creates many problems for analysis: for example, many small castes have in fact already disappeared.

Assumption (5) marks a radical departure from the traditional situation, although it is today generally agreed that the old ideology of hierarchy must be rejected. For the ethnic activists, introducing real equality implies removing the special status of Hinduism and introducing measures of positive discrimination to overcome the entrenched, privileged position of the Brahmans. For those who oppose such measures it is enough that such privilege is no longer upheld by law, and they see the status of Hinduism in the Constitution as a simple reflection of the majoritarian position of Hindus in the country. The census statistics on religion are bitterly contested, with non-Hindus, especially Buddhists, claiming that the number of Buddhists has been deliberately massaged down in successive censuses and that Hinduism has been used as a default category into which anyone who does not insist that they are something else is placed.

The argument about equality between what were previously hierarchically ranked social units reappears *within* different groups. For example, the Gurungs have two ranked divisions which many Gurung activists now claim to have been foisted upon them by Brahmans (Macfarlane 1997). The Newars of the Kathmandu Valley have a complex caste hierarchy of twenty or more castes in the largest settlements (Kathmandu, Lalitpur and Bhaktapur) (Gellner & Quigley 1995). Newar cultural and ethnic activists have long sought to bring about more 'unity' and were therefore dismayed when, in the aftermath of 1990, many Newar castes, and especially the largest, peasant caste, the Jyapus, began to organize caste associations which threatened that unity. This soon generated other organizations (Newa De Dabu, Newa Mahaguthi) that attempted to bring together all the different Newar organizations, including these caste associations, on the basis of equality, just as NEFEN aims to bring together all Nepal's 'nationalities' (*janajati*) on the basis of equality.

Similar arguments setting those who wish for unity on an individualist basis against those who argue that true unity can only be achieved by the recognition of previously stigmatized constituent parts occur both at the national and at the intra-ethnic level. At the national level, those against granting ethnic rights argue that conceding them would encourage communalism and undermine nationalism. They are countered with the argument that the best way to build national unity is to strengthen the constituent parts of the nation, namely the ethnic groups; otherwise, they argue, the inbuilt inequalities of the present situation will eventually lead to the emergence of ethnically based violence as in Sri Lanka or the former Yugoslavia. In exactly the same way, Newar ethnic activists who are unhappy at the emergence of caste associations within the Newars are faced with the argument that only by recognizing the distinct and previously stigmatized identity of large groups like the Jyapu cultivator caste can their sense of identity as Newars and as Nepalis be properly founded; and there is, it is argued, no contradiction or conflict in asserting, and feeling pride, in these various identities, each of which operates at a different level.[11]

Despite these differences, all agree that ethnic groups and castes exist. The facts that there are numerous intermarriages, that there are many marginal cases of people who do not fit easily into one of the categories, or belong to more than one, are treated as insignificant exceptions. Nationalists still argue that there is a common culture (at least in the hills, if not extending to the Tarai), but do not carry the argument against the ethnic activists onto a more conceptual level. They do not try to argue that hybridity is a more appropriate concept for understanding the history and development of Nepal, that ethnic or caste purity are ideological figments which hide a history of intercaste mixing. Concern with hybridity, as Friedman (1997: 72) remarks, has remained restricted to a few cosmopolitan intellectuals. Instead the debate in Nepal is largely about statistics: is more than 90 per cent of the country Hindu, or is the true figure (including only Brahmans and Chetris) 30 per cent? It was only after the census of 1990 that figures were released for different castes and ethnic groups. Debates over the figures are bound to intensify.

The position of those who oppose the demands of ethnic activists today has been succinctly summarized by Krishna B. Bhattachan. He claims that there are thirteen 'fallacies' or 'myths' which the ruling class has propagated over the last 200 years and which have marginalized ethnically based demands:

1. Inter-caste and ethnic harmony or unity in diversity is a main feature of Nepalese society;
2. Social and cultural diversity is a problem, not a resource, for development;
3. Bahuns and Chetris have contributed most in the process of the making of the Nepali State;
4. Positive discrimination/reservation system/affirmative action, federalism, right to self determination/self-rule/local level autonomy disintegrates Nepal;
5. Equality of opportunity shall take care of all kinds of inequalities;
6. The economic success of the Thakalis, Mananges [sic], and Sherpas are not because of State policies;

7. If ethnic groups are backward it is because of their choice to remain in their own cultural cocoons;
8. Nepali language and Hindu religion have been accepted spontaneously by all ethnic groups;
9. Either everyone or no one is indigenous in Nepal;
10. Ethnic line [that is, pushing the ethnic line] invites riots, violence and disintegration;
11. There is no correlation between ethnicity and development and/or under-development;
12. Ethnic issue is a Western import/support with a motivation of destabilization in Nepal;
13. Ethnic problem is non-existent but it has been over inflated by some ethnic leaders to self-serve their narrow interests. (Bhattachan 1997: 119–20)

Conclusions

I have outlined three different models of the relationship between culture and political incorporation, corresponding to three periods of recent Nepalese history: the hierarchical, caste-based model of the Rana period; the citizen-based, developmental and culturally homogenizing model of the Panchayat period; and the as yet unrealized, and perhaps unrealizable, multicultural, 'different but equal' model of the ethnic activists of today.[12] All three models entered Nepal from outside and were reworked to suit local conditions. Expectations of the government were, of course, very different in these three historical periods. In the Rana period, the government made demands (of corvée labour, taxes, participation in rituals) and the people obeyed; after the devastating earthquake of 1934 many refused to take the government assistance offered for rebuilding their homes because they believed that it was sinful to take the king's property. Today, by contrast, after several decades of developmentalist, top-down ideology, which has inculcated the idea that Nepal is one of the world's poorest countries, people have come to believe they have a right to government and foreign aid to provide for basic needs – an expectation which is still far from being met.

The three models I have depicted are, it must said, heuristic: the first two were certainly dominant in the periods referred to, but they were not uncontested and they were not adhered to equally by everyone. The second and third models, though both claim or claimed to be founded in the specificities of Nepali history and society, are strongly influenced by norms introduced from outside South Asia. The first two models were imposed from above, whereas the third is being claimed by activists and has so far largely been resisted by the state.[13]

In all three models, the position of Hinduism, and the relation of other religious traditions to it, is central. Hinduism was the main means of legitimation for the Rana regime, and the law of the country was framed explicitly in Hindu terms. All other religious traditions had to accept these terms, and even Muslims are governed by Hindu-derived family law (Gaborieau 1993). In the Panchayat period, the state was still proud to call itself the only Hindu kingdom in the world, and the official doctrine was that Buddhism, Jainism and Sikhism were 'branches' of Hinduism; only a minority of Buddhist activists were seriously offended by this. In practice, secularism was pervasive, and the role of Hinduism in actual government was less than, for example, that of Islam in Pakistan (Gaborieau 1982). Today the continued official status of Hinduism in the Constitution, and the lack of recognition of Nepal as a multi-religious country, is highly controversial. One of the principal aims of ethnic activists is to try to construct a national anti-Hindu coalition across all the divisions of religion, geography, language, culture and politics.

How far, and in what ways, the third, multiculturalist model should be put into practice is, I have tried to show, a matter of crucial and immediate concern in Nepal. How far should the state go in recognizing different cultural groups and giving them rights as groups?[14] In a symbolic sense the state has already recognized that the country is divided into sixty-nine castes and ethnic groups of vastly differing sizes. Some have their own language and some do not, but all are assumed to have their own cultural traditions worth representing in a National Ethnographic Museum. Given the figures in the 1990 census, it would be hard for the state not to go some way towards acknowledging diversity.[15] At the same time such an approach is necessarily fraught with difficulties. Any attempt to grant serious recognition to cultural rights requires hard choices about which cultural units to accept and which to overlook; whatever choices are made, someone is bound to be offended.

In the Nepalese case a new national tradition might usefully include a stress on both cultural and biological hybridity. If the elite could abandon its traditional concern with purity, there might be much to gain. Whelpton (1997: 73) has suggested that it is time for the royal house 'to reclaim its Magar heritage' – in other words, to acknowledge that it is descended not only from prestigious Rajput forebears in India, but also from the Magar 'tribe'. Gurung heroes of Nepali history, written out of Panchayat history books, could be reincluded in official accounts (Onta 1996). Primary teachers in government schools could be permitted to use the local language alongside Nepali in order to explain the (Nepali-language) school textbooks, as currently happens in the one existing Newari-language school.

Another radical move might help, though it is perhaps naïve to expect the Nepalese state to embark on a conceptual innovation that has not been tried, or even to my knowledge suggested, in the 'developed' West, either among census-takers or among the arbiters of ethnic monitoring.[16] In order to defuse the numbers game, people could be permitted to tick more than one box in the questions on ethnic or caste identity or on religious affiliation; for many people ticking both 'Hindu' and 'Buddhist' boxes would be a truer reflection of their actual religious practice and, given encouragement to do so, there might be many who would prefer to claim a dual ethnic identity, or none at all (like the pre-conflict Bosnians who returned their ethnic group in Yugoslav censuses as 'human being' and the US citizens who wrote in 'earthling').[17] Thus, alongside a strategic admission that distinct cultural traditions exist within Nepal, all of which, as many now argue, should be acknowledged as authentically Nepali, the government could simultaneously push the idea that it is legitimate, indeed meritorious, for individuals to claim allegiance to more than one such tradition or to none. Different cultures would then have rights, but only individuals would be able to claim those rights, with no one being able to force another into a cultural straitjacket. This would require the brave conceptual leap of reversing millennia of stress on the value of purity and the shame of mixture, but it would have the virtue of carrying the battle effectively against the ethnic activists who have, in practice, accepted the traditionalist model of separate groups while rejecting its hierarchical and integrationist components. Such a strategy would also have the merit of reinforcing an old, relatively tolerant South Asian tradition of making matters of linguistic and cultural choice effectively the decision of the household, subject only to local opinion.

Whichever solutions are attempted, it is clear that Nepalis face a predicament that is common in many other places. At the very time when many minor cultural differences are being eroded and when it makes sense to speak of an emerging global culture, other cultural differences are being politicized as never before. A large part of this has to do with the replacement of hierarchical ways of thinking about cultural difference with egalitarian ones, at least within formal and public forms of political discourse, and a key causal factor here is the power that democratic political rituals give to previously suppressed majorities.

ACKNOWLEDGEMENTS

I would particularly like to thank Joanna Pfaff-Czarnecka and John Whelpton, whose work and comments have helped me to formulate the argument of this paper. Rajendra Pradhan, D.P. Martinez, Declan Quigley, seminar audiences in Harvard and Edinburgh, and the editors of this volume have all offered perceptive and constructive criticisms which I have done my best to take on board.

Whether one restricts oneself to detached analysis or indulges in offering advice as well, there is bound to be fierce criticism from some quarters, so it may not be wholly redundant to insist that I alone should be held responsible for the shortcomings which undoubtedly remain, as well as for the opinions expressed.

NOTES

1 Pérez de Cuellar *et al.* (1995: 282).
2 This is the title of Kukathas' interesting article (1992). For a recent attempt to provide a typology of cultural rights, including a critique of some of Kukathas' ideas, see Levy (1996).
3 For a small sample of the critiques, see Appadurai (1986), Marriott (1992), Quigley (1992), Raheja (1988).
4 There has been some attempt to express the equality of all India's communities in the selection of its presidents: three Brahmans have been interspersed with a high-caste Hindu, two Muslims, a Sikh, a middle-caste Hindu, and a low-caste southern Hindu. But in one sense the unequal, or at least different, treatment of its citizens is also ensured because they do not all live under the same civil law: the price of obtaining Muslim leaders' allegiance to the new Indian state was to permit the continuation of the British colonial practice of separate personal legal codes for Muslims, Hindus, Christians, Parsis, and Jews (Sikhs counted as Hindus). Although much modified from the colonial era, Muslim leaders have resisted fiercely anything that might seem like an encroachment on Muslim difference in this area. Today the secular status of the Indian Republic is, in fact, highly controversial, because it is questioned by the BJP, currently the largest political party, which would like to give Hinduism special status.
5 There was no primer or 'little red book' of Panchayat ideology, but the elements I have listed can be found in school textbooks and were the themes taken up on official holidays and in politicians' speeches.
6 For interesting accounts of the Panchayat ideology, see Borgström (1980), Gaborieau (1982), and Pigg (1992).
7 For accounts of this movement, see Bonk (1990), Brown (1996), Hacchethu (1990), and Raeper and Hoftun (1992).
8 From the official English translations of the 1962 Constitution (modified in 1980) and 1990 Constitution (Gellner 1997: 6).
9 This followed the report of the Government Commission on Policy towards National Languages (Rastriya Bhasa Niti Sujhav Ayog). For details, see Gellner (1997: 6) and Sonntag (1995).
10 See Gellner *et al.* (1997) for more on the new term, *janajati*, and on NEFEN. NEFEN defines *janajati* and *adivasi* as 'falling outside the Hindu 4

varna scheme' and 'indigenous', respectively. They are taken to have an identical reference in the Nepali context.

11 This argument is examined in greater detail in Gellner (1999).

12 In drawing up these three models, my indebtedness to the work of Pfaff-Czarnecka (1997, 1999) should be clear. In terms of Walzer's typology of states (1997), the Rana regime was a sub-species of multinational empire; the Panchayat regime was an attempt to forge a nation-state on the basis of the Parbatiyas' language and culture; and the multiculturalists of today are aiming at some form of consociation.

13 It would be wrong to assume that these models were internally entirely consistent or without tensions. The Rana model had problems welding a geographically and culturally disparate country into a single hierarchical order; numerous anomalies perforce remained. There was also a contradiction between its forthright traditionalism and the first hesitant steps that were taken during the Rana period to build a sense of national identity and to propagate Nepali as the national language. The Panchayat model was undeniably modernizing and moved in the direction of individual rights. But the inheritance of ancestral property remained collective: all extant male heirs had and still have a right to an equal share of inherited property. Daughters had no such right, and it is in the post-1990 era that the first attempts to introduce corrective legislation have been made. The multiculturalist model is by no means the only or dominant one after 1990. Conventional surveys of human rights focus entirely on individual rights (Upadhyaya *et al.* 1997), and it is left to the ethnic activists to argue for collective rights.

14 The Maoist rebels have promised a high degree of ethnic autonomy and many ethnic activists are tempted by these promises, as well as by the ever new depths of corruption to which politicians of all political parties seem determined to sink, to throw in their lot with them.

15 In December 1998 the Ministry of Local Development did indeed announce that official status would be given to sixty-one *janajati* groups. A National Committee for Development of Nationalities, chaired by the Minister for Local Development, has been set up to target development programmes, scholarships, research, cultural programmes and seminars at the members of these groups.

16 According to newspaper reports the 2001 UK census will include the categories 'Irish' and 'mixed race' for the first time.

17 Friedman (1997) is contemptuous of such discourses of hybridity, considering them implicated in the essentialism they reject; he also points out that the adoption of such discourses by the elite in Central America has been a means of defusing ethnonationalist resistance from below. On the US census, see Yanow (1998).

REFERENCES

Allen, N.J. 1997. Hinduization: The Experience of the Thulung Rai. In *Nationalism and Ethnicity in a Hindu Kingdom: The Politics of Culture in Contemporary Nepal.* (Eds.) Gellner *et al.* Amsterdam: Harwood.

Appadurai, A. 1986. Is Homo Hierarchicus? *American Ethnologist* 13, 745–61.

Bhattachan, K.B. 1995. Ethnopolitics and Ethnodevelopment: An Emerging Paradigm in Nepal. In *State, Leadership and Politics in Nepal*. (Ed.) D. Kumar. Kathmandu: CNAS.

Bhattachan, K.B. 1997. People/Community-Based Development Strategy in Nepal. In *Developmental Practices in Nepal*. (Eds.) K.B. Bhattachan & C. Mishra. Kathmandu: CNAS/Friedrich-Ebert-Stiftung.

Bhattarai, B. 1990. *Nepal: A Marxist View*. Kathmandu: Jhilko.

Bonk, T. 1990. *Dawn of Democracy: People's Power in Nepal*. Kathmandu: FOPHUR.

Borgström, B.E. 1980. *The Patron and the Pancha: Village Values and Panchayat Democracy in Nepal*. New Delhi: Vikas.

Brown, T.L. 1996. *The Challenge to Democracy in Nepal: A Political History*. London: Routledge.

Burghart, R. 1996. *The Conditions of Listening: Essays in Religion, History and Politics in South Asia*. (Eds.) C.J. Fuller & J. Spencer. Delhi: OUP.

Dumont, L. 1980. *Homo Hierarchicus: The Caste System and its Implications*. Chicago: Chicago University Press.

Friedman, J. 1997. Global Crises, the Struggle for Cultural Identity and Intellectual Porkbarrelling: Cosmopolitans versus Locals, Ethnics and Nationals in an Era of De-hegemonisation. In *Debating Cultural Hybridity: Multi-cultural Identities and the Politics of Anti-Racism*. (Eds.) P. Werbner & T. Modood. London: Zed Books.

Gaborieau, M. 1982. Les Rapports de Classe dans l'Idéologie officielle du Népal. *Purusartha* 6, 251–90.

Gaborieau, M. 1993. *Ni Brahmanes, ni Ancêtres: Colporteurs musulmans du Népal*. Nanterre: Société d'Ethnologie.

Gellner, D.N. 1997. Ethnicity and Nationalism in the World's Only Hindu State. In Gellner *et al.* (Eds.), *Nationalism and Ethnicity*.

Gellner, D.N. 1999. From Cultural Hierarchies to a Hierarchy of Multiculturalisms: The case of the Newars of the Kathmandu Valley, Nepal. In *Multiculturalism: Modes of Coexistence in South and Southeast Asia*. Washington DC: Sasakawa Peace Foundation.

Gellner, D.N. and D. Quigley (Eds.). 1995. *Contested Hierarchies: A Collaborative Ethnography of Caste among the Newars of the Kathmandu Valley, Nepal*. Oxford: Clarendon.

Gellner, D. N., J. Pfaff-Czarnecka and J. Whelpton (Eds.). 1997. *Nationalism and Ethnicity in a Hindu Kingdom: The Politics of Culture in Contemporary Nepal*. Amsterdam: Harwood.

Gilbert, K. 1992. Women and Family Law in Modern Nepal: Statutory Rights and Social Implications. *Journal of International Law and Politics* 24, 729–58.

Hacchethu, K. 1990. Mass Movement 1990. *Contributions to Nepalese Studies* 17:2, 177–201.

Höfer, A. 1979. *The Caste Hierarchy and the State in Nepal: A Study of the Muluki Ain of 1854*. Innsbruck: Universitätsverlag Wagner.

Hutt, M. 1988. *Nepali: A National Language and its Literature*. New Delhi: Sterling.

Joshi, B.L. and L. Rose. 1966. *Democratic Innovations in Nepal: A Case Study of Political Acculturation*. Berkeley: University of California Press.

Kandangwa, N. 1996. The Policies and Programmes of the Political Parties on the Janajati/Indigenous Peoples Question [in Nepali]. In *Nepal Janajati Mahasangh Smarika 2053*. Kathmandu: NEFEN.

Kukathas, C. 1992. Are There any Cultural Rights? *Political Theory* 20, 105–39; reissued in 1995, *The Rights of Minority Cultures*. (Ed.) W. Kymlicka. New York: Oxford University Press.

Levy, J.T. 1996. Classifying Cultural Rights. In *Ethnicity and Group Rights*. (Eds.) I. Shapiro and W. Kymlicka. New York and London: New York University Press.

Macfarlane, A. 1997. Identity and Change among the Gurungs (Tamu-mai) of Central Nepal. In Gellner *et al.* (Eds.), *Nationalism and Ethnicity*.

Marriott, M. 1992. *India Through Hindu Categories*. Delhi: Sage.

Michaels, A. 1997. The King and the Cow. In Gellner *et al.* (Eds.), *Nationalism and Ethnicity*.

Onta, P. 1996. Ambivalence Denied: The Making of *Rastriya Itihas* in Panchayat Era Textbooks. *Contributions to Nepalese Studies* 23:1, 213–54.

Pérez de Cuellar, J. *et al.* 1995. *Our Creative Diversity: Report of the World Commission on Culture and Development*. Paris: UNESCO.

Pfaff-Czarnecka, J. 1993. The Nepalese Durga Puja Festival or Displaying Military Supremacy on Ritual Occasions. In *Anthropology of Tibet and Nepal*. (Eds.) C. Ramble & M. Brauen. Zürich: Ethnological Museum.

Pfaff-Czarnecka, J. 1997. Vestiges and Visions: Cultural Change and the Process of Nation-Building in Nepal. In Gellner *et al.* (Eds.).

Pfaff-Czarnecka, J. 1999. Debating the State of the Nation: Ethnicization of Politics in Nepal. A Position Paper. In *Ethnic Futures: The State and Identity Politics in Asia* (Eds.) J. Pfaff-Czarnecka, D. Rajasingham-Senanayake, A. Nandy and E.T. Gomez. New Delhi: Sage.

Pigg, S.L. 1992. Inventing Social Categories through Space: Social Representations of Development in Nepal. *Comparative Studies of Society and History* 34, 491–593.

Quigley, D. 1992. *The Interpretation of Caste*. Oxford: Clarendon.

Raeper, M. and M. Hoftun. 1992. *Spring Awakening: An Account of the 1990 Revolution in Nepal*. Delhi: Viking.

Raheja, G.G. 1988. *The Poison in the Gift: Ritual, Prestation, and the Dominant Caste in a north Indian Village*. Chicago: Chicago University Press.

Rana, P.S.J.B. 1998. The Evolution of Nepalese Nationalism. In *Contemporary Nepal*. (Eds.) P.S.J.B. Rana and D.N. Dhungel. Delhi: Vikas.

Sakya, K.M. 1990. Secularism in the National Assembly [in Nepali]. *Dharmakirti* 12:2, 9–10.

Shaha, R. 1982. *Essays in the Practice of Government in Nepal*. New Delhi: Manohar.

Sonntag, S.K. 1995. Ethnolinguistic Identity and Language Policy in Nepal. *Nationalism and Ethnic Politics* 1, 108–20.

Upadhyaya, K.P. *et al.* 1997. *Human Rights Year Book 1997*. Kathmandu: INSEC.

Van der Veer, P. 1994. *Religious Nationalism: Hindus and Muslims in India.* Berkeley: University of California Press.

Walzer, M. 1997. *On Toleration.* New Haven and London: Yale University Press.

Whelpton, J. 1983. *Jang Bahadur in Europe: The First Nepalese Mission to the West.* Kathmandu: Sahayogi.

Whelpton, J. 1991. *Kings, Soldiers and Priests: Nepalese Politics and the Rise of Jang Bahadur Rana, 1830–57.* New Delhi: Manohar.

Whelpton, J. 1997. Political Identity in Nepal: State, Nation, and Community. In Gellner *et al.* (Eds.).

Yanow, D. 1998. American Ethnogenesis and the 1990 Census. In *Democracy and Ethnography: Constructing Identities in Multicultural Liberal States.* (Ed.) C.J. Greenhouse. Albany: State University of New York Press.

9 Advancing indigenous claims through the law: reflections on the Guatemalan peace process

Rachel Sieder and Jessica Witchell

Introduction

In December 1996 a negotiated peace settlement between insurgent and government forces in Guatemala brought to an end over three decades of armed conflict. Although this had not been fought over ethnic claims for autonomy or self-determination, the historical marginalization of, and discrimination against, the majority indigenous Maya population was one of the underlying causes of the war and remains one of the country's central political problems. After 1990 indigenous organizations began to emerge and lobby for greater participation and rights for indigenous people on the basis of ethnic entitlement. Supported by the UN and other international actors, such demands found expression within the framework of the negotiated settlement. The Agreement on the Identity and Rights of Indigenous Peoples, signed by the insurgent *Unidad Revolucionaria Nacional Guatemalteca* (URNG) and the Guatemalan government in March 1995, represents an official commitment to improving the political representation and socio-economic participation of indigenous peoples. However, this document, whilst seen to be representing indigenous demands 'on the ground', was at the same time shaped by the language of international human rights and multiculturalist discourses.

In this chapter we argue that recourse to legalistic strategies and discourses to strategically further the aims of indigenous movements shapes the ways their aspirations are represented. Indigenous identities in Guatemala are effectively being narrated or codified through dominant legal discourses, specifically those of international human rights law and multiculturalism. This has resulted in the projection of an essentialized, idealized and atemporal indigenous identity, the movement's leaders often perceiving such essentializing as tactically necessary in order to secure collective rights for indigenous people. These tendencies are most evident in the manner in which indigenous legal norms

201

and practices, or 'customary law', have been represented. Influenced by international discourses on indigenous rights, activists have claimed that customary law operates at the community level according to a 'harmonious' world view particular to indigenous peoples. Such claims of authenticity have become intrinsic to demands for indigenous authorities and legal practices to be given greater political space as part of the wider process of state reform. However, such conceptions ultimately fail to reflect the complexity and power dynamics of social relations, especially in the wake of the armed conflict. We argue here that discourses, strategies and legal frameworks which reify stereotypes of harmonious and 'traditional' indigenous communities risk further marginalizing indigenous people from national processes, and may even deny access to justice to the most disadvantaged sectors within the indigenous population. Instead of such reifications of cultural stereotypes, the development of a democratic and multicultural rule of law requires flexible and dynamic conceptions of indigenous peoples within society which allow for integrated reform strategies respectful of cultural differences.

Globalization and legal and cultural pluralism

In contrast to an earlier legal anthropology linked to the colonial enterprise, which analyzed indigenous legal orders as something entirely distinct and separate from national state law, much recent anthropological investigation is concerned with the way in which the legal ideas and processes of subordinate groups are constrained and shaped by dominant legal frameworks.[1] Focusing on the imbrication of different legal orders, such research analyzes relations of domination, accommodation and resistance.[2] These approaches maintain that legal pluralism should be understood not as a plurality of separate and bounded cultural systems, but rather as a plurality of continually evolving and interconnected processes enmeshed in wider power relations. This underlines the need to analyze local beliefs and practices within their broader social, political and economic context and to understand law as a social construct, rather than as a universal or essentialized category.

Geertz asserts that normative orders must be seen as cultural systems and advocates a reading of law as culture. According to his interpretation, legal orders contain systems of symbols and meaning through which structures of ordering are formed, communicated, imposed, shared and reproduced. Law is therefore like a language, a 'distinctive manner of imagining the real' (1983: 173), and as such determines which events and interpretations are taken up as 'legal facts'. Conley and O'Barr have argued that the specific legal discourse of the state transforms everyday social discourse in order to conform to abstract legal categories and conventions, a process that Geertz has referred to as the 'skeletonization of fact' (Geertz 1983; Conley & O'Barr 1990). The law itself is by no means unproblematic or neutral. Normative and legal ideas are predominantly shaped by dominant groups and tend to legitimize particular ideologies, asymmetrical power relations, and conceptions of personhood and agency. Legal orders map out specific formulations of interests and understandings of disputes, as well as the regulatory patterns for settling them. Dominant modes of thought are thus symbolically represented in the 'rule of law', through which central concepts such as 'property' and 'the individual' are projected, systematically excluding those who do not conform.

Yet while such fixed categories are essential to the perpetuation and legitimacy of the law, in practice rules and concepts are open to interpretation. Although state law projects itself as an all-encompassing social ordering system, anthropologists have long documented the ways in which multiple alternative normative orders operate at the margins of official legal regimes.[3] Legal systems can therefore be understood as contested sites of meaning, where dominant ideas and values provide the framework for contestation and for advancing alternative understandings and practices (Starr & Collier 1994). In this way law is constantly negotiated and reshaped in a dynamic dialectic between hegemonic projections and counter-hegemonic actions (Santos 1987; Stammers 1999).[4]

As Starr and Collier have pointed out, not only anthropologists assume that legal orders are cultural systems; people continually treat legal systems as appropriate vehicles for asserting, creating and contesting identities. Within nation-states, legal orders and national identities are mutually defining and continually shaped by historical processes. Dominant conceptions of personhood define which groups or persons are entitled to rights and duties as citizens (Harris 1996). In any state the construction and meaning of the rule of law can therefore be understood as a contested process involving negotiation over which rights should be granted to different individuals and groups, and which obligations are required of them. While the effective exercise of rights and obligations generally depends on relative degrees of power, the *codification* of rights, for example within a national constitution, is in itself singularly important because it shapes the formal parameters and spaces for popular mobilization and struggle. In the case of Guatemala, the 1996 peace settlement agreed in principle to redefine the nation state as 'multi-ethnic and pluri-cultural'. Until that point the liberal ideology of state law had effectively marginalized indigenous groups from national identity and from the dominant politico-legal order. In the current process of political transformation, ideas of legal pluralism, human rights and indigenous rights have become resources for indigenous groups, and the law itself has become a central mechanism to express and formalize multicultural, multi-ethnic relations.

Throughout the world, globalized political values such as human rights and multiculturalism are increasingly taken up and vernacularized in particular social contexts, often providing important leverage for opposition movements in their struggles to extract greater concessions from national states. Human rights themselves are not a fixed given; instead their form and content are continually negotiated in specific social and historical contexts. Binion (1995) has argued that human rights are not universal 'natural' rights, but rather politically-contested entitlements that gain strength and legitimacy precisely because they are framed in universalist language (see also Dembour 1996). As Stavenhagen (1996: 148–78) has pointed out, the conceptual and theoretical construction of human rights reflects the historical asymmetries and inequalities of human society. While human rights are founded on the principles of equality and non-discrimination, in practice this entails a core of basic human rights around which a periphery of human rights exists for specific categories of people (for example, children, women, workers, migrants, refugees, ethnic minorities or indigenous people). While seeking to protect those categories of people that are struggling to be recognized as equally 'human' and deserving of rights, the articulation of specific rights to those categories through the international human rights regime also serves to codify and shape those identities within asymmetrical relations of power.

In recent years international legal agreements for the recognition of indigenous peoples' rights have been framed in a discourse of special rights and multiculturalism, rather than in a universalist discourse of human rights *per se*. Indeed the struggle for recognition of specific rights for indigenous peoples involves a challenge to the hegemonic human rights discourse, which is based exclusively on ideas of universalism. Multiculturalist approaches challenge the cultural hegemony of dominant groups by arguing for special recognition of previously excluded cultural and ethnic rights (Turner 1993). They aim to combat discrimination via official recognition of cultural differences, and to promote positive discrimination with the aim of creating inclusive, multi-ethnic and multicultural democratic institutions. Multiculturalism offers a critique of the difference-blindness inherent in classical liberal conceptions of rights and citizenship, where rights and obligations are focused exclusively on the individual, arguing that the existence of universal human rights alone is insufficient to protect and advance the rights of indigenous peoples. Young, who has advanced the concept of 'differentiated citizenship' (1990; 1995), and Kymlicka (1995a; 1995b) have challenged the classical liberal idea of a rule of law encompassing universal rights and obligations that apply to everyone in the same way. They argue that this may both suppress the specificities of identity by not recognizing difference, and also fail to correct historical wrongs which have denied rights to oppressed or marginalized groups of the population (in this case, indigenous peoples).

While not officially part of the Universal Declaration on Human Rights, the 'right to self determination of peoples' was included in the 1966 UN Covenant on Civil and Political Rights (Stamatopolou 1994). Although this occurred within the historical context of decolonialization, in recent decades indigenous populations have increasingly fought for recognition as 'peoples' in order to gain the right to self-determination. In Latin America, indigenous claims for self-determination have generally been expressed as demands for greater representation, recognition of difference and federal or regional autonomy arrangements, rather than as aspirations for separate statehood (Díaz-Polanco 1997; Sieder 1999). However, this process has involved the shaping of identities around the terms 'indigenous' and 'peoples' in a mutually constitutive relationship between indigenous movements, national and international law, and inter-governmental institutions. The term 'indigenous' is itself conceptually based around the relation of the original population to that of their colonizers. The construction of an indigenous identity can in one sense be understood as a reaction to the historical projection of the Indian as the 'other', subjected to policies of assimilation or eradication. The distinctive criteria for indigenous populations are therefore primordialism and cultural difference (Saugestad 1993); in order to gain the right to self-determination, indigenous movements evoke the language of historical continuity, on which they stake their claim to collective identity.

In 1982 the UN set up a Working Group on Indigenous Populations, which seeks dialogue with indigenous populations (strategically electing not to call them peoples) with the aim of codifying their rights in a declaration. The UN envisages that this internationally sanctioned legal instrument will serve to advance the codification of indigenous rights in national constitutions and legal systems. Through its local, national and international human rights promotion and monitoring agencies, the UN has extended the dictum of universal human rights to cover the rights of historically marginalized indigenous peoples. While this new formulation is in part a response to indigenous resistance, it has also undoubtedly played a part in shaping and creating indigenous identity and organization, strengthening the assertion and creation of indigenous identities at the international level under the banner of human rights. The International Labour Organisation (ILO)'s Convention 169 also has great influence on processes of political and constitutional reform as it is legally binding in domestic law for those governments that choose to ratify it. Convention 169 favours recognition of the right of indigenous and tribal peoples to continued existence and development along the lines that they themselves determine, although the emphasis remains firmly on social, economic, political and cultural development *within* the framework of the nation-state. The Convention also explicitly recognizes the rights of indigenous peoples to use their traditional legal practices, or customary law, within their own communities. The debate has now moved away from whether or not indigenous collective rights are legitimate towards how they can be realized within the framework of a unitary state. Article 31 of the UN draft Declaration on the Rights of Indigenous Peoples, concerning the right of indigenous people to control their own development, goes further than the ILO Convention. It provides that:

Indigenous peoples, as a specific form of exercising their right to self-determination, have the right to autonomy or self-government in matters relating to their institutional and local affairs, including culture, religion, education, information, media, health, housing, employment, social welfare, economic activities, land and resources management, environment and entry by non-members, as well as ways and means for financing these autonomous functions.[5]

The Organization of American States (OAS) has also put forward a draft declaration on the question of indigenous rights. This draws on recent experiences of legal and constitutional reform throughout Latin America, which have made increasing reference to multi-ethnicity and multiculturalism (Van Cott 2000; Yashar 1996). Rather than emphasizing self-determination, it embodies a new form of integrationism in which the focus is less on political autonomy than on emphasizing indigenous participatory and decision-making structures and institutions as integral to the remaking of the national polity. With regard to the right to autonomy in local affairs, the declaration emphasizes the recognition of indigenous law within the state's legal, economic and social systems. While underlining the right of indigenous peoples to strengthen their own judicial systems, the OAS declaration views these as an integral part of the overall national politico-legal structure (Plant 1998).

Through their increased participation in the international arena, the demands of indigenous peoples are shaped by international institutional processes and international manners of 'imagining the real'. There is now a recognized place for indigenous peoples on the international stage. This position is strategically beneficial, enabling them to articulate their demands, albeit in an appropriated format. However, this increased participation of indigenous peoples also acts to legitimize the expansion and reproduction of the international institutions themselves and the legal discourses they produce. Demands which have arisen out of indigenous peoples' lived experience are now committed, through the strategic recourse to such international institutional channels, to the maintenance of those same powers and are constrained and shaped accordingly. In other words, cultural processes are fluid and receptive to the wider environment and power relations; transnationalism – linking peoples through economics and politics – has interacted with local cultural processes throughout the world (Merry 1997). As Santos (1987) notes, the legal context is now characterized by inter-legality and the mixing of cultural codes, while global discourses become part of the local vernacular and constantly acquire new meanings.

Surely, as Wilson (1997) emphasizes, the issue is now not whether it is right for supposedly bounded cultural entities to interact, as the relativists would have it, or the insistence on universal values, but rather *how* these different cultural processes interact in practice. During the 1990s, cultural diversity became a basis for challenging, revising and relativizing the ideas and values held by dominant groups in attempts to construct a multi-ethnic social and political order throughout Latin America. We argue here that multiculturalist approaches to political reform have tended to favour and encourage a subaltern politics based on identity, in which an essentialized concept of culture merges with that of ethnic identity in particular contexts and struggles. This in turn reflects the 'romancing of otherness' (Turner 1993) observable within international legal discourses. As indigenous struggles interact with dominant discourses, they appear to become more essentialist in response to the reductionist orientation of law. However, while the outcome of these interactions may be to present a seemingly atemporal, fixed notion of collective identity in order to claim rights, this is precisely because of the strategic invocation of rights language rather than any pre-existing ontological 'culture'.

The Guatemalan context

Centuries of discrimination have engendered a pervasive local culture of accommodation and resistance in Guatemala, which has enabled the Maya to avoid the fate of assimilation or destruction which has met many indigenous peoples elsewhere in Latin America. Approximately 60 per cent of Guatemala's population of 10.2 million is indigenous, including some 21 different Mayan linguistic communities and two small non-Mayan indigenous groups, the Xinca and the Garifuna. The remainder of the population is *mestizo* or *ladino* (non-Indian), mixed-race descendants of Spanish settlers and members of other immigrant groups which colonized Guatemala after the sixteenth century. The highly unequal distribution of resources has a marked ethnic dimension – a product of the historical subjection of indigenous people to an exploitative economic system and a political culture of racism and exclusion. Rural communities continue to form the mainstay of indigenous culture. However, while most Mayan families continue to depend to some degree on subsistence agriculture for their survival, less than 3 per cent of the population owns 70 per cent of all arable land. According to recent UN figures, 80 per cent of the overall population lives in poverty, while 90 per cent of all indigenous people lives in poverty, and 76 per cent in extreme poverty (PNUD 1998). Indigenous people are more educationally disadvantaged; some 50 per cent of the population is illiterate (making Guatemala the second most illiterate country in Latin America), but this figure rises to 75 to 80 per cent for indigenous people, increasing to approximately 90 per cent for Mayan women, more than 60 per cent of whom are monolingual (Minority Rights Group 1994: 40).

Following independence from Spain, the consolidation of liberal ideologies among ruling elites during the latter part of the nineteenth century intensified pre-existing pressures on indigenous lands and labour. The triumph of universalist ideals did not imply the extension of full citizenship status to all groups. Instead, in the context of an agro-export boom, liberal notions of equality before the law provided ideological justification for the removal of historic protections traditionally afforded to indigenous people by the Crown, conservative regimes, and the Catholic Church, and their forced assimilation on highly disadvantageous terms. Thousands of acres of indigenous common lands were expropriated as 'unproductive' and the indigenous population was increasingly prohibited or impeded from using its own customs and languages. Dominant, non-indigenous elites justified forced indigenous labour and cultural assimilation in terms of nation-building ideologies which emphasized the need to 'civilize the Indian'. (Indigenous people remained subject to forced labour requirements until 1944, when legislation enforcing debt servitude was formally abolished.)

During a ten-year period of reformist government between 1944 and 1954, indigenous men were granted voting rights and benefited from a programme of agrarian reform. The introduction of trades unions and political parties throughout rural Guatemala gave many Mayans access to local political office. However, following the CIA-backed overthrow of the government of Jacobo Arbenz in 1954, the political exclusion of indigenous people increased as the state was militarized within the anti-communist framework of the Cold War. Throughout the 1960s Mayan communities radicalized, a consequence of Church-backed development initiatives, the ideological influence of liberation theology, and an increasingly desperate struggle for land and economic survival (Le Bot 1995). By the late 1970s violent state repression forced activists attempting to secure land and fairer wages underground. Many younger Mayans subsequently joined the guerrilla movement which, in contrast to its 1960s *foquista* precursor, was committed to incorporating indigenous people into the armed revolutionary struggle. However, the poorly-armed guerrillas were unable to defend their supporters in the rural highlands against the full brunt of military violence.

The defining feature of the armed conflict of the 1980s was the army's forced integration of the Maya into a national counter-insurgency project. The violence employed by the military to destroy the guerrillas' social base totally transformed the countryside and closed down any space for popular social organization. Tactics ranged from periodic sweeps by death squads and 'disappearances' to massacres and physical destruction of entire hamlets. Over 150,000 people were killed during this period, hundreds of villages disappeared and many others were reorganized under military auspices.[6] Hundreds of thousands of Mayan men were forced by the army to organize paramilitary civil defence patrols, charged with local surveillance and 'defence' of communities against the guerrillas (Popkin 1996). These impositions aggravated local divisions and gave pre-existing conflicts a lethal edge as villagers denounced each other to the army as guerrilla sympathizers. This had the effect of destroying the pre-existing networks of meanings and understandings that had hitherto governed everyday social relationships (Zur 1994). Religious divisions also increased as army repressive measures against Catholic catechists prompted ever greater numbers of Maya to convert to Protestant sects. The civil war in effect constituted an all-out assault on indigenous culture and identity: as one Maya-Q'eqchi' elder described it, 'With the war we lost our memory'.[7]

A limited political space was opened by the military-endorsed return to civilian rule in 1985 (Schirmer 1998). Although human rights violations and the militarization of rural areas continued, the organization of civil opposition groups slowly increased towards the end of the decade. The 1985 Constitution officially recognized the multi-ethnic nature of the country, containing five Articles (Articles 66–70) which referred specifically to the 'protection of ethnic groups'. Mayan activists slowly began to campaign for the state to live up to its constitutional commitments to respect and promote indigenous culture, languages and forms of organization. Yet in the latter half of the 1980s it was principally organization around human rights that brought indigenous people into the political arena. By 1986 over 85 per cent of members of the Mutual Support Group (GAM), founded in 1984 by families of the disappeared, were Mayan women. In 1988 the widows' organization CONAVIGUA was set up, its 11,000 strong membership almost totally Maya. The membership of the anti-civil patrol organization, the Ethnic Council *Runujel Junam* (CERJ), and of CONDEG, set up in 1989 to represent displaced populations in the cities and rural areas, was also predominantly indigenous. These human rights organizations, which benefited considerably from strong links with international human rights organizations and other non-governmental organizations (NGOs), were broadly aligned with the armed left, but also exercised a degree of autonomy and independence from them.

The repression of indigenous identity during the war generated an increased awareness of indigenous rights within the peace process in the 1990s. In the wake of the armed conflict, a pan-Mayan movement emerged which began to contest existing conceptions of national identity and citizenship (Warren 1998; Nelson 1999). This drew inspiration and support from an increasingly transnational indigenous people's movement in the Americas, which emerged around the 1992 quincentenary of the Spanish Conquest. Its growing strength also reflected the fact that indigenous rights had come to occupy the agenda of non-governmental and inter-governmental organizations in the international arena, not least the UN which, in 1994, installed an observer mission in Guatemala to monitor human rights violations and verify the peace accords. Indeed, the 1992 award of the Nobel peace prize to Guatemalan Mayan activist Rigoberta Menchú Tum was a clear signal of increasing global endorsement of indigenous claims. During the 1990s demands for indigenous rights and idealized projections of 'Mayan values' constituted a newly articulated discourse affecting social relations and framing much of the debate around democratization in Guatemala. The Mayan movement, supported by the UN mission and several international institutions, gradually strengthened its capacity to put forward proposals for national reform. While human rights issues remained crucial, indigenous intellectuals and popular organizations increasingly concentrated their efforts on reconstituting Mayan identity, drawing on cultural elements such as language and devising innovative interpretations of

Mayan traditions. For example, the para-legal NGO Defensoría Maya has consistently advocated greater recognition and application of 'Mayan Law' as a means to remedy the lack of access to justice experienced by indigenous people (Defensoría Maya 1999). The discourse used to advance such demands illustrates the strategic essentializing deployed by indigenous leaders:

> Our method is to facilitate the application of the Mayan judicial system for the solution of conflicts. Litigants discover what they have lost through centuries of assimilation. They realize that our system is effective, not bureaucratic, it is truly conciliatory and not based on corruption, trickery or denigration. Neither is it discriminatory, exclusive or coercive. (Chuj Waljo'q, March 1997, our translation)

> Mayan Law is a judicial system whose norms and principles facilitate harmonious relations between members of society, and between the Mayan, Garifuna, Xinca and Ladino peoples, according to our worldview. (Chuj Waljo'q, February 1997)

Initiatives throughout the country to rebuild the social fabric destroyed by the war, including the reconstitution of local authorities or conflict resolution procedures, have been framed in terms of ethnic specificities. For example, in Northern Quiché, where the counter-insurgency war left a legacy of division and land conflicts between Ixil and K'iché villages, Defensoría Maya has deployed a strategy for conflict-resolution based on attempts to reconstruct an 'imagined community' of harmonious inter-ethnic relations among Mayan peoples. In their publications they call for 'the reconstitution of the social fabric of the communities of the Ixil and K'iché peoples . . . involving the rediscovery of family and communal nuclei to initiate harmonious coexistence . . . [and] the recovery of the historical memory of Indigenous Peoples' (Chuj Waljo'q, March 1997). Indigenous leaders have increasingly emphasized the importance of Mayan spirituality and worldviews, stressing the need to actively rebuild both local communities and the nation-state by drawing on the imagined values of a shared pre-colonial Mayan past.

> The [military] repression meant the destruction of the millenarium systems of the Mayan people. However, our system of organization and law for the resolution of conflict has very deep roots; our own mechanisms practiced in our communities on a daily basis for centuries. In this way we have been able to survive physical and psychological trauma and maintain our identity. (Chuj Waljo'q, April 1997)

By revitalizing and creating a shared past, or 'imagined community' (Anderson 1983), indigenous activists have responded to an acute form of ethnic discrimination and the destruction wrought by war. Within the current political context it is also used to lobby for greater rights for the indigenous population by drawing on ideas of multiculturalism and ethnic entitlement. However, the creation of such 'foundational myths' is also a reflection of the essentialized view of indigenous peoples advanced within international rights discourses and the reductionist nature of current legal frameworks for recognizing indigenous rights.

Elevating Culture: the Agreement on the Identity and Rights of Indigenous Peoples

The efforts of international organizations such as the UN and ILO to secure greater recognition of indigenous rights dovetailed with the efforts of indigenous and popular organizations in Guatemala to advance their claims within the national peace process. In the course of the negotiations indigenous groups were formally recognized as 'peoples', affording them new status and rights in international law and framing novel ways of conceiving national reform. The 1995 Agreement on the Identity and Rights of Indigenous Peoples was greatly influenced by international human rights declarations and covenants, as well as by the increased direct participation of the indigenous movement as a whole in the political process. The initial draft of the agreement was proposed by the umbrella organisation, Co-ordination of the Organizations of the Mayan People of Guatemala (COPMAGUA), and subsequently amended by the multi-sectoral Assembly of Civil Society (ASC) before being presented to the negotiating table. It was signed by government and URNG representatives on 31 March 1995 and represented a singular success in the Mayan struggle for inclusion in a broad democratic process.

The central demands set out in the agreement relate to constitutional recognition of the Mayan, Garifuna and Xinca peoples and to a redefinition of the Guatemalan nation as culturally plural, multi-ethnic and multi-lingual. This echoes multicultural and new integrationist approaches that insist on the need for measures to combat discrimination as part of building more inclusive nation-states. The agreement calls for the constitutional and legal recognition of Mayan organizational forms, political practices and customary law, as well as recognition of the cultural and socio-economic rights of indigenous peoples. Its language mirrors that of international declarations and covenants, and indeed explicitly states that the government should promote policies to implement provisions set out in international law regarding indigenous peoples; for example, ILO Convention 169. The agreement in effect elevates culture as a medium through which equal representation may be fought for. As a legal discourse, it tends to essentialize and codify cultural values and practices. For example, the agreement states:

The development of national culture is inconceivable without recognition and promotion of the culture of the indigenous peoples. Thus, in contrast to the past, educational and cultural policy should be orientated to focus on recognition, respect and encouragement of indigenous cultural values.[8]

Specifically recognizing the legitimacy of indigenous customary law, the agreement states that indigenous legal systems are rooted in a particular worldview 'based on the harmonious relationship of all the elements . . . [that] has been passed down from generation to generation'.[9]

The traditional norms of indigenous peoples have been and continue to be an essential element for the social regulation of the life of the communities and, consequently, for the maintenance of their cohesion.[10]

In addition to recognizing the existence of 'traditional' legal norms and practices within indigenous communities, the agreement explicitly commits the state to respect them as long as they do not violate fundamental human rights or national laws. It states that judges and legal officials must take into account local legal custom, and sets out requirements for the provision of legal defence in indigenous languages.

The agreement therefore assumes that essentialized categories of 'culture' and 'customary norms' are entities that can somehow be codified within the state system. However, far from being 'natural' phenomena, these categories reflect the reorganization of ethnic identity to fit international human rights norms and practices. The consensual 'harmony' and historical continuity so often promoted in indigenous discourses are not an accurate representation of social reality: what it in fact reflects is the contemporary reorganization of the past as the means to secure certain political gains in the present. There are no qualities that are inherently Mayan; what we are witnessing is rather the process by which certain qualities are constructed as such. As anthropologists have long argued, culture can no longer be seen as a bounded entity that is separate from other influences. Rather, cultural processes are involved in a matrix of dialectical relations and identities reconstructed and maintained through processes of change. To present Mayan identities and practices as rooted in tradition and as somehow autonomous from the state is to ignore the mutually constitutive relationship between state practices and indigenous identities. Popular systems of justice are formed in the social spaces which exist at the peripheries of the dominant legal orders and as such the nature and capacity of their ordering is shaped within the dynamic of asymmetrical power relations. Before accepting claims that customary norms are rooted in a 'harmonious' indigenous worldview, present-day local practices should be considered in their historical and social context.

Mayan custom as law?

Decades of authoritarian government, discriminatory and exclusionary practices, and the impunity from legal redress enjoyed by powerful actors have profoundly and negatively affected Guatemalans' belief in the rule of law. Most of the population continues to view the legal system as arbitrary, corrupt and ineffective. Indigenous leaders have relied upon dissatisfaction with state law as justification for their demands for the codification of customary law as a means to secure greater local autonomy. However, rather than constituting some kind of self-contained legal sphere, recent ethnographic investigation has shown that customary law exists in a dynamic and mutually constitutive relationship with state law.[11] Policies favouring the establishment of hermetically sealed, 'separate but equal' jurisdictions of state courts and their indigenous equivalents would run the risk of further marginalizing indigenous groups from the national polity. In addition, and particularly in the wake of the armed conflict, such formulations could ultimately prejudice the human rights of individual members of indigenous groups by effectively legitimizing the authoritarian exercise of power by dominant groups within indigenous communities as 'tradition' or 'custom'.

During the most acute years of the violence and counter-insurgency in the early 1980s, informal practices for local conflict resolution became increasingly punitive as a consequence of the authoritarian structures and practices instituted throughout the country by the army. In rural areas the paramilitary civil patrols and military commissioners operated as highly coercive extra-judicial arbitration systems sponsored by the armed forces. Sanctions included detaining suspected guerrilla sympathizers in water-filled pits, torture, beatings, forced labour and often death. While military commissioners were abolished in 1995 and civil patrols demobilized weeks after the final peace agreement was signed, the legacy of militarization in indigenous communities, as in the country as a whole, will take much longer to eradicate. The prolonged militarization of local politics and the use of violence to resolve conflicts during the war has undoubtedly influenced how people approach dispute resolution. In many villages and municipalities relations are far from consensual; often people live side by side with fellow villagers who were directly responsible for the rape, torture and murder of their family members. Communities are therefore divided by the legacy of violence, authoritarianism and militarization left by the armed conflict. In such contexts, local norms and practices can contain highly oppressive features. In some instances, entire families of suspected miscreants have been forcibly evicted from their villages. In the absence of an effective judicial process and with crime indicators rising since the end of the war, reports have also increased of villagers dispensing summary justice and mob-lynching individuals suspected of robbery, rape or membership of organized criminal gangs. Most lynchings have occurred in the regions of the country worst hit by the counter-insurgency violence during the 1980s, even though these areas have comparatively low levels of criminality (MINUGUA 1998).

Discourses, strategies and policies which tie customary law to a reified imaginary of 'traditional' and 'harmonious' indigenous communities are problematic in other ways too. Even before the armed conflict, inter-generational disputes and religious conversion had undermined communal cohesion throughout the Guatemalan countryside. As a consequence of the processes of displacement, exile and resettlement throughout the 1980s and 1990s, many indigenous people now live far from their place of birth in new villages comprised of people from different areas and linguistic groups, with different customs. Indigenous knowledge systems and established practices were shattered by the war and are now being refashioned. The gradual reduction of military control over the countryside has facilitated greater social space for community politico-legal ordering and, in turn, for local structures and practices to become more conciliatory. Common mechanisms include extended dialogue, moral sanctions based on shame, the acknowledge-ment of error by the offender, and restitutive sanctions involving compensation for the victim and the community. The process is generally geared towards re-establishing peaceful coexistence within the community as a whole, which is actively promoted by indigenous organizations and activists. In some cases certain state-imposed institu-tions, such as infrastructural 'improvement committees' established at village level, have been appropriated as new spaces for local conflict-resolution. In others, returned refugees have adapted the organizational structures they developed while in exile in Mexico. Within the post-war context, indigenous people are devising innovative means of resolving local conflicts: for example, in Northern Alta Verapaz Catholic villages of displaced Q'eqchi' have constituted a regional Council of Elders to provide spiritual advice on community matters. The elders draw on images of 'traditional Mayan law' as a point of reference, well aware that a harmonious Mayan legal order is an aspiration rather than the reflection of a complex, dynamic and often highly conflictive social reality. This constitutes an example of what Slater (1997: 63) has pointed to as the use of 'submerged signifiers, meanings and practices of previous periods' as a starting point for rethinking justice. These examples illustrate that customary legal practices are not fixed or 'traditional', but rather highly relational, changing according to shifting local, national and international contexts. As Van Cott has observed, their authenticity derives not from their millenarian nature, but 'rather from their . . . adoption in the absence of effective access to state justice' (2000: 212).

Current efforts to secure recognition of customary law and strengthen community-based norms and practices are part of the wider historic struggle of indigenous groups for justice, autonomy and representation. The strengthening of local mechanisms for resolution of disputes has the potential to contribute to a more democratic and culturally sensitive rule of law in Guatemala. However, because such processes are often framed within an essentialist cultural discourse, they may effectively shape and constrain many popular aspirations. Such contradictions are most evident with regard to gender, where essentialist discourses emphasize the 'complementarity' of Mayan men and women, minimizing existing gender discrimination or justifying the de facto exclusion of women from holding community office, public schooling, or tenure of property. Such views, however, are increasingly challenged by indigenous women, whose experience of internal displacement, war and refuge has led them to transcend traditional boundaries. Formerly monolingual women learnt Spanish and literacy skills in exile; interaction with church agents and human rights NGOs encouraged a greater awareness of national and international norms of human rights, prompting women refugees to present their demands on the international stage (Mama Maquín 1999). The large number of widows left by the armed conflict organized to provide for their families and discover the fate of their relatives, with the consequence that women increasingly occupied public spaces traditionally reserved for men. Many now question their traditionally subordinate and marginal role in community decision-making and demand cultural rights which include more preferential treatment for Mayan women. In addition, a growing consciousness by indigenous women of their own legal rights and attempts to 'resist the structures of domination which characterize their everyday lives' (Lazarus-Black 1991: 120) is reflected in recourse to national law for cases of domestic abuse and conflict. This indicates an unwillingness to be judged solely according to the authority of men in their communities.[12] A gendered analysis of customary law underlines the fact that, like any form of law, it is a historically bounded construction determined by contested power relations both within indigenous communities and between those communities, the state and dominant interests. Incorporation of customary fora and practices into the judicial system will not, of itself, guarantee women's access to justice.[13] Reform measures must therefore ensure that indigenous authorities and conflict-resolution practices do not discriminate against less advantaged groups such as women.

If legal reform to recognize customary law in the wake of the 1996 peace settlement fetishizes or reifies 'custom' or 'tradition' as law, in effect it will essentialize dynamic institutions and practices. Instead it should be based on the recognition of indigenous people's right to determine their own systems of conflict resolution, provided these are respectful of the rights to representation and dissent of all individual community members. Rather than a concession by the state to indigenous peoples, recognition of 'customary law' should be conceived of as part of a wider effort to develop effective and culturally sensitive forms of justice for the entire population. In the event, elite opposition to recognition of indigenous rights in Guatemala increased after the peace settlement was signed in December 1996. In May 1999 a clause agreed in a multi-party forum proposing constitutional recognition of the right of indigenous people to use their customary law was rejected, along with fifty other constitutional amendments, in a controversial popular referendum on a constitutional reform package aimed at implementing the peace agreements.[14] However, ILO Convention 169 and the 1995 Agreement on the Rights and Identity of Indigenous Peoples are binding on the Guatemalan state. International donors remain committed to the terms of the peace settlement and to advancing indigenous rights, and indigenous organizations continue to bring pressure to bear on both the government and international institutions to force the former to meet the agreements concluded during the peace negotiations. The complex and controversial question of how indigenous customary law will be incorporated into the judicial system is therefore likely to remain on the political agenda.

Conclusion

The 1995 Agreement on the Identity and Rights of Indigenous Peoples places much emphasis on cultural rights as a basis for political, social and economic claims for inclusion in the Guatemalan state. This elevation of 'culture' as a means of recognition and inclusion of indigenous peoples has been used to combat a deep-rooted legacy of discrimination within Guatemalan society and reflects the desire to create a genuinely multi-ethnic democracy. However, such strategies, inspired by international discourses of multiculturalism, have also encouraged indigenous activists to present an essentialized vision of a harmonious and millenarian Mayan culture as a means of securing greater autonomy and representation. We have argued here that the political discourse of Mayan culture in Guatemala is best understood as what Roseberry has described as a 'social and discursive construction and imagination' (1996: 83), which subaltern groups use as a counter-hegemonic mechanism to contest domination.[15] Rather than deriving from any primordial or a priori 'culture', identities are in fact historically created and recreated through mutually constitutive interactions between different actors, contexts and ideas – in this case between the Guatemalan indigenous movement, international actors, the peace process, and human rights and multiculturalist discourses.

Examination of the Guatemalan case has wider relevance for discussions about multiculturalism and legal reform in Latin America and elsewhere. First, it illustrates the ways in which local demands and processes are shaped and constrained by international frameworks for claiming rights. As people across the globe increasingly appeal to international human rights law and international institutions to further their claims for justice, the tendency of subordinated groups to elaborate 'primordial authenticities' and to claim rights on the basis of culture is likely to increase.[16] However, as we have emphasized here, indigenous movements do not represent bounded or 'traditional' cultural formations, but are in fact transnationalized phenomena representing what are often highly dynamic communities undergoing accelerated processes of change. In fact, as De la Peña signals for the case of Mexico (1999), growing international migration has meant that cultural identities themselves have increasingly become transnational or post-national. De la Peña rightly points to the breakdown in the link between territory, peoples and states that has resulted from globalization (1999: 21). In contexts where rights entitlement is increasingly based on 'culture', such developments pose difficult questions about how to adapt and reform the political, legal and economic structures of the nation-state. Certainly they indicate that official strategies based on granting limited autonomy to 'traditional' rural indigenous communities are problematic at best.

Second, the Guatemalan case indicates the difficulties inherent in recognizing rights based on 'culture' at a time when discourses of human rights and gender rights are increasingly part of the vernacular in local contexts. Multiculturalist legal frameworks advanced by international institutions such as the UN and the ILO have encouraged indigenous movements throughout Latin America to advance essentialist projections of identity. However, indigenous women across the continent have appropriated discourses of human rights and women's rights and increasingly challenged essentialist discourses of gender complementarity or harmony (Sierra 1999; Hernández & Garza 1997).

In practice, the division between cultural rights and human rights is often over-stated. Yet when conflicts do emerge, as in the case of gender, the challenge is how to ensure that indigenous communities govern themselves in a manner that is tolerant of difference without legitimizing external imposition by state authorities or 'new colonialism' in the name of equality or human rights.[17]

Third, the Guatemalan case points to the wider, unresolved tensions between indigenous demands for political autonomy and claims for greater inclusion and the construction of a multicultural democracy. Indeed these tensions are clearly reflected in the different international instruments and draft conventions which attempt to codify indigenous rights. Indigenous movements throughout Latin America are now calling for integration into the nation-state on their own terms, but the issue of autonomy continues to be problematic for ruling elites.[18] The increasing recognition of multiculturalism by Latin American governments in recent years is undoubtedly a significant advance compared to ethnocentric and racist nation-building ideologies of the past (Diaz-Polanco 1997; Stavenhagen 1996). However, it can also be understood as a new form of assimilation or integration within what remain highly asymmetrical power relations. The legal recognition of 'customary law' may ultimately constitute an extension of state jurisdiction to accommodate and shape normative orders which previously existed at its margins. As Speed and Collier (2000) have highlighted in their discussion of indigenous rights in Chiapas, Mexico, in practice states continue to reserve the right to determine which indigenous 'customs' can and cannot be recognized.[19] The key challenge is how to ensure the effective participation of indigenous peoples in state decisions and policies which affect them.

Ultimately, whatever new legal ordering emerges from current efforts to make Latin American states 'multi-ethnic' and 'pluri-cultural', it will have to address ever-increasing demands to reverse the profound social and economic marginalization of indigenous peoples since the Spanish Conquest. Cultural rights cannot be separated from social and economic processes, and any meaningful steps towards a multicultural democratic order must address these issues.

ACKNOWLEDGEMENTS

Rachel Sieder would like to thank Jane Collier, Ven de la Cruz, Edgar Esquit, Carlos Flores, Iván García, Roger Plant, René Poitevín, John Watanabe and Judith Zur for their comments and encouragement. Both Rachel Sieder and Jessica Witchell are grateful to Jane Cowan and

Richard Wilson for their helpful observations on an earlier version of this paper.

NOTES

1 The extent to which different normative orders can be categorized as 'legal' depends on whether or not they have been identified as such by the social actors themselves. (For further discussion see Tamanaha 1993.)

2 Falk Moore 1986; Griffiths 1997; Hirsch 1998; Merry 1988, 1992, 1997; Moore 1998; Nader 1980; Starr and Collier 1989.

3 In general, normative systems operating at the margins of state law tend to be more embedded in the cultural and social processes of the everyday. Local systems of social mapping are oriented towards details of the particular and thus direct attention to action as perceived 'on the ground' (Santos 1987). In such contexts there is less distinction between law and fact (or 'local knowledge') (Geertz 1983). Dispute resolution mechanisms are generally geared towards reinforcing those 'social relationships', as opposed to abstract 'contractual' ones. Conley and O'Barr (1990) attribute this distinction between rule-based and popular normative systems to the fact that the latter have remained reflexive to social status and networks of contextually rooted social relations.

4 For a particularly useful discussion of hegemony see Roseberry (1994) and (1996).

5 Working Group, supra note 31, in Stamatopoulou 1994:78.

6 See Carmack 1992; Manz 1988; Stoll 1993; REMHI/ODHAG 1999.

7 Fieldnotes, Puribal village, Alta Verapaz. February 1996.

8 AIDPI, Section III, paragraph 2.

9 AIDPI, Section I, paragraph 2(iii).

10 AIDPI, Section IV, part E, paragraph 1.

11 See for example Dary 1997; Esquit and García 1998; Sieder 1997; Universidad Rafael Landívar 1998.

12 Such action by indigenous women in Guatemala is not new; see Sieder (2000). Other studies have suggested that women turn to state courts in order to contest gender hierarchy: see June Starr (1989) on rural Turkey; Jane Collier (1973) on Zinacantán, Mexico.

13 In her study of legal pluralism and gender in Rajasthan, India, Erin Moore (1993, 1998) found that where village conflict resolution structures were incorporated into the lower levels of the state judicial system, women continued to be denied access to justice. Within the village customary courts men blocked women's appeals, and state courts tended to return domestic conflicts to the villages for resolution. Mandatory representation of women in customary courts was legislated for, but did not happen in practice.

14 It was proposed that the relevant Article (Article 203) of the 1985 Constitution be reformed to include the following additional paragraph:

> The state recognizes indigenous customary law, understood as the norms, principles, values, procedures, traditions and customs of indigenous peoples, for the regulation of their internal affairs and [also recognizes] the validity of their decisions when these are

voluntarily submitted to [by the parties to a dispute] and when they do not violate fundamental human rights defined in the national legal system, international treaties and conventions on human rights signed and ratified by Guatemala, or the rights of third parties. (Centro de Estudios de Guatemala (1998), authors' translation.) On the referendum and its implications see Arnson (1999).

15 Roseberry (1996: 83) maintains that 'As such communities are imagined, symbols of distinctiveness and authenticity are selected and appropriated, within a social field marked by inequality, hierarchy, and contention. Languages of ethnicity, religion, and nationalism draw upon images of primordial associations and identifications, but they take their specific and practical forms as languages of contention and *opposition*.'

16 Yashar (1996) has argued that in Latin America indigenous organizing on the basis of cultural identity is a response to the imperfect democracies throughout the region and the effects of neoliberal reforms, which have reduced pre-existing corporatist benefits for peasant communities.

17 Speed and Collier (2000) have analyzed how state authorities in Chiapas have manipulated a discourse of human rights in order to constrain indigenous claims for autonomy.

18 For a comprehensive analysis of Mexican experiences of autonomy see Burguete Cal y Mayor (1999).

19 See Van Cott (2000) for discussion of recognition of customary law in the Bolivian and Colombian cases.

REFERENCES

AIDPI (Acuerdo de Identidad y Derechos de los Pueblos Indígenas). 1995. United Nations, Guatemala.

Anderson, B. 1983. *Imagined Communities: Reflections on the Origins and Spread of Nationalism*. London: Verso.

Arnson, C. (Ed.). 1999. *The Popular Referendum (Consulta Popular) and the Future of the Peace Process in Guatemala*. Working Paper No. 241, Woodrow Wilson Center Latin American Program, Washington DC.

Binion, G. 1995 Human Rights: A Feminist Perspective. *Human Rights Quarterly* 17, pp 509–526.

Burguete Caly Mayor, A. (coord.). 1999. *México: Experiencias de Autonomía Indígena*. Document of the International Working Group on Indigenous Affairs, Denmark.

Carmack, R. (Ed.). 1992. *Harvest of Violence: the Maya Indians and the Guatemalan Crisis*. Norman and London: University of Oklahoma Press.

Centro de Estudios de Guatemala. 1998. *Las Reformas Constitucionales Aprobadas por el Congreso de la República el 14 y 15 de octubre de 1998*, http://www.c.net.gt/ceg.

Chuj Waljo'q, monthly bulletin of the Defensoría Maya, Guatemala, March 1997.

Collier, J. 1973. *Law and Social Change in Zinacantan*. Stanford: Stanford University Press.

Conley J.M. and W.O'Barr. 1990. *Rules versus Relationships: The Ethnography of Legal Discourse*. Chicago: University of Chicago Press.

Dary, C. 1997. *El Derecho Internacional Humanitario y el Orden Jurídico Maya.* FLACSO, Guatemala.

Defensoría Maya. 1999. *Suk'b'anik: Administración de Justicia Maya. Experiencias de Defensoría Maya.* Guatemala: Editorial Serviprensa.

De la Peña, G. 1999. Territorio y ciudadanía étnica en la nación globalizada. *Desacatos: Revista de Antropología Social* Vol.1. CIESAS, Mexico, pp.13–27.

Dembour, M.B. 1996. Human Rights Talk and Anthropological Ambivalence: the Particular Context of Universal Claims. In *Inside and Outside the Law: Anthropological Studies of Authority and Ambiguity,* (Ed.) O. Harris. London: Routledge.

Díaz-Polanco, H. 1997. *Indigenous Peoples in Latin America: The Quest for Self-Determination.* Boulder and Oxford: Westview Press.

Donnelly, J. 1989. *Universal Human Rights in Theory and Practice.* Ithaca, NY and London: Cornell University Press.

Esquit, E. and I. García. 1998. *El Derecho Consuetudinario, la Reforma Judicial y la Implementación de los Acuerdos de Paz.* FLASCO, Guatemala.

Falk Moore, S. 1986. *Social Facts and Fabrications: Customary Law on Kilimanjaro, 1880–1980.* New York and Cambridge: Cambridge University Press.

Fuller, C. 1994. Legal Anthropology: Legal Pluralism and Legal Thought. *Anthropology Today* 10:3, 9–12.

Geertz, C. 1993. Fact and Law in Comparative Perspective. In *Local Knowledge.* London: Fontana Press.

Griffiths, A.M.O. 1997. *In the Shadow of Marriage: Gender and Justice in an African Community.* Chicago and London: Chicago University Press.

Harris, O. 1996. Introduction: Inside and Outside the Law. In *Inside and Outside the Law: Anthropological Studies of Authority and Ambiguity.* London: Routledge.

Hernández, A. & A.M. Garza. 1997. En Torno a la Ley y la Costumbre: Problemas de Antropología Legal en los Altos de Chiapas. In *Tradiciones y Costumbres Jurídicas en Comunidades Indígenas de México.* (Eds.) R. I. Estrada Martínez and G. González Guerra. Comisión Nacional de Derechos Humanos, Mexico.

Hirsch, S.F. 1998. *Pronouncing and Persevering: Gender and the Discourses of Disputing in an African Islamic Court.* Chicago and London: University of Chicago Press.

Kymlicka, W. 1995a. *Multicultural Citizenship.* Oxford: Clarendon Press.

Kymlicka, W. (Ed.). 1995b. *The Rights of Minority Cultures.* Oxford: Oxford University Press.

Lazarus-Black, M. 1991. Why Women Take Men to Magistrate's Court: Caribbean Kinship Ideology and Law. *Ethnology* 30:2, 119–134.

Lazarus-Black, M. and S.F. Hirsch (Eds.). 1994. *Contested States: Law, Hegemony and Resistance.* New York and London: Routledge.

Le Bot, Y. 1995. *La guerra en tierras mayas: comunidad, violencia y modernidad en Guatemala (1970–92).* Fondo de Cultura Económica, Mexico.

Mama Maquín. 1999. *Nuestra Experiencia ante los Retos del Futuro: Sistematización del Trabajo de las Mujeres de Mama Maquín durante el Refugio en México y su Retorno a Guatemala.* Chiapas, Mexico: Editorial Fray Bartolomé de las Casas.

Manz, B. 1988. *Refugees of a Hidden War*. Albany, NY: University of New York at Albany.

Merry, S.E. 1988. Legal Pluralism. *Law and Society Review* 22, 869–96.

Merry, S.E. 1992. Anthropology, Law and Transnational Processes. *Annual Review of Anthropology* 21, 357–79.

Merry, S.E. 1997. Legal Pluralism and Transnational Culture. In *Human Rights, Culture and Context*. (Ed.) R. Wilson. London: Pluto Press.

Minority Rights Group. 1994. *The Maya of Guatemala*. Minority Rights Group, London.

Minugua (United Nations Mission for Guatemala). 1998. Unpublished data on lynchings in Guatemala.

Moore, E.P. 1993. Gender, Power, and Legal Pluralism: Rajasthan, India. *American Ethnologist* 20:3, 522–42.

Moore, E.P. 1998. *Gender, Law, and Resistance in India*. Tucson: University of Arizona Press.

Nader, L. 1980. *Harmony Ideology, Justice and Control in a Zapotec Mountain Village*. Stanford: Stanford University Press.

Nagengast, C. 1994. Violence, Terror, and the Crisis of the State. *Annual Review of Anthropology* 23, 109–136.

Nelson, D.M. 1999. *A Finger in the Wound: Body Politics in Quincentennial Guatemala*. Berkeley, Los Angeles and London: University of California Press.

Plant, R. 1998. Ethnicity and the Guatemalan Peace Process: Conceptual and Practical Challenges. In *Guatemala After the Peace Accords*. (Ed.) R. Sieder. Institute of Latin American Studies, London.

PNUD (United Nations Programme for Development) and Mesa Nacional Maya de Guatemala. 1998. *Situación de Pobreza del Pueblo Maya en Guatemala*. Guatemala: Mimeo.

Popkin, M.L. 1996. *Civil Patrols and their Legacy: Overcoming Militarization and Polarization in the Guatemalan Countryside*. The Robert F. Kennedy Memorial Center for Human Rights, Washington DC.

REMHI/ODHAG. 1999. Recovery of Historical Memory Project, The Official Report of the Human Rights Office. In *Guatemala Never Again!* Archdiocese of Guatemala. Latin American Bureau and Catholic Institute for International Relations, London.

Roseberry, W. 1996. Hegemony, Power and Languages of Contention In *The Politics of Difference: Ethnic Premises in a World of Power*. (Eds.) E.N. Wilmsen and P. McAllister. Chicago and London: University of Chicago Press.

Roseberry, W. 1994. Hegemony and the Language of Contention. In *Everyday Forms of State Formation: Revolution and the Negotiation of Rule in Modern Mexico*. (Eds.) G. Joseph and D. Nugent. Durham and London: Duke University Press.

Santos, B. De Souza. 1987. Law: A Map of Misreading. Toward a Post-Modern Conception of Law. *Journal of Law and Society* 14:3, 279–302.

Saugestad, S. 1993. Indigenous Peoples. National Models, and Recent International Trends. In National Institute of Development Research and Documentation (NIR), Working Paper No. 64, University of Botswana.

Schirmer, J. 1998. *The Guatemalan Military Project: A Violence Called Democracy*. Philadelphia: University of Pennsylvania Press.

Sieder, R. 1997. *Customary Law and Democratic Transition in Guatemala*. Institute of Latin American Studies, London.

Sieder, R. 1999. Rethinking Democratization and Citizenship: Legal Pluralism and Institutional Reform in Guatemala. *Citizenship Studies* 3:1, 103–118.

Sieder, R. (2000). 'Paz, progreso, justicia y honradez': Law and Citizenship in Alta Verapaz During the Regime of Jorge Ubico. *Bulletin of Latin American Research* 19, 283–302.

Sierra, M.T. (forthcoming). Derecho indígena y mujeres: viejas y nuevas costumbres, nuevos derechos. In *Debates Actuales en los Estudios de Género*. (Coords.) S.E. Pérez-Gil. and P. Revelo. Mexico, CIESAS-INN.

Slater, D. 1997. Spatialities of Power and Postmodern Ethics: Rethinking Geopolitical Encounters. *Environment and Planning: Society and Space* 15, 55–72.

Speed, S. and J.F. Collier. 2000. Limiting Indigenous Autonomy in Chiapas, Mexico: The State Government's Use of the Discourse of Human Rights. *Human Rights Quarterly* 22, 877–905.

Stamatopoulou, E. 1994. Indigenous Peoples and the United Nations: Human Rights as a Developing Dynamic. *Human Rights Quarterly* 16, 58–81.

Stammers, N. 1999. Social Movements and the Social Construction of Human Rights. *Human Rights Quarterly* 21:4, 980–1008.

Starr, J. and J. Collier (Eds.). 1989. *History and Power in the Study of Law: New Directions in Legal Anthropology*. Ithaca, NY and London: Cornell University Press.

Starr, J. 1989. The Role of Turkish Secular Law in Changing the Lives of Rural Muslim Women, 1950–1970. *Law and Society Review* 23:3, 497–523.

Stavenhagen, R. 1996. Indigenous Rights: Some Conceptual Problems. In *Constructing Democracy: Human Rights, Citizenship, and Society in Latin America*. (Eds.) E. Jelin and E. Hershberg. Boulder and London: Westview Press.

Stoll, D. 1993. *Between Two Armies in the Ixil Towns of Guatemala*. New York: Columbia University Press.

Tamanaha, B. 1993. The Folly of the 'Social Scientific' Concept of Legal Pluralism. *Journal of Law and Society* 20:2, 192–217.

Tennant, C. 1994. Indigenous Peoples, International Institutions and the International Legal Literature. *Human Rights Quarterly* 16, 1–57.

Turner, T. 1993. Anthropology and Multiculturalism: What is Anthropology that Multiculturalists Should be Mindful of it? *Cultural Anthropology* 8:4, 411–429.

URL (Universidad Rafael Landívar). 1998. *El Sistema Jurídico Maya: Una Aproximación*. URL, Guatemala.

Van Cott, D.L. 2000. A Political Analysis of Legal Pluralism in Bolivia and Colombia. *Journal of Latin American Studies* 32:1, 204–237.

Warren, K. 1998. *Indigenous Movements and their Critics: Pan-Mayan Activism in Guatemala*. Princeton: Princeton University Press.

Wilson, R.A. 1997. Human Rights, Culture and Context: An Introduction. In *Human Rights, Culture and Context: Anthropological Perspectives*. (Ed.) R.A. Wilson. London: Pluto Press.

Wilson, R.A. 2000. Reconciliation and Revenge in Post-Apartheid South Africa:

Rethinking Legal Pluralism and Human Rights. *Current Anthropology* 41:1, 75–98.

Yashar, D. 1996. Indigenous Protest and Democracy in Latin America. In *Constructing Democratic Governance: Latin America and the Caribbean in the 1990s.* (Eds.) J.I. Domínguez and A.F. Lowenthal. Baltimore: John Hopkins University Press.

Young, I.M. 1990. *Justice and the Politics of Difference.* Princeton: Princeton University Press.

Zur, J. 1994. The Psychological Impact of Impunity. *Anthropology Today* 10:3, 12–17.

10 Rights as the reward for simulated cultural sameness: the Innu in the Canadian colonial context

Colin Samson

Introduction

It is only relatively recently that nation-states have concerned themselves with explicating the nature of the 'rights' of various indigenous, ethnic and minority groups, both internationally and within their borders. This concern for the human and other rights of peoples around the world has largely occurred in the era following formal decolonization. There was little attention given to such issues by European or other states during the height of European expansion, and it has only been in the wake of the Second World War with the legacy of a *European* holocaust, that such concerns attained international prominence with the adoption of the Universal Declaration of Human Rights in 1948. Since then, a host of international bodies, Non Governmental Organisations (NGOs) and academics have begun seriously to confront the problems that surround the recognition, protection and abuse of rights.

Because political discussions and academic debates over the nature and content of these rights occur in what is generally regarded as a post-colonial era, there has been little thought given to two important dimensions of rights struggles: the persistence of colonialism in many areas of the world, and the nature of cultural difference in regard to the extension of rights. Colonialism, if it is considered at all, is treated as a historical backdrop to the more pressing business of engaging in largely academic debates. Thus, many authors in the field are at pains to examine whether human and other rights in contemporary nation states should be labelled 'universal' or 'relative' (see Wilson 1996, Handwerker 1997, Zechenter 1997, Nagengast 1997), and/or 'collective' or 'individual' (see Thompson 1997). In their desire to focus on the principles that are thought to underlie *theories* of rights and rights claims, many such accounts fail to question the legitimacy of the states themselves in regard to particular populations. Because relatively few authors discuss the imposition of sovereignty, states are constituted as the potential guarantors and abusers of a range of 'rights' that culturally diverse populations are subject to.[1]

What is missing from most contemporary discussions is any notion of how to understand the political status of peoples who have not been decolonized and for whom the nation-states that exercise authority over them and their lands do so without their consent. Many tribal and indigenous peoples obviously fall into this category. In the Americas, European states did not relinquish authority or control over the native inhabitants or their land, as they did in Africa, Asia and the Indian subcontinent. In North America, for example, native peoples have never been given any meaningful opportunities to decide the terms of their political, economic, cultural and social conditions (Morris 1992: 56). The only form of political autonomy which native North Americans have been permitted is that which has been granted to them by the states that took their lands, and which are based on the coloniser's models of representative government and democracy. In all of the processes adopted by the US and Canadian courts and legislatures, including most famously, the treaty, natives[2] have never been allowed the option of *not* ceding their autonomy. The only point subject to debate was the terms under which they surrendered it.

Now that a great deal of time has passed since the frontier days, there is a common public perception that natives are now integrated or absorbed, albeit as political marginals, within Canada and the US. As a result, they are seen not to constitute a politically separate, and hence colonised, population. Conveniently, this integrationist assumption has been incorporated into government policy. It has also featured in many liberal discussions that treat indigenous peoples as 'minorities' and that unquestioningly accept the authority of the settler state as legitimate (see Tully 1995: 53, Samson 1999). On the other hand, some social scientists have undertaken research in which natives in Canada were directly understood as colonised peoples (see Brody 1975; 1981; Watkins 1977). To a certain extent this trend continues, but, as I will illustrate, social science in Canada figures prominently in the service of the colonial policies of the state itself. Generally, the balance is tipped towards ignoring or downplaying the colonial relations between Canada and natives.[3]

While the US and Canadian states claim authority over native peoples, the political relationships between states and natives is still a unique one. No other groups have the same direct relationships with the Federal governments. In Canada, the Federal government has a 'fiduciary responsibility' for native peoples, while in the US the Marshall doctrine of the Supreme Court in the 1830s that Indians are 'dependent domestic nations' still holds. These legalities constitute natives as a separate category of citizen. By doing so, the law, itself imposed, exposes the colonial nature of the relationship between the state and native peoples. Several aboriginal groups in Canada have not ceded territory to the state by treaty and were not included in the numbered treaties that were concluded in the nineteenth century. These groups are judicially deemed to have 'aboriginal title' to lands occupied since 'time immemorial', but such title is an inferior status to Canadian sovereignty and has been by-passed relatively easily. Aboriginal title has been scant defence against industrial encroachments and the imposition of Euro-Canadian social institutions, including the state, in native affairs.

The only possible legal option open to native groups that have not signed treaties and do not wish that their land be appropriated by 'developers' is the Comprehensive Land Claims process. The prime objective of this, a latter-day treaty process, is to 'extinguish' aboriginal title in exchange for state-guaranteed rights in certain areas and cash compensation. Several tribal organisations are now undertaking Comprehensive Land Claims negotiations with the Federal and Provincial governments. However, active Comprehensive Land Claims negotiations do not prevent the sale and development of land under negotiation. Thus far, natives have been fairly powerless to prevent mega-projects such as mines and dams on land under negotiation. As Forer (1979: 112) writes of a Potawatomi legal case in the US in 1972: 'Imposed law forces its subjects to seek their rights within the constraints of an alien and hostile legal system without the option of relief from the system.' Under such circumstances, the relationship is colonial rather than postcolonial.

Moving to the question of culture, if we are to examine the extension of rights to colonised peoples within the state, then we must also confront the possibility that it is not simply the law that is imposed, but also personal and cultural identity. This means that in order to receive rights, colonised people are culturally transformed in the discourses and procedures of the state. For such purposes, they are required to adopt a particular view of themselves and of the world that fits with the rights-conferring political machinery of the state.

'Culture', as the now repentant new wave of anthropologists are at pains to point out, is hardly a tenable concept since it implies that groups of people are homogenous, separate and bounded. While this critique is a necessary corrective to the primitivizing still-lifes that anthropologists composed of American Indians and other non-Europeans, one need not assume therefore that natives and non-natives are the same. As the recent writings of Gerald Vizenor (1994, 1998) demonstrate, one can be opposed to 'paracolonial' anthropological renderings of culture at the same time as maintaining a dynamic sense of native difference in stories, survival, memories, humour, motion and sovereignty. For Vizenor, a native absence is connoted by anthropological studies of natives, while presence is apparent in native sovereignty – a quality that is never static and includes, but also transcends, territory. The simulation, the 'Indian', that is created in the compositions of anthropology and public policy, signifies the absence of the native.

Although never absolute or determining, both colonialism and the sense of difference are present for many of the peoples of the subarctic, the area of concern in this chapter. The term 'colonialism' is especially applicable to the contemporary experiences of peoples who, until very recently, have been living as hunters, and for whom hunting, and the worldview, social forms and spiritual values attached to it are active and present engagements. Their sense of difference exists not necessarily as some sort of static inheritance, but as modified by their own shifting stories, the migrations of the animals, the freeze-up and thaws of each new season, and the 'two worlds' of hunting camps and government-sponsored settlements, where contact with the assimilationist colonial institutions is most intense.[4]

These differences are active, present and palpable. Yet, as I will show, cultural sameness is not only assumed but required in the extensions of 'rights' to natives in Canada. In fact, it is only through simulating themselves as the same that native peoples can have such rights recognized. In this chapter, I will examine how both colonialism and the assumption of cultural sameness operates in the conferring of particular rights upon the Innu people of the Labrador-Quebec peninsula. By relating some accounts of landmark events in relations between the Innu and the Canada, I will show how various extensions of rights have demanded cultural sameness. Three phases in the recent history of the Innu will be recounted: Newfoundland's sedentarization drive of the 1950s; the initial industrialization of Innu land, which paved the way for; contemporary efforts being made by the Canadian state to recognize certain 'rights' of the Innu through the Environmental Impact Assessment of a nickel mine on their land at Voisey's Bay.

Civilization on the northward march

Until the twentieth century, European settlement of the Labrador-Quebec peninsula was limited to scattered missionaries, trappers and fishermen. As a consequence, Europeans exerted less influence over a longer period here than anywhere else outside of the very far north. Although they have been in contact with traders and missionaries since the seventeenth century, the Innu lived as permanent nomadic hunters until the second half of the twentieth century. While traders and missionaries influenced them, neither were successful in persuading them to abandon the fundamental beliefs and practices associated with hunting. For example, despite the urgings of priests to the contrary, the Innu accepted only temporary and contingent forms of leadership under the *utshimau* ('first man') in the hunt (Henriksen 1973). They placed a high value on personal autonomy, sharing and gender egalitarianism, and were even considered to be 'communistic' by one anthropologist (Leacock 1994).

However, what has affected them most profoundly is the division of their lands. As a response to French-British competition for timber and furs, the Judicial Committee of the Privy Council in London drew a border to separate Quebec and Labrador in 1927. This split members of the same Innu families on either side: some automatically became 'Canadians', while their relatives were to be aboriginal occupants of a British home rule colony of Newfoundland (including Labrador), which did not enter the Canadian confederation until 1949. Although natives were not even mentioned in the Articles of Confederation, soon after Newfoundland's admission to Canada, the new Provincial authorities pursued a vigorous sedentarization policy towards the nomadic Innu, who at this time were travelling and hunting widely across the peninsula. By the end of the 1960s their efforts had resulted in the formation of two settlements in Labrador, Sheshatshiu and Utshimasits or Davis Inlet.

According to the testimony recorded in the Innu Nation volume, *Gathering Voices* (1995), and many conversations I have had with *Tshenut* (elders), the Innu went along with settlement in the context of (ultimately unfulfilled) promises, priestly persuasion and 'gifts' such as welfare. Oblivious to, and uninterested in, Innu understandings of their lands, the Newfoundland authorities explicitly followed a Social Darwinist view of inter-ethnic relations. They perceived the Innu as backward and destined to extinction unless they were persuaded, or forced, to adopt Euro-Canadian habits of sedentary community life and to abandon the beliefs and practices that had made them successful inhabitants of the subarctic boreal forests and barrens.

A great deal of the government story is revealed in the correspondence and memoranda of Walter Rockwood, Director of Northern Labrador Affairs for the Provincial government of Newfoundland from the mid-1950s to 1964.[5] With Oblate priests and the International Grenfell Association,[6] the Provincial government was the prime sponsor of the sedentarization policy. Rockwood's goal was to transform 'the Indians' into productive workers. He forcefully articulated the need for 'economic rehabilitation' of the Innu on many occasions and exerted a great deal of energy in devising and advocating schemes to channel them into 'productive' activity. This always involved some type of wage labour. Only a few years after the destructive and abortive relocation of the Innu to Nutak to chop wood for the Inuit (see Assembly of First Nations, 1993), the government advocated settled relocation to areas of labour demand, such as Schefferville and Wabush, where mines had been established. The nomadic hunting activities of the Innu, although alluded to, were not generally considered 'productive' activities. The Innu were thought to have only one salvation to save them from 'loafing' around the trading posts and depots at North West River and Davis Inlet, and collecting the welfare relief which was suddenly granted to them by the Province on account of their 'lack of employment.' As Rockwood wrote with great urgency in 1956, 'Unless a strong positive approach is adopted *now* there is a danger that the Indians will become loafers whose only aim is to extract more and more handouts from the government; indeed there is grave danger that this stage has already been reached' (Roche, 1992, *emphasis in original*).

Fur trapping was one answer to 'loafing'. Trapping and other essentially make-work schemes such as a cod fishery were encouraged by Rockwood and others in the 1950s and 1960s, in part to enable Innu to qualify for unemployment insurance rather than the more stigmatized welfare relief. This then engaged the Innu in hunting animals for sale rather than use in order that they could obtain unemployment benefit. In the process hunting was transformed into 'work', an economic activity, useful as the means to procure unemployment insurance. Unemployment became preferable not only because it paid marginally more, but because it signified that the recipient 'worked' rather than 'loafed'. For the Provincial government, such schemes were a means of assimilation: they discouraged 'loafing' and promoted settled, regular and predictable behaviour. In 1962, Dr Paddon, the Grenfell Association doctor at North West River, wrote a gruff letter to Rockwood, arguing that the lack of integration into the market economy was 'the heart of the whole Indian problem' (Roche 1992).

Housing construction had begun at North West River in 1957, but not seriously until 1968 at Davis Inlet under Rockwood's successor Ross King. Housing schemes seem to have proceeded through the efforts of the priest, who represented 'the Indians' and selected a 'chief' to expedite the extraction of consent. Once the Provincial government decided to go ahead with housing, a rental purchase plan was introduced whereby the heads of households were issued with lumber as an 'advance' to actually construct the house. All those receiving houses through what was called the Indian Housing Agreement were required to sign a contract stating that they were to live in the house for a period of ten years. At the end of this time, if the house was deemed to have been kept in a good state of repair, the 'homeowner' received title to it.

Through this contrivance, the Innu were suddenly 'given' private property and lured into sedentary life. This sleight of hand resulted in the Innu shifting from collectively using and occupying an area the size of France, to being individual rent-to-buy tenants in shacks. In this masterstroke the Newfoundland authorities created the impression of being attentive to individual Innu housing needs, while simultaneously creating the conditions which would make it more difficult for them to continue their collective hunting activities on the land as a whole. The conferring of a 'right' here came at the expense of a massive loss of land occupancy.

The correspondence of government and church authorities in Labrador at mid-century rings through with cries for 'integration' of 'the Indian' as the only possible salvation. In 1955, Rockwood made a prophetic statement relating to the inevitability of assimilation:

But one fact seems clear, – Civilization is on the northward march, and for the Eskimo and the Indian there is no escape. The last bridges of isolation were destroyed with the coming of the airplane and the radio. The only course now open, for there can be no turning back, is to fit him as soon as may be to take his full place as a citizen in our society. (Roche 1992).

Left to their own devices, the Innu would ultimately become extinct or live a miserable life on the edges of white society. Rockwood provided an evocative rendition of this in a June 1959 memorandum in which he compared the Innu to the extinct Beothucks of Newfoundland, killed off completely by European disease and violence:

For the Indians and many of the Eskimos, there is no easy, short term solution, unless it be the solution found for the aborigines of Newfoundland more than a century ago. They, the Beothucks, have been no bother since June 6 1829. The writer does not advocate this solution for the Labrador Indians, but it would be almost kinder than to allow them to live off the garbage dumps, and become prey to unscrupulous persons (Roche 1992).

For the Newfoundland authorities, there could be no other future for Labrador outside of industrial development. The society shaped by it, and implied in their visions, was a uniform one in which difference had to be obliterated. As Rockwood expressed it, 'What the future holds for us, it should also hold for them' (Roche 1992). The task the authorities set for themselves was to brace the Innu for the appropriation of the land. Their method of doing this was to found 'communities'. By 1968 the last Innu inhabiting the interior of Labrador were settled at Davis Inlet or Utshimasits on Iliukoyak Island. The creation of the village of Pukuat-shipu for the last remaining group of tent dwelling Innu in Quebec marked the completion of sedentarization in 1971.

The events of the period from 1949 to the end of the 1960s show that while the authorities did not couch any of their aboriginal policies in terms of 'rights', they believed that sedentarization would facilitate the extension of certain benefits to the Innu. These benefits would include rights to housing, healthcare, work, welfare and schooling, and would be incumbent upon the induction of the Innu into a more advanced society. The key to the creation of sameness was therefore the destruction of nomadism and its replacement with the conferral of particular 'rights' within a colonial political order. Thus, the Innu were urged to swap 'loafing' for 'working', hunting for settlement, the Animal Gods for the Christian God, and their language for English. Native 'rights' could only be guaranteed if the natives ceased to be natives. Consequently, nefarious schemes involving welfare, housing contracts, and the appointment of 'chiefs' by the priests were used as levers to eventually settle the Innu.[7]

Ten thousand years behind

The subsequent, early 'development' of the waters and lands of the Labrador-Quebec peninsula represent a second phase of colonial relations with the Innu. This, however, was not accompanied by any specific concern for Innu rights, despite the fact that sedentarization was precipitated directly in the context of the industrialisation of Innu hunting and trapping areas.[8]

Although the climate and terrain of Labrador had been regarded by Europeans as unattractive, bleak and inhospitable (see Leacock and Rothschild 1994: xxi–xxiv), the potential yield of natural resources had not gone unnoticed. These resources became an explicit rationale for the gradual extension of British and then Canadian control over the territories. In 1959, Walter Rockwood described Labrador as 'a young giant . . . fast approaching maturity' (Roche, 1992).

One of the most significant landmarks for the Innu was *Patshetshunau* (Steam rising), an enormous waterfall, taller than Horseshoe Falls at Niagara, which could be seen and heard from more than ten miles away. The construction of a hydroelectric plant, completed in 1972, turned the waterfall into a trickle; flooded Lake Meshikimau, with the loss of Innu and settler trap lines, equipment and hunting grounds (see Plaice 1990: 36); altered the water levels in the rivers, lakes and brooks, and thereby drastically changed the habitat for the waterfowl, fish and fur-bearing mammals of the area. Sir Winston Churchill, who was involved in establishing Brinco, the company that constructed the dam, referred to the damming as 'putting a bridle' on the waterfall. For him, Brinco was 'a great imperial concept' (Rowe, 1985: 30, 39). In the process, Churchill was posthumously memorialised when the hydroelectric complex and the nearby settlement was named Churchill Falls. The Newfoundland government named the massive body of water created by the flooding Smallwood Reservoir, in honour of the first Newfoundland Premier, Joey Smallwood, who travelled to London in the 1950s to negotiate with Churchill.

Profit-making from the land was conceived in connection with a projected primitivity of 'the Indians'. In a book celebrating the project, Smith (1975: vi) draws upon this combination of vast natural richness and astonishing primitiveness – ten thousand years behind Europeans – as the backdrop to the 'largest construction job ever tackled by a private company anywhere':

Summer comes late to Labrador, and the first snows of winter follow swiftly on its fleeting heels. Gaunt and empty, a place of ancient rock and rivers, of lakes and swamps and stunted, tattered trees, it has never been an easy land to live in. Few men have even tried the experiment: the earliest traces of human habitation found on the Labrador plateau go back only a thousand years. And in those comparatively recent times, the men who roamed that wilderness had no tools more advanced than the chipped flints wielded by the cave-dwellers of Europe ten thousand years before (Smith 1975: vi).

The only native trace here is of wandering savages wielding chipped flints. Even this faint and risible presence dissolved altogether in the deal that was cut between the Newfoundland authorities and the Hydro-Quebec utility company. No Innu was ever consulted about this project.

Up to this point, the early 1970s, two main assumptions had been made by Canadian authorities about Innu 'rights': that they could only be safeguarded through coercing and cajoling the hunters to abandon their nomadic ways and live in villages, and that once this was achieved, they had no specific rights to the land worthy of consideration. The only meaningful rights the Innu had were conferred upon them as assimilation measures. As a result of various Federal judicial rulings on native land rights over the last thirty years, however, methods of rights conferral have more recently been modified by a number of different policies. As it pertains to the Innu, the latest phase of industrialisation of the Labrador-Quebec peninsula has been accompanied by bureaucratic methods of consultation over the environmental impact of particular industrial projects. The bestowing of rights in regard to such projects

involves the state making overtures to Innu political bodies to 'participate' in the evaluation of the environmental impact of such projects.
This thereby makes them collaborators in a political process in which
they are set up as consultants to a new appropriation of land that they
have never formally relinquished. Differences between Canada and the
Innu as regards the use of the land, its meaning and the ways in which
conflict should be settled are swept aside under the state imposition of a
single process that I will describe below.

A fatal strategy

While projects such as the Churchill Falls hydroelectric complex proceeded without any native consultation or participation, since the early
1970s, Canada has implemented a series of Environmental Impact
Assessments (EIAs) procedures to consider the effect of proposed
industrial developments on the social and physical environment. Even
this, however, is merely administrative – as opposed to legislative, as in
the US – and operates at the discretion of Federal ministers (Notzke
1994: 264–5). If ministers agree to it, final permission for a proposed
development is permitted on completion of the required scientific
studies on the possible effects of the development. In the short history of
the procedure, native people have only very recently been included as
participants – and only then as an afterthought, since developers, the
scientific community and the general Canadian public have been the
primary constituents (Notzke 1994: 270). At present, native populations
in areas faced with industrial developments are simply one 'interest
group' among others, such as settlers, the Provincial government and
industrialists who are also taken into account by EIAs. Their 'rights' are
not specifically enumerated, but are considered along with those of other
interests in the EIA procedure.[9]

   Despite Churchill Falls and the Goose Bay airbase, from which
military jets soar at tree level over the Labrador-Quebec peninsula, Innu
people are still able to hunt and live on the land. Utshimasits is close to
good hunting grounds, enabling virtually the whole population to enjoy
the life of the country, *nutshimit*. In Sheshatshiu, the Outpost Programme permits at least half of the population to spend up to several
months of the year in the country. Thus, even though sedentarization
has undoubtedly changed the character of the *nutshimit* life, it has not
eliminated nomadic hunting. In many ways, the resistance of Innu
people to processes of incorporation, assimilation and land appropriation is reflected in their continuing attachment to the land, despite the
personal devastation that has accompanied sedentarization.[10]

However, the hunters are continually tested and violated by intrusions onto the land with the encouragement of the Provincial and Federal governments. By 1996, mining companies and numerous prospectors had purchased 250,000 claim stakes on Innu (that is, aboriginal title) land in Labrador (Innu Nation 1996b) from the Provincial government. As a result of discoveries from stakes at Voisey's Bay in 1994, an area known to the Innu as Emish, about 75 km from Utshimasits, has become the site of a multi-billion dollar mining operation. Again, the Innu were never consulted even though this is land on which many were born, where burial sites are located, and where the animals and fish on which many Innu depend are to be found. In February 1995 Innu Nation served an eviction notice on Archean Resources and Diamond Fields, two of the companies involved in establishing the mine, and a joint Innu-Inuit protest was held at the site in 1997. The message from both of these actions was ignored and preparations for the mine have been deterred only by decreases in the world price for nickel and wrangling between the mining company and the Provincial government over the location of a smelter.

The Innu Nation Task Force on Mining Activities (Innu Nation 1996a: 49) summarized the feelings of people surveyed in the two communities as follows:

Some people talked about it [mining at Emish] as Innu culture being destroyed. Others said it would be lost and still others described it as the culture eventually disappearing. *Some thought the consequences of this could be fatal.* A number worried about the future of the Innu. They said the future of their children and generations to come was very uncertain. Some thought their grandchildren would be lost like other Native children across Canada who have lost their language and their culture, and who don't know their ancestry. They were worried that their children would no longer think of themselves as Innu and think like whitemen. (*Emphasis added.*)

The main concern was that, as Innu, they would remain invisible to the company. Their sense that the mining company was adopting a fatal strategy towards them was underlined by the belief that mining would wreak immense ecological damage, polluting air, land and water and destroying much of the habitat of the animals on which the survival of hunting and the beliefs and practices based on it depends. In the presence of open cast mining, the smaller animals and fish would simply become extinct in the area. Larger animals such as the caribou would change their migration route to avoid the mines. Bears would be attracted to the site when they should be hibernating. Even those who saw jobs as a benefit acknowledged the potentially catastrophic cultural and ecological consequences of mining.

The EIA for the Voisey's Bay mine, as set out in the final guidelines, required the proponent, the Voisey's Bay Nickel Company, to submit a Environmental Impact Statement. This needed to include documentation of public consultation, a full description of the project, factors that could alter its plans for the project, the current state of the environment, potential environmental effects, possible beneficial effects and mitigating measures, including provisions for accidents and monitoring. In doing this, the proponents were asked to take into account 'traditional ecological knowledge' as well as Western scientific concepts such as 'sustainability' and 'biodiversity'.

Regardless of the actual outcome of the EIA for the Voisey's Bay mine, the imposition of the process itself symbolises appropriation of the land as a *fait accompli*. It assumes that Canada already has the right to adjudicate how 'aboriginal title' land can be used. This is reinforced by the imposition of Western scientific methodology, which is governed by certain ethnocentric assumptions: that land, animals and people can be abstracted and commodified; that accumulated measurements can produce relevant predictions; and that 'risk' can be assessed and managed. Even the seemingly magnanimous inclusion of 'traditional ecological knowledge' as relevant data merely reinforces colonial dominance. In the Innu communities, traditional 'ecological knowledge' is gathered and supervised primarily by non-Innu researchers who employ social science methods which comprise of various kinds of interviews with the *Tshenut*, as well as film documentation and map-drawing. The interview responses of those surveyed are then collated into a format which can be fed into the EIA panel. Thus oral knowledge of the land, the wildlife and the waters is translated into documents, written in English, to be considered by a panel of white experts.

While it is supposed to convey the impression that difference is respected, 'traditional ecological knowledge' is of course a Euro-Canadian, rather than a native, creation. It is a simulation of hunting, a representation that has no real referent, an absence rather than a presence.[11] Hunting wisdom emerges in immediate and direct experience with the land, the animals and the stories. All that is known is contingent. Knowing is an active process; it is always dynamic. Truth is found in real experience, including dreams, stories and visions, not in the abstractions or objectifications of social science. Knowing in hunting actively resists the kind of generalization and codification presupposed by 'traditional ecological knowledge'. Thus, 'the hunter, alive to constant movements of nature, spirits, and human moods, maintains a way of doing things that repudiates a firm plan and any precise or specified understanding with others of what he is going to do. His course of action is not, must not be, a matter of predetermination' (Brody 1981: 37). Hunting is motion, movement, contingency, and the avoidance of firm plans. The EIA simulates it by encapsulation as 'traditional ecological knowledge'. What was fluid, changeable and non-material becomes forced into contributing to a predictive objective of a colonial state.

As Shapcott (quoted in Notzke 1995: 263) argues, '[T]he values of the dominant culture are so embedded in the process of EIA . . . that alternative values cannot even be considered'. The imposition of the process and its ethnocentric methods effectively reduces natives to onlookers in the processes that will radically alter their land and futures. Although the Innu communities were encouraged to participate in the various EIA studies, they have had no authority to determine how their views would be considered. That authority is vested in the panel. The final guidelines for the Voisey's Bay EIA – reached, again, through a seemingly 'fair' process of 'consultation', but drawn up by the panel of consultants – specifically and categorically excluded any consideration of the land claims of the Innu and the aboriginal title to the Voisey's Bay land. Although the EIA could have considered these factors – and indeed several submissions, including those of Innu Nation and third parties, including myself, urged the panel to attend to land claims first – such pleas were ignored.

Like most other EIAs, the Voisey's Bay impact assessment was entirely *ex post facto*. At the time of the EIA implementation, the mining site had been identified, drilling had begun, workers and managers had been employed, the Provincial and Federal governments had promoted the enterprise, millions of dollars had been invested, and indeed the company openly referred to the area as its 'property'. Moreover, primarily the 'proponents' of the project fund the EIA studies – in this case the Voisey's Bay Nickel Company, a subsidiary of Inco, and the government. According to the company's own records, some $14 million has been devoted to conducting the EIA. By comparison, Innu Nation was allocated $136,000 to organise its case for the EIA. Newfoundland Premier Brian Tobin tirelessly lobbied for the project, inferring in numerous television and newspaper interviews that environmental approval was merely a formality. It was little surprise, then, that in 1999 the government finally gave the mining company the green light and ignored key recommendations of the panel.

'Functionally de-link the deliverables'

The invitation to participate in environmental impact studies on industrial developments within their territories is difficult for native groups to refuse. If they do not involve themselves, they risk having their land simply appropriated without ever putting on record their objections. However, at a cultural level, the cost of participation is that it demands the adoption of political institutions and ways of thinking that are commensurate only with the objectives of the state. Hence, across North America native political bodies were created by the state to become opposite parties in negotiations. The US and Canada demanded that natives adopt institutions that would become miniature images of the state itself: the effect, and often the intention, was to destroy existing patterns of social organisation.

As the stakes have risen, native groups have felt it necessary to solicit assistance from non-native advisers. In regard to the EIA, these intermediaries are employed to undertake a wide range of studies such as baseline research to assess the current conditions of the land and waterways, the locations, numbers and habitats of the local wildlife, the collection of 'traditional ecological knowledge' and the documentation of various social and demographic indices of the people themselves. In addition, lawyers are hired at great expense to advise on legal matters.

In 1996 I was invited by the Innu leadership to participate in a two-day meeting in Sheshatshiu to discuss strategy on a series of environmental and social impact studies to be fed into the EIA. After making a $500,000 one-off payment to Innu Nation, the Voisey's Bay Nickel Company, as the 'proponents' of the mine, financed both the meeting itself, including the air fares and payments for all of the participants, and the EIA studies. A Mennonite volunteer who had been resident in Sheshatshiu for two years drew up the agenda. Discussions of particular subjects were strictly limited by time parameters set out on the agenda. In attendance over the two days were several Euro-Canadian and European 'experts' – predominantly environmental scientists and anthropologists – a small section of the Innu Nation leadership, and a few *Tshenut* from Sheshatshiu and Utshimasits. The overwhelming majority of the Innu in the two villages were unaware that the meetings were taking place.

The first morning's events opened with the Mennonite telling the delegates that the Voisey's Bay Nickel Company had decided to fund the meeting in order that some clear 'outputs' would be achieved. From the start, it was apparent that fundamental questions of land use and rights to land were outside the remit of the meeting, even though the land in question had never been ceded to Canada and as 'aboriginal title' land was the subject of Comprehensive Land Claims negotiations. After the representatives of the mining company had provided a thumbnail sketch of the history of the mining activities, and peripherally asserted the need for significant 'progress' on land rights, an expert advising the Innu side laid down what he believed was a shared assumption: that it was impossible for the Innu to stop the mine. Although there was some debate over that position, including my own remark that this position could create a self-fulfilling prophecy, the meeting proceeded, at least for the bulk of the experts, as if it were true.

As the meeting proceeded each set of contributions was translated to the *Tshenut* into *Innu-aimun*, the Innu language. This proved difficult for the translator because of the incomensurability of words and concepts: 'process', 'deliverables' and 'work-scoping', for example, have no equivalent in *Innu-aimun*. With time, the voices that were heard were increasingly those of the white experts. The language used became more abstract and scientific. At one point an expert called for the need to 'functionally de-link the deliverables'. The silences of the Innu, particularly the *Tshenut*, stood in stark contrast to the vocal animation of the experts. After sitting patiently for two days the *Tshenut* were asked their views. Akat Piwas was the first to speak:

What the Innu say should not be translated into Western science. It should be taken in the context of what is being said. We have no real information on Voisey's Bay. There are stories told by Innu of water that is polluted flowing into Voisey's Bay as well as other negative impacts. This needs to get out and be shared. The impacts on the land as expressed by Innu people have to be brought out.

Dominic Pokue, also silent and patient for two days, offered his perspective:

Tshenut care that their children and grandchildren will have land to sustain them. The area is close to the hearts of the Utshimasits people, but this will be no factor in the decision-making arena of the government. It's crazy for us to pretend otherwise. The project has already started. The project is here and that's a fact. It is important to collect information and have on record the opinions of Tshenut and put this on paper. But let's not pretend that there is no mine. Already wildlife is being affected, but white people don't see it and this is going to be rammed down our throats no matter what we say.

Akat Piwas then continued:

Dominic is right. There is a place where Innu people used to get arctic char when they were hungry. Now they don't go there anymore. This may be because they think that oil and lubricants have contaminated the water. In Spring people went to an area near Voisey's Bay and found a decline in the wildlife. There were no black bear, porcupine or other animals. Before there was a lot to be hunted. This will not happen when the mine is in place. I can predict myself what will happen to the Innu without going through all of these studies that we are talking about today. There will be a loss of culture. Young people will not know their way of life. Our children will be walking on the pavement, not the barren ground.

For the *Tshenut* the signs were ominous. Mining would lead to a decline in wildlife, contamination of the environment and the loss of ways of being and thinking. This is what needed to be said and 'put down on paper', as Dominic Pokue pointed out. Yet it never was. After the *Tshenut* had said their piece, people from both communities expressed their concerns about dealing with these important issues when so many people were suffering from the trauma of alcohol, gas sniffing, suicide and abuse. According to David Nui, a man from Utshimasits, the healing process was failing badly. It was, he asserted, necessary for people to heal before they could do anything else. He did not know how people would cope if mining started. While he spoke, Mary May Osmond whispered to a small group of us that the whole affair was like handing a dying man a dinner menu. All of these testimonials reflected a willingness to confront both mining and the EIA procedures themselves by rejecting Western science, attaching a different cosmic vision to the land, imagining ethnocide and environmental devastation, and setting the decision-making over the mine in the context of the current collective trauma experienced in Sheshatshiu and Utshimasits.

The experts quickly brushed aside these unsettling observations as the meeting resumed its scientific and technical tone. The movement away from the heartfelt and politically explosive reflections of the Innu participants was swift. Any time to dwell on what the *Tshenut* and others had said was killed by the urgings of one adviser to identify people with the relevant 'skill sets' necessary for particular aspects of the EIA studies. What was needed, he enthusiastically asserted, was an administrator who could be 'bossy' enough to keep researchers 'in line'. The appointee would have to be able to work well with an aboriginal person, and have knowledge of both 'good' Western social science and traditional ecological knowledge. The Mennonite facilitator signalled that this line of discussion was going in the right direction. The process, he said, had been 'long and unwieldy'. There was a need, now, at nearly five o'clock on the final day, to move ahead smoothly by identifying a process to 'operationalize a proposal'. Helpfully, another white expert volunteered to access the community and come up with a 'boiler plate'.

Over the course of the two days, these discussions became something like the *fables du ricochet*, stories in which the narrator constantly evades the hearer's questions. In this case, the expert narrators' monologues were conveyed without ever taking account of the hearers' thoughtful but often melancholy responses. The thick abstract jargon of social and environmental science turned both people and land into objects. As humans, the Innu were barely visible beneath the smoke of reason. The identification of abstractions, such as 'key elements', 'key objectives',

'assessing costs of purchasing data' and 'arriving at a community participation profile', became the ultimate concerns. According to one
expert, it was up to the Innu Nation to get a larage enough budget from
the mining company and then 'integrity will flow'. As the huddled and
now silent people from Utshimasits became backdrops, the untranslat-
able verbosity gave way to more concrete talk about particular 'outputs'.
These were framed in terms of the need for more time to conduct the
studies in question and an increased budget to pay the environmental
consultants, many of whom were in the room, who would carry out the
required research. Nothing from what any of the *Tshenut* had said was
factored into the 'outputs'. They were invisible – only the pretexts for
the meeting.[12]

Several months later a job advertisement appeared on the internet:
'Wanted. Coordinator for a Participatory Research project with Communities of Utshimasits and Sheshatshiu, Labrador.' The job required
the holder to be conversant with 'community development and facili-
tation', 'training skills', 'video documentation' and 'computer bases'.
Interested persons were to apply to an office in Saskatoon, thousands of
miles away from Labrador.

The meeting over the environmental and social impact studies provides one example of a contemporary colonial process in which rights-
giving occurs at the expense of much greater losses of cultural autonomy
and land. Unlike Rockwood's civilizing project of sedentarization, or the
decision-making which resulted in the Churchill Falls hydroelectric
complex, the Innu were brought into the decision-making, but only in a
nominal sense did they 'participate'. The general expert consensus on
the impossibility of stopping the mine, and their seeming blindness
towards the catastrophic visions of the *Tshenut* and other Innu, lent
weight to the opinion, which became a dictum, that the mine was
inevitable. The emphasis of the advisers on technical compliance with
the procedures, larger budgets and scientific methodologies then reinforced a fatalism that could have only produced despondency among
the Innu.

Conclusion: rights as a reward for simulated sameness

Although contemporary procedures for the recognition of native rights
are couched in the politically correct language of participation and
citizenship, a deep fatalism underpins them. Burdensome government
policies such as Environmental Impact Assessment for the evaluation of
potential industrial developments on such land and Comprehensive
Land Claims ultimately rest on the European notion that the sovereignty

of the state is a paramount assertion of territorial occupation to which native peoples *must* defer, even though they have not signalled their consent. This assertion guarantees that native deference is integral to the very procedures that were created and are implemented by non-natives. They are carried out in the master languages of English or French, and are governed by a Western liberal protocol that is alien to many of the peoples subject to them. The EIA and other such policies presuppose one Euro-Canadian authority that in the final instance is backed by the threat of violence. If this were not enough, even the advisers to aboriginal parties often urge them to believe that they are doomed as a culturally distinct group and can only ever hope to tinker with the eco-friendliness of development.

How does this occur? From the invention of the treaty through to the EIA, the sealing of agreements from which rights flow could only be achieved through the simulation of the native as an 'Indian', the closure of difference and the contrivance of sameness. In this vein, Gerald Vizenor (1998: 148) tells us that 'the *indian* named in treaties was a perversion of native transmotion', and that native

sovereignty is in the visions of transformation: the humor of motion as survivance over dominance; the communal movement to traditional food sources; dreams and memories as sources of shared consciousness; the stories of reincarnation, out of body travel; the myths and metaphors of flying; communal nicknames and memories of migration; the spiritual and herbal powers to heal and locate lost souls (Vizenor 1998: 184).

By contrast, European sovereignty, which as Taussig (1997. 125) observes, is 'not belief so much as make-believe', permits the state to magnanimously confer various 'rights'. In the colonial context, these extensions of rights related to land and native peoples always reserved final authority to the state. In the case of the many natives who have not signed any treaties, sovereignty is surely make-believe, resting on none of the formalities believed to signify sovereignty. There have been no cessions, consent, military conquests, Hobbesian covenants, or social contracts. The conferring of rights, then, occurs even though the beneficiaries have not relinquished the autonomy that is required by the 'extinguishment' convention.[13] and by constitutional precedents such as the Royal Proclamation of 1763 and the instrument of Indian policy it created, the treaty, by which the state is required to negotiate native cessions before imposing authority over their lands.

Under contemporary conditions of colonial bureaucratic authority, representations of 'Indians' as 'loafing' evolutionary precursors to Western civilisation have become unnecessary. The racist and assimilationist justifications used mid-century in Labrador to move 'the Indians' into villages are redundant. Now the state nurtures and advertises 'participation' in Canadian civil society as evidence of multicultural democracy.[14] Social Darwinism as a political doctrine, legitimizing European expansion, has already served its purpose. It is no longer broadcast as an imperious march of civilization, but instead is silently enveloped in the deep fatalism that always denies difference, and always proclaims that the march will proceed whether the Innu like it or not.

Tracing the parallel movement in anthropology to the post Second World War era, Fabian (1983: 144–6) suggests that a kind of 'public' or 'international' Time came into anthropological discourse. This concept of Time provided a simultaneity of experiences of Europeans and Others that was construed as politically and ideologically neutral. Meanwhile, ethnographic and theoretical anthropology continued to produce images of cultural distance. 'Distance, in turn', writes Fabian, 'is what the forces of progress need so that it may be overcome *in time*' (1983: 146).

It is this *overcoming* that is incarnated in the current procedures for the recognition of native rights in Canada.[15] These turgid and deadening formalities force a compression of the distance between natives and the state. They homogenize aboriginal peoples with others as citizens, even 'first nations', of the nation state. Those represented by the simulation 'first nations' can only be the recipients of rights and the objects of procedures for the conferring of rights. They cannot impose their own procedures for recognizing Canada's 'claims' to their land. All statements of what rights are, who is accorded them and how they should be negotiated can only be authorised by the state. This transparently colonial policy forces compliance through simulating sameness. The question of this case is not so much about whether 'culture' has any place in rights discourses, but how the denial of cultural difference can be used to suppress native aspirations for the right to be different.

ACKNOWLEDGEMENTS

This article is based on fieldwork conducted from 1994 to 1999 in Sheshatshiu and Utshimasits. I gratefully acknowledge the help, advice, translation skills and constant good humour of the people in the two communities. My visits to the communities were funded by a 1995 RISM Landes Fellowship from the Research Institute for the Study of Man and an Institutional Research Grant from the Canadian High Commission. The Research Promotion Fund and the Fuller Bequest at the University of Essex provided initial funding for the project. I have benefitted especially from the helpful comments and inspiration of

Daniel Ashini, Sheila Blake, John-Pierre Ashini and Anthony Jenkinson of Sheshatshiu; George Rich, Mary Angela Pijogge, Sam Pijogge and Christine Cleghorn of Utshimasits; Jane Hindley and Andrew Canessa of the University of Essex; Rampaul Chamba of the University of California at San Diego; Heidi Grainger of the University of Liverpool; Adrian Tanner of Memorial University, Newfoundland; Gerald Vizenor, Ernest Landauer and David Minkus of the University of California at Berkeley; the editors of this volume, two anonymous referees, Nicola Gray, and James Wilson.

NOTES

1 Weber (1995: 2) notes this tendency as particularly prevalent among International Relations theorists. Tully (1995: 53) recognizes the same in liberal theorists of citizenship rights such as Kymlicka, Walzer and Resnick.

2 Following the usage employed by Anishinaabe scholar Gerald Vizenor (1994, 1997), I use the word 'native' throughout to denote indigenous peoples. The terms 'indigenous' and 'aboriginal' are also used interchangeably with 'native'.

3 This is the case in a recent textbook on anthropology and aboriginal peoples, in which colonialism is mentioned only rarely, and when it is, it usually applies to some sort of injustice meted out to natives, such as 'welfare colonialism' *within* the state (Hedican, 1995).

4 This theme of 'two worlds' is commented on in Henriksen (1973) for the late 1960s, and more recently in the BBC documentary, *Two Worlds of the Innu* (Wilson, 1994).

5 This correspondence is collected in Roche (1992). This document is not page numbered, and cannot be referenced precisely. References are taken from individual memoranda, letters and statements in the collection.

6 The International Grenfell Association was philanthropic organization founded in the 1890s by Wilfred T. Grenfell to provide health and spiritual services, originally for the fishermen of the Labrador coast but later concerning itself in wider social engineering for the whole of Labrador, including the native population.

7 Only in retrospect have these procedures been condemned as gross violations of the rights of the Innu. For example, an Assembly of First Nations (1993: 57) report on the relocation of Utshimasits noted that 'the federal and Newfoundland governments have repeatedly failed to meet even the most minimum human rights standards in relation to the Mushuau ['barren ground'] Innu'.

8 This was true for most of the Labrador–Quebec peninsula. Apart from the mining activities, the air base and the sawmills mentioned by Rockwood and his confederates, Charest (1982: 424) notes that sedentarization was precipitated directly in the context of the industrialization of the hunting and trapping areas of the Montagnais of Bersimis in Quebec.

9 The EIA treatment of aboriginal peoples as simply one 'interest group'

among others contradicts the spirit of international human rights conventions. For example, it is not surprising that Canada has not ratified or implemented instruments of international law such as ILO Convention 169 concerning indigenous and tribal peoples in independent countries. Article 13 spells out obligations on the part of states to '. . . respect the special importance for the cultures and spiritual values of the peoples concerned of their relationship with the lands and territories, or both as applicable, which they occupy or otherwise use, and in particular the collective aspects of this relationship'.

10 The Labrador Innu communities have extremely high suicide rates, as well as high infant mortality rates, epidemics of children sniffing gas and mass adult alcoholism (see, Samson, Wilson and Mazower 1999).

11 'Traditional ecological knowledge' would be, in Gerald Vizenor's terms, a simulation, a celebration of the *indian*, which is a native absence. The EIA procedures engage in exactly the opposite of that which he recommends. Hence, 'the point here, in the absence of natives, is to counter the enterprise of reason that sustains the *indian* as a social science simulation of modernity' (Vizenor 1998: 56).

12 The indifference shown by the white experts to the points of view of the *Tshenut* and other Innu is similar to the attitudes of white bureaucrats in the hearings on the Alaska pipeline documented by Brody (1981: 256–270) in the Indian communities of Northeastern British Columbia two decades ago.

13 This convention itself has been roundly criticized by human rights organisations (see Samson *et al*, 1999), as well as the UN Committee on Human Rights in April 1999. The UN recommended that Canada abandon the practice of extinguishing inherent aboriginal rights as incompatible with the International Covenant on Civil and Political Rights.

14 For example, the Canadian Multiculturalism Act of 1988, 'commits the Government of Canada to assist communities and institutions in bringing about equal access and participation for all Canadians in the economic, social, cultural, and political life of the nation'.

15 Thus, even recent 'concessions' to natives such as the 1997 Supreme Court *Delgamuukw* decision, which spells out the content of 'aboriginal title', and the state approval of the Inuit territory of Nunavut (see Perry 1996: 159), reserve most subsurface mineral rights and other economic prerogatives to the state.

REFERENCES

Assembly of First Nations. 1993. *Violations of Law and Human Rights by the Governments of Canada and Newfoundland in Regard to the Mushuau Innu: A Documentation of Injustice in Utshimasits (Davis Inlet)*. Submission to the Canadian Human Rights Commission. Assembly of First Nations, Ottawa.
Brody, H. 1975. *The People's Land: Inuit, Whites and the Eastern Arctic*. Vancouver: Douglas & McIntyre.
Brody, H. 1981. *Maps and Dreams*. New York: Pantheon.
Charest, P. 1982. Hydroelectric Dam Construction and the Foraging Activities

of Eastern Quebec Montagnais. In *Politics and History in Band Societies*. (Eds.) E. Leacock & R. Lee. Cambridge: Cambridge University Press.

Fabian, J. 1983. *Time and the Other: How Anthropology Makes Its Object*. New York: Columbia University Press.

Forer, N. 1979. The Imposed Wardship of American Indian Tribes: A Case Study of the Prairie Band of Potawatomi. In *The Imposition of Law: The Social Consequences of Imposed Law*. (Eds.) S. Burman and B. Hurrell-Bond. London: Academic Press.

Handwerker, W.P. 1997. Universal Human Rights and the Problem of Unbounded Cultural Meanings. *American Anthropologist* 99:4, 799–824.

Hedican, E. 1995. *Applied Anthropology in Canada: Understanding Aboriginal Issues*. Toronto: University of Toronto Press.

Henriksen, G. 1973. *Hunters in the Barrens: The Naskapi on the Edge of the White Man's World*. St. John's: Institute of Social and Economic Research Press.

Innu Nation and Mushuau Innu Band Council. 1995. *Gathering Voices: Finding Strength to Help Our Children*. Vancouver: Douglas & McIntyre.

Innu Nation. 1996a. *Between a Rock and A Hard Place*. Innu Nation, Sheshatshiu.

Innu Nation. 1996b. *A Matter of Respect: Mineral Exploration in Nitassinan*. Innu Nation, Sheshatshiu.

Leacock, E. 1995. The Montagnais-Naskapi of the Labrador Peninsula. In *Native Peoples: The Canadian Experience*. (Eds.) R.B. Morrison and C.R. Wilson. Toronto: McClelland & Stewart.

Leacock, E and N. Rothschild. 1994. *Labrador Winter: the Ethnographic Journals of William Duncan Strong*. Washington DC: Smithsonian Institution Press.

Morris, G. 1992. International Law and Politics: Toward a Right to Self-Determination for Indigenous Peoples. In *The State of Native America: Genocide. Colonization and Resistance*. (Ed.) M.A. Jaimes. Boston: South End Press.

Nagengast, C. 1997. Women. Minorities. and Indigenous Peoples: Universalism and Cultural Relativity. *Journal of Anthropological Research* 53:3, 349–369.

Notzke, C. 1994. *Aboriginal Peoples and Natural Resources in Canada*. North York, Ontario: Captus Press.

Perry, R. 1996. *From Time Immemorial: Indigenous Peoples and State Systems*. Austin: University of Texas Press.

Plaice, E. 1990. *The Native Game: Settler Perceptions of Indian/Settler Relations in Central Labrador*. St. Johns: Institute for Social and Economic Research Press.

Roche, J. 1992. *Resettlement of the Mushuau Innu 1948 and 1967: A Collection of Documents from the Provincial Archives of Newfoundland and Labrador and the Centre for Newfoundland Studies*. Innu Nation, Sheshatshiu.

Rowe, F. 1985. *The Smallwood Era*. Toronto: McGraw-Hill Ryerson.

Royal Commission on Aboriginal Peoples. 1996. *Looking Forward, Looking Backward*. five volumes. Minister of Supply and Services Canada, Ottawa.

Samson.C. 1999. The Dispossession of the Innu and the Colonial Magic of Canadian Liberalism. *Citizenship Studies* 3:1, 5–26.

Samson, C., J. Wilson, and J. Mazower, 1999. *Canada's Tibet: The Killing of the Innu*. Survival International, London.

248   *Colin Samson*

Smith, P. 1975. *Brinco: The Story of Churchill Falls*. Toronto: McClelland & Stewart.
Taussig, M. 1997. *The Magic of the State*. New York: Routledge.
Thompson, R. 1997. Ethnic Minorities and the Case for Collective Rights. *American Anthropologist* 99:4, 775–798.
Tully, J. 1995. *Strange Multiplicity: Constitutionalism in an Age of Diversity*. Cambridge: Cambridge University Press.
Vizenor, G. 1994. *Manifest Manners: Postindian Warriors of Survivance*. Hanover, NH: Wesleyan University Press.
Vizenor, G. 1998. *Fugitive Poses: Native American Indian Scenes of Absence and Presence*. Lincoln: University of Nebraska Press.
Watkins, M. (Ed.). 1977. *Dene Nation: The Colony Within*. Toronto: Toronto University Press.
Weber, C. 1995. *Simulating Sovereignty: Intervention, the State, and Symbolic Exchange*. Cambridge: Cambridge University Press.
Wilson, J. 1994. *The Two Worlds of the Innu*. BBC2 documentary film. Broadcast 7 August.
Wilson, R. 1996. Human Rights. Culture and Context: An Introduction. In *Human Rights. Culture and Context*. (Ed.) R. Wilson. London: Pluto Press.
Young, I.M. 1990. *Justice and the Politics of Difference*. Princeton: Princeton University Press.
Young, I.M. 1995. Polity and Group Difference: A Critique of the Ideal of Universal Citizenship. In *Theorizing Citizenship*. (Ed.) Ronald Beiner. New York: New York University Press.
Zechenter, E. 1997. In the Name of Culture: Cultural Relativism and the Abuse of the Individual. *Journal of Anthropological Research* 53:3, 319–338.

Index

CPSIA information can be obtained at www.ICGtesting.com
Printed in the USA
LVOW07s0329251014

410431LV00001B/42/P